THE POETRY OF RELIGIOUS SORROW
IN EARLY MODERN ENGLAND

In early modern England, religious sorrow was seen as a form of spiritual dialogue between the soul and God, expressing how divine grace operates at the level of human emotion. Through close readings of both Protestant and Catholic poetry, Kuchar explains how the discourses of "devout melancholy" helped generate some of the most engaging religious verse of the period. From Robert Southwell to John Milton, from Aemilia Lanyer to John Donne, the language of "holy mourning" informed how poets represented the most intimate and enigmatic aspects of faith as lived experience. In turn, "holy mourning" served as a way of registering some of the most pressing theological issues of the day. By tracing poetic representations of religious sorrow from Crashaw's devotional verse to Shakespeare's weeping kings, Kuchar expands our understanding of the interconnections between poetry, theology, and emotion in post-Reformation England.

GARY KUCHAR is Assistant Professor in the Department of English at the University of Victoria in British Columbia, Canada. He is the author of numerous articles on early modern literature and of *Divine Subjection: The Rhetoric of Sacramental Devotion in Early Modern England* (2005).

THE POETRY OF RELIGIOUS SORROW IN EARLY MODERN ENGLAND

GARY KUCHAR

CAMBRIDGE
UNIVERSITY PRESS

CAMBRIDGE UNIVERSITY PRESS
Cambridge, New York, Melbourne, Madrid, Cape Town, Singapore, São Paulo, Delhi

Cambridge University Press
The Edinburgh Building, Cambridge CB2 8RU, UK

Published in the United States of America by Cambridge University Press, New York

www.cambridge.org
Information on this title: www.cambridge.org/9780521896696

First published 2008

Printed in the United Kingdom at the University Press, Cambridge

A catalogue record for this publication is available from the British Library

Library of Congress Cataloguing in Publication Data

Kuchar, Gary, 1974–
The poetry of religious sorrow in early modern England / Gary Kuchar.
p.   cm.
Includes bibliographical references and index.
ISBN 978-0-521-89669-6 (hardback)
1. English poetry–Early modern, 1500–1700–History and criticism.
2. Christian poetry, English–Early modern, 1500–1700–History and criticism.
3. Grief in literature.   4. Theology in literature.   5. Philosophy in literature.
6. Religion in literature.   7. Literature and society–England–History–16th century.
8. Literature and society–England–History–17th century.
9. Loss (Psychology) in literature.   I. Title.
PR508.R4K83 2008
821'.3093828–dc22
2008012203

ISBN 978-0-521-89669-6 hardback

For Erin E. Kelly
and in memory of Sylvia Bowerbank, 1947–2005.

Contents

Acknowledgments

This book began while I enjoyed the support of a Social Sciences and Humanities Research Council of Canada postdoctoral fellowship. I would like to thank Marshall Grossman and the Department of English at the University of Maryland College Park for supporting the postdoctoral phase of this project. More recently, the book has benefited from the support of the Faculty of Humanities at the University of Victoria and from many colleagues and friends. Patrick Grant and Ed Pechter kindly commented on large portions of the manuscript at various stages. Andrew Griffin, James Knapp and Grant Williams helpfully responded to parts of the manuscript and have provided enormously appreciated friendship and dialogue. Melinda Gough offered very useful feedback on an early version of Chapter 3. Mary Silcox and David Clark continue to be implicit interlocutors in my work: my discussions of apostrophe constitute responses to several conversations with David and my interest in Lanyer was inspired by Mary's engaging approach to *Salve Deus*. The influence of Sylvia Bowerbank also remains strong here and it is my hope that this book does something to honor her memory. The members of the early modern studies group at the University of Victoria helpfully commented on an early version of Chapter 6. I am grateful to Jennifer Clement, Lowell Gallagher, Kenneth Graham, and Arthur Marotti, for inviting me to try out portions of this project at the Renaissance Society of America, a Clark Library Conference on early modern Catholicism, a session on George Herbert at the Canadian Society for Renaissance Studies, and an MLA panel on devotional poetry. Questions and comments from numerous participants at these conferences find responses here, especially some questions on Crashaw from Richard Rambuss. The anonymous readers at Cambridge University Press offered extremely rigorous comments on the manuscript, and Clare Zon offered patient and skilled editing. I would also like to acknowledge the support of my chair, Robert Miles and associate dean, Claire Carlin, as well as the intellectual camaraderie and good humor I share with many other colleagues and friends who have been sources of ongoing dialogue about my work, especially Michael Best, Luke Carson, Ronald Corthell, Chris Douglas, Gordon Fulton, Ian Higgins, Ken Jackson, Janelle Jenstad, Allan Mitchell, Linda Morra, Stephen Ross, and Lincoln Shlensky. Many of my students have also been teachers to me, especially Nina Belojevik, Veronica Bishop, and Alison Knight. My research assistants, Katie Paterson and Peter Perkins, have been of great help. My parents, Joseph and Beverley Kuchar, continue to be a source of wonderful support. Most of all, I would like to thank Erin Kelly for making writing about sorrow much more enjoyable than it probably ought to have been and for reminding me during the composition of this book that there is more to life than compunction. Erin's contributions to this book are too many to cite.

An early version of Chapter 3 appeared as "Andrew Marvell's Anamorphic Tears," *Studies in Philology* 103.3 (2006), 345–81; Chapter 4 appeared as "Aemilia Lanyer and the Virgin's Swoon: Theology and Iconography in *Salve Deus Rex Judaeorum*," *English Literary Renaissance* 37.1 (2007), 47–73 and Chapter 5 appeared as "Petrarchism and Repentance in John Donne's *Holy Sonnets*," *Modern Philology* (February 2008); I am grateful to the editors of these journals for permission to reproduce this material and to the anonymous readers for their helpful comments.

Abbreviations and notes on texts

OED   *Oxford English Dictionary* (2nd edn)

SD   *The Sermons of John Donne*, ed. and introd. George R. Potter and Evelyn M. Simpson (Berkeley: University of California Press, 1957). References are given in the text by volume and page number.

The Complete Poetry of Richard Crashaw, ed. George Walton Williams (New York: W. W. Norton, 1970). References to "The Weeper" are from this edition and are given in the text by stanza number. Except when noted otherwise I cite the 1648 version of "The Weeper." Other references to Crashaw's poems are from this edition and are indicated as either line or stanza numbers in the text.

   The Complete English Poems of John Donne, ed. C. A. Patrides (London: Dent, 1985). Except when noted otherwise, references to Donne's *Songs and Sonets* are from this edition and are given by line numbers.

   The Variorum Edition of the Poetry of John Donne, volume 6: *The Anniversaries* and the *Epicedes and Obsequies*, ed. Gary A. Stringer (Bloomington: Indiana University Press, 1995). References to *An Anatomy of the World. The First Anniversary* are given in the text by line numbers. I have modernized the use of u and v in citations of this text. Citations from the critical apparatus of this edition are given by page numbers and are cited in the notes as *Variorum Edition: Anniversaries*.

   The Variorum Edition of the Poetry of John Donne, volume 7 part I: *The Holy Sonnets*, ed. Gary A. Stringer (Bloomington: Indiana University Press, 2005). Except when noted otherwise, references to the *Holy Sonnets* are from this edition and are given in the text by sequence (Original, 1635, Westmoreland, or Revised) and by line numbers.

   George Herbert: The Complete English Works, ed. Ann Pasternak Slater (New York: Alfred A. Knopf, 1995). Except when noted otherwise, references to Herbert's poetry are from this edition and are given by line numbers in the text.

Aemilia Lanyer, *Salve Deus Rex Judaeorum*, ed. Susanne Woods (New York and London: Oxford University Press, 1993). References to Lanyer are from this edition and are given in the text by page and line numbers. Page and line numbers are separated with a semi-colon.

Andrew Marvell: The Complete Poems, ed. George deF. Lord (New York: Alfred A. Knopf, 1984). References to Marvell's poetry are from this edition and are cited in the text by line numbers.

John Milton, *Paradise Lost*, ed. Alastair Fowler, 2nd edn. (London: Longman, 1998). References to *Paradise Lost* are from this edition and are cited in the text by book and line numbers.

William Shakespeare, *King Richard II*, ed. Charles Forker, Arden 3rd Series (London: Thomson Learning, 2002). References to the play are from this edition and are given in the text by act, scene, and line numbers.

William Shakespeare, *The Sonnets and Narrative Poems*, ed. Sylvan Barnet (New York: Signet, 1964). References to *Venus and Adonis* are from this edition and are cited in the text by line numbers.

The Poems of Robert Southwell S.J., ed. James H. McDonald and Nancy Pollard Brown (Oxford: Clarendon Press, 1967). References to Southwell's poems are from this edition and are given in the text by line numbers.

Except when noted otherwise, references to the Bible are from a modern spelling edition of the King James version.

All italics in quotations are original except where marked.

Introduction: Of Sighs and Tears

Christianity is nothing if not a vast technology of mourning. From David's psalms, to Jeremiah's lamentations, to Jesus' weeping, to Magdalene's tears, Christian scripture draws much of its power of fascination as a religious and literary document from its representations of grief. The fascination elicited by these and other scriptural depictions of sacred sorrow is testified to by the many devotional and artistic traditions they helped engender. In such traditions, Christians are encouraged to generate, temper, interpret, and signify a bewildering array of different forms of mourning – many of which are thought to constitute the very medium by which God makes himself present to the soul. While traditions of religious sorrow are especially characteristic of the later middle ages, post-Reformation culture did not exorcise itself of the medieval fascination with sacred grief so much as it complicated what was already a complex set of practices. The European Reformations introduced into devotional life a series of competing discourses about how one should make sense of the most intimate aspects of one's religious experience as affective in nature. In early modern England, as in virtually all parts of medieval and Renaissance Europe, religious sorrow remained ubiquitous – be it the godly sorrow that works repentance, the sadness for Christ's agony, called *compassio*, or the despair of perceived damnation. Yet despite, or perhaps because of, the ubiquity of such forms of sorrow in early modern England, literary critics have remained primarily interested in more secular forms of melancholy, especially the kinds one finds on the public stage. While the recent turn to religion in literary studies has begun to correct this, we still do not understand the cultural work performed by discourses such as the "poetry of tears," nor do we adequately comprehend the literary power wielded by such traditions.

The Poetry of Religious Sorrow in Early Modern England seeks to explain the cultural and literary significance of poetic depictions of Christian grief from Robert Southwell's *St Peters Complaint* (1594) to Milton's *Paradise*

I

Lost (1674). My primary goal is to demonstrate how poems which explore religious sorrow have a tendency to address the most pressing theological, metaphysical, and literary issues in the post-Reformation era. In other words, I seek to explain how in the process of expressing what repentance, *compassio*, or despair feel like as lived experiences, early modern English poets find themselves addressing the most vital doctrinal and philosophical issues of the post-Reformation period. As a result, poems which explore these issues reveal a great deal about the dynamic relations between theological commitment, poetic practice, and faith as felt experience in the period.

The theological complexity and poetic vitality that are characteristic of many Renaissance accounts of sacred grief are made possible by the way religious sorrow operates within Christian thought as a discourse rather than just as a theme. In early modern England, as in Christian culture more broadly, religious grief is not simply one or another affective state; it is a set of discursive resources which allow writers to express the implications that theological commitments have on the lived experience of faith. Thus, while it may not be shocking to discover that early modern poems on devout sorrow engage questions about salvation or soteriology, it is surprising to learn that such poems also address questions of identity and difference, time and finitude, Eucharistic presence, the gendering of devotion, the nature of testimony, and how one predicates God. Yet all of these determinative issues, and others, get addressed in early modern poetry through the lens of religious sorrow. Properly understood, devout sorrow is less an emotional state than it is a language – a grammar of tears, so to speak.[1]

And like any language spoken for 1,600 years across many countries, the language of Christian sorrow developed various dialects – the differences among them becoming most significant within western Christianity in the post-Reformation period. The language of sacred sorrow becomes increasingly complicated in the wake of post-Reformation conflict, not only through Reformation debates over justification but also through the development of competing literary and artistic traditions. In the post-Reformation era, the art of interpreting one's sorrow can be excruciatingly complex as competing doctrines and literary – exegetical traditions collide and intersect. Poems about Christian sorrow are often theologically contentious because poets seek to understand "holy mourning" within one rather than another theological or devotional code; or, more radically, poems can be contentious because they interrogate rather than passively versify traditions of religious sorrow, sometimes demystifying them, sometimes mourning their passing, sometimes expressing their enormous power. In other cases, poems can be creatively syncretic, drawing together doctrines and genres normally thought to be antithetical to one another. As a result of shifting religious contexts, and the contests of meaning taking place between them, one of the primary tasks of early modern religious poetry is to give expression to the complexity of devout grief as an experience while, in most cases, seeking to work towards a coherent interpretation of it.[2] It is a key claim of this book that the poetry of religious sorrow derives much of its literary power from this complex and dynamic theological context. Given the doctrinally charged nature of religious sorrow, poems on the topic reveal a great deal about their authors' theological preoccupations, their oftentimes agonistic relationship to previous poets or traditions, and about the lived experience of early modern faith.

The conceptual flexibility of devout sorrow as a discourse, rather than a set of static affects, rests on the way it is viewed as a particular form of communication – the way it is understood as a key component of what Augustine calls *homo significans*. The Latin emblematist Herman Hugo encapsulates this point in his 1624 work, *Pia Desideria*, when he declares: "My longing sighs a mystick Language prove."[3] According to this widely held view, religiously mediated sorrow is not one species of emotion among others, but rather it is the most elemental form in which a suppliant's relationship to God is "set forth." In other words, devout sorrow is understood in early modern English poetry, and religious culture more generally, primarily as a mode of divine communication and only secondarily as an autonomous psycho-physiological experience. That is to say, the emotional dimension of devout sorrow as a set of personal "feeling tones" is subordinated to the intersubjective dimensions of sorrow as a sacred language. John Hayward articulates this view in his 1623 treatise, *Davids Tears*, when he asserts that "teares are the language of heaven; they speake strongly to God, hee heareth them well ... Therefore ... whensoever I sin, I will write my supplication for pardon with tears."[4] By depicting religious grief as a "language," early modern culture insisted on the dialogical nature of the phenomenon. In a state of sacred grief, Hugo and Hayward imply, one is speaking and being spoken to, one is both calling and being called; and the conversation taking place is thought to be more important than any other conversation one will ever have, for it expresses nothing less than the status of one's soul. Bearing such a linguistic view of religious grief in mind, the title of this book refers not only to poetic depictions of religious sorrow, but also to the way that devout grief is understood in the period *as* a kind of "divine poetry," as a "grammar," revealing – at the level of affect – what Luther calls "the Alien Word."

The significance of devout sorrow as a discourse reflects its enormous conceptual and historical complexity. As a theological concept and a devotional theme, devout grief emerges out of a rich history of scriptural, literary, devotional, exegetical, iconographical, and doctrinal traditions. This complexity provided early modern poets with a sophisticated language for expressing the increasingly complicated experience of sorrow itself. As well, the discourse of holy mourning offered the necessary resources for reflecting on the most significant issues of the post-Reformation period, not only those issues directly affecting the *ordu salutis*, but also basic theological questions about the relation between the human and the divine. In this way, post-Reformation controversies helped shape how poets predicate the relation between the orders of nature and grace – giving rise, in the process, to the kinds of intertextual relations with previous poets and traditions which occur in and between works such as George Herbert's *The Temple* and Richard Crashaw's *Steps to the Temple*.

2 CORINTHIANS 7

The practice of employing holy mourning as a medium for addressing theological questions is made possible by the way godly sorrow is first theorized by St. Paul. Virtually all post-scriptural depictions of devout sorrow, be they penitential or Christological, owe something to the modality of sorrow St. Paul speaks of in 2 Corinthians 7. In this passage, Paul begins the long process of theorizing many of the Old Testament exhortations to holy sorrow in Christian terms.[5] Thus in order to understand the literary and cultural significance of poetic depictions of godly grief in Renaissance England, it is first necessary to see how Christian exegetes interpret the concept of godly sorrow that Paul forwards.

In the second letter to the Corinthians 7:9–11, St. Paul justifies the sadness he inspired in his auditors in a previous letter by distinguishing between two kinds of sorrow: one that is according to God and one that is according to the world:

Now I rejoice, not that ye were made sorry, but that ye sorrowed to repentance: for ye were made sorry after a godly manner, that ye might receive damage by us in nothing. For godly sorrow worketh repentance to salvation not to be repented of: but the sorrow of the world worketh death. For behold this selfsame thing, that ye sorrowed after a godly sort, what carefulness it wrought in you, yea, *what* clearing of yourselves, yea, *what* indignation, yea, *what* fear, yea *what* vehement desire, yea, *what* zeal, yea *what* revenge!

From patristic commentaries to Reformation exegeses, St. Paul's distinction between two fundamental modalities of sorrow is not understood as deciding between two emotions or sensations (like pain or anger), but between two distinct ways of attuning oneself to God – two different orientations toward the Word. As a result, the distinction functions as much more than a static opposition between emotions; it serves as a medium for addressing different existential comportments. In *The City of God*, for example, Augustine distinguishes between Christian and Stoical disciplines by claiming that for pagan philosophers such as Cicero the wise man cannot be sad, while the wise Christian is defined by the way he "laments what he ought to be" but is not.[6] Adducing 2 Corinthians 7, Augustine argues that grief is not simply an affect, but a way of making oneself available to oneself as an object of knowledge. According to Augustine's model of the Christian subject, a supplicant knows herself as a Christian by knowing that God knows the character of her sadness.

Like Augustine, John Chrysostom offered a highly influential account of the way Paul "philosophizeth" about sacred sorrow or *penthos*.[7] The Greek father placed particular emphasis on the existential implications of 2 Corinthians 7, suggesting that godly sorrow reveals the basic modalities of Christian experience as such. According to Chrysostom, godly sorrow reveals the states of care and fear which produce a "clearing" of the soul, a vindication on the order of a verbally expressed defense or *apologia*. The *apologia* of the soul that occurs through godly sorrow grounds the general view of devout melancholy as a language. Through this *apologia*, the Christian undergoes a radical change in how he experiences himself as an object of God's gaze and judgment:

"For behold" [Paul] saith, "this self-same thing, that ye were made sorry after a godly sort, what earnest care it wrought in you" ... Then he speaks of the certain tokens of that carefulness; "Yea," what "clearing of yourselves," towards me. "Yea, what indignation" against him that had sinned. "Yea, what fear." (ver. II) For so great carefulness and very speedy reformation was the part of men who feared exceedingly ... "Yea, what longing," that towards me. "Yea, what zeal."[8]

Augustine's and Chrysostom's views of the Christian soul as essentially sorrowful in nature get richly developed in medieval traditions of affective piety. Medieval practices are often characterized by the way they express the experience of God's love as complexly bound up with conflicting emotions of joy and sorrow, emotions which counter-intuitively coexist at one and the same moment. This combination of opposing feelings in one state led the late fifth-century commentator John Climacus to coin the neologism *charmolypi* or joy-sorrow as a way of denoting *penthos*.[9] Such terms denote the way that godly sorrow was thought to inscribe the inscrutable paradoxes of Christian faith, particularly the simultaneous coexistence of God in man. From such a perspective, one understands the mysteries of incarnationist thought at the level of affect rather than just at the level of cognition. According to the eleventh-century commentator John of Fecamp, for example, the excessive abundance of God's love often expresses itself as weeping, thereby revealing the soul's claim to grace through an affectively mediated form of divine proclamation as in the following petition for tears: "give me a visible sign of your love, a wet fountain of continually flowing tears, that these very tears also may clearly proclaim your love to me and that they may say how much my soul loves you since because of too much sweetness of your love, my soul cannot keep itself from tears."[10] In such accounts, tears are a virtual form of *kerygma* – a proclamation of the divine will whose excessive force overflows the soul's limited ability to contain or bear the overpresence of *amor Dei*.

Early modern conceptions of devout grief come in the wake of such patristic and medieval responses to 2 Corinthians 7. John Donne, for example, develops the epistemological implications that Augustine and Chrysostom see in Paul's thought when he claims that devout grief works on the soul as though the sorrowing soul were "a window, through which [God] may see a wet heart through a dry eye" (*SD* 6.49). Viewed this way, godly sorrow is a means of deepening one's sense of being an object of the deity's gaze – as in James 4:9–10: "Be afflicted, and mourn, and weep ... Humble yourselves in the sight of the Lord, and he shall lift you up." For Donne, this phenomenon of feeling oneself "in the sight of the Lord" is profoundly and unknowably mysterious. As a result, he adds "wonder" to the end of Paul's "chain of Affections," emphasizing that godly sorrow is a primary means by which God communicates himself to the human soul:

according to that chaine of Affections which the Apostle makes ... godly sorrow brings a sinner to a care; He is no longer carelesse, negligent of his wayes; and that care to a clearing of himselfe, not to cleare himselfe by way of excuse, or disguise, but to cleare himselfe by way of physick, by humble confession; and then that clearing brings him to an indignation, to a kind of holy scorne, and wonder, how that tentation could work so. (*SD* 8.206)

By placing wonder at the end of Paul's "chain of Affections," Donne conforms to the longstanding view that devout melancholy "is subject to the law of the secret."[11] The opacity of godly sorrow as a phenomenon leads Donne to describe it as a "tentation" or spiritual trial leading to a wondrous recognition of the limits of human understanding and thus to a deepened sense of what lies beyond and before such understanding.

The mysteriousness of godly sorrow that Donne acknowledges both causes and results from the way the Christian subject is thought to be carried away by godly sorrow's transformative force, its reorienting power. In the experience of such sorrow, the supplicant is taken into areas of experience that have nothing, or little, to do with intention. One does not generally will godly sorrow into happening any more than one wills oneself to fall in love. It happens to us, more than because of us. At best, one prepares for it, readying oneself for its arrival so as to be appropriately hospitable should it come. This is what is meant by the common idea that godly sorrow is a gift, a *donum lacrimarum* or *gratia lacrimarum*. The exact nature of this gift constitutes a central crux of post-Reformation thought: Can such a gift be refused or lost? Does its reception lead to an intrinsic transformation of the soul or does it signal how God extrinsically perceives the soul? And if such a gift brings one closer to God, how does the process work exactly? How, for example, does it alter one's experience of time? If one does not directly will godly sorrow into happening, in what sense, if any, does it involve a retrospective choice? And what is the temporal modality of retrospective "choosing" exactly? Such questions exert significant pressure on both the rhetorical forms and devotional/theological themes of early modern religious poetry.

KENOSIS

From early Christianity on, the vindication of the soul by means of godly sorrow occurs through another kind of "clearing" than the *apologia* that Paul speaks of in 2 Corinthians 7. Godly sorrow is also thought to work by emptying the soul in a way that imitates Christ's kenosis in Philippians 2:7, his voiding of his divinity during the Incarnation: "God emptied [*ekenosen*] himself, taking the form of a servant."[12] Donne links the work of godly sorrow expressed in Corinthians to the ethos of self-emptying predicated on Philippians when he declares that

my holy tears, made holy in his Blood that gives them a tincture, and my holy sighs, made holy in that Spirit that breathes them in me, have worn out my Marble Heart, that is, the Marbleness of my heart, and emptied the room of that former heart, and so given God a *Vacuity*, a new place to create a new heart in. (*SD* 9.177)

This emptying of the soul through godly sorrow is understood by Donne and other influential commentators not just as a purification in the sense of a moral cleansing, but also as a change in one's existential relation to and conceptual reorientation towards God. According to such accounts of Paul, godly sorrow empties the Christian soul so that a fundamental reconstitution of being and thus a new way of perceiving the world can occur. Godly sorrow is thus bound up with the work of the negative in two closely related senses: it destroys the old, worldly person, clearing the way for a regenerate soul; and in doing so, it renders palpable the abyssal difference between human and divine, even as it draws them together. In other words, godly sorrow deepens the Christian's sensitivity to the otherness of God as a way of generating a paradoxical form of intimacy with him. In many early modern poems on godly sorrow, as in many exegetical commentaries, this process of coming to know God by not knowing him occurs through the work of the negative, through the grammatical operations of negation. As a result, godly sorrow is understood first and foremost as a mystery of grace, a "tentation" that is believed to be one of the most intimate and determinative encounters with the will of God. The notion that godly sorrow performs the work of the negative makes it an ideal concept for exploring how the difference between human and divine is felt as a lived experience rather than as an abstract postulate. Through the kenotic language of godly sorrow, the grammar of tears is thought to signify God's presence within the soul while, at the same time, deepening one's experience of his radical difference from all forms of empirical apprehension.

The communicative dimensions of godly sorrow make possible the wide range of discursive uses to which it is put in early modern poetry. Because godly sorrow is a dynamic concept with theological, epistemological, literary, psycho-sociological, and ethical consequences, it functions as a nodal point or key *topos* through which poets address other doctrinal and literary issues which might not seem directly related to it. The articulation of these consequences in early modern poetry and the agon between poets and traditions that occurs in the process are the subjects of this book.

That important intellectual work gets carried out in discussions of godly sorrow is evinced by John Donne's extraordinary sermon on John 11:35 "Jesus Wept." In this sermon, Donne sees Christly sorrow as requiring a more radical conception of identity than the one offered by scholasticism: "To conceive true sorrow and true joy, are things not onely contiguous, but continuall; they doe not onely touch and follow one another in a certain succession, Joy assuredly after sorrow, but they consist together, they are all one, Joy and Sorrow. *My tears have been my meat day and night*, saies *David*" (*SD* 4.343). In this passage, Donne flouts the Aristotelian principle of identity that A is not not A that Thomas Aquinas uses in order to account for the paradox of pleasurable grief. According to Aquinas, remembering sad things "causes pleasure, not in so far as sad things are the contrary of pleasurable, but in so far as one is now delivered from them."[13] Sadness and joy may coexist accidentally, says Aquinas, but they cannot coincide substantially. Despite his deep sympathies with Aquinas, Donne insists that godly sorrow cannot be understood through Aristotelian logic or the mediations of time; it is grasped through the paradoxes of incarnation or not at all. Donne thus sees godly sorrow as a sensation in which the mysteries of the Incarnation are acknowledged at the level of affective experience rather than known through cognitive apprehension. By offering a more radically paradoxical account of godly sorrow than that offered by the categories of the *via antiqua*, Donne presents what is, in effect, a Protestant deepening of the kind of paradoxical thinking visible in medieval monastic traditions – the sort of thinking that led Climacus to coin the term *charmolypi*. For Donne, as for Luther and the monastic tradition in which the German Reformer was first schooled, godly sorrow is an incarnationist language that speaks the Christian paradoxes which confound human thought.

To put this another way, godly sorrow is a discourse that allows writers to theorize how the relationships between divine and mundane worlds are registered at the level of affect. According to Nicetas Stethatos, for example, writing in the early Greek tradition, godly sorrow both reveals and works to overcome the disjunctions between flesh and spirit. Devout tears, he insists, are gateways between the human and the divine:

Tears are placed as a frontier for the mind between corporeity and spirituality, between the state of passion and the state of purity. As long as one has not received this gift [of tears], the work of his service remains in the outward man and there is no way that he can acquire even the smallest sense of the service hidden in the spiritual man. But when he begins to leave the corporeity of this world and to pass into the realm which is within visible nature, he will immediately arrive at this grace of tears. From the very first stage of this hidden life his tears will begin, and they will lead him to the perfect love of God. And when he arrives there he will have such an abundance of them that he will drink them with his food and drink, so perpetual and profuse are they. That is a certain sign for the mind of its withdrawal from this world and of its perception of the spiritual world.[14]

Godly sorrow is thus a liminal site; it deepens the Christian's awareness of the mortality of the flesh as a paradoxical way of opening a path beyond it. In this respect, holy mourning names the affective modalities of repentance – the emotional dynamics of re-orientating the subject from a worldly to a spiritual comportment, from a visible to an invisible reality. These dynamics are understood as the linguistic means by which one establishes a relation with the radical interiority of a God who is, as Augustine says, "more inward than my most inward part, higher than the highest element within me" (*interior intimo meo et superior summo meo*).[15]

In the wake of post-Reformation controversy, the process of knowing oneself as a Christian subject through the communicative power of godly sorrow is opened to reinvention and question. The poetry of religious sorrow in early modern England participates in this opening of the question of what it means to experience oneself as a subject of faith through the medium of holy affects. Poets such as Herbert, Donne, and Marvell help reinvent the language of godly sorrow for a culture that is highly aware of, and is thus wrestling over, its many dialects.

COMPUNCTION

Throughout the middle ages and Renaissance, the change in existential orientation identified with godly sorrow often goes by the name "compunction," which Origen defines as a "lasting affliction of the soul fed by the consciousness of sin and by the traces it leaves in the soul."[16] According to Gérard Vallée, monastic conceptions of *compunctio* constitute a key bridge between medieval and Reformation cultures insofar as monastic doctrines of compunction closely relate to Luther's notion of *Anfechtung* or spiritual tribulations testing the status of one's soul. This bridge between medieval and Reformation devotional cultures is primarily located, Vallée claims, in "a certain quality of the experience of God … that type of experience [which] emphasizes the passive element in man's relation to God and [which] underlines the fact that man is being acted upon from outside." In such an experience, "God's action predominates, disconcerting man and spurring him on."[17] Vallée's assertion is borne out by a key similarity in both Protestant and Catholic poems on godly sorrow in early modern England: almost all poems on the topic emphasize kenotic passivity as the experiential attitude proper to the reception of justifying grace; one must undergo a pricking, broaching, or wounding of the heart before anything salvific can follow.

While Protestant and Catholic poets share this emphasis on kenotic passivity, there are important doctrinal and formal differences between them. These differences arise from the very proximity between a certain post-Tridentine Catholic view which asserts that the gift of compunction must be passively accepted in order to be salvific, and a certain Protestant view which says that such receptive passivity is an irrevocable sign of grace. Such subtle, but nonetheless significant, differences give rise to struggles between competing doctrines and literary traditions – struggles that take place within single poems as well as between and among poems. Writing in the shadow of nuanced theological polemic, seventeenth-century religious poets develop new ways of thinking about godly sorrow as a language. Seeking to accommodate the unprecedented doctrinal and devotional complexities of a post-Reformation world, early modern religious poets in England expand and change the formal strategies used for expressing and interpreting devout melancholy. One of the claims this book makes is that the complex theological history subtending the many "sighs and tears" we find in the devotional verse of Herbert, Southwell, and Donne, as well as in less devotional works such as *Richard II*, *Venus and Adonis*, and *Paradise Lost*, endows the poetic conventions informing such works with doctrinal and experiential density that is often over-looked. If we wish to understand how Renaissance poets "think with tears," we must attend more carefully to how depictions of godly and ungodly sorrow serve as a way of addressing the most doctrinally pro-vocative issues in post-Reformation England. By doing so, we will begin grasping how poetic accounts of religious sorrow focus some of the most crucial dilemmas facing early modern subjects of faith.

PSALM 42 AND THE TRANSLATION OF GRIEF

As several of the passages we have seen indicate, the biblical psalms provide much of the vocabulary informing the early modern lexicon of godly sorrow. This is especially true of poetic depictions of devout grief in the period. While the seven Penitential Psalms are important sources for Renaissance accounts of holy mourning, Psalm 42 appears to play an even more important role.[18] The influence of Psalm 42 on discourses of godly sorrow goes back at least as far as chapter 7 of John Climacus' discussion of the *donum lacrimarum* in *The Ladder of Divine Ascent* (which opens with a sequence that glosses the psalm in the context of 2 Corinthians 7) and continues at least until the Reformation.[19] The reasons for Psalm 42's influence on Reformation religious culture are evinced by John Durant's

1653 sermon on *Spiritual Dejection*, when Durant takes it as an example of the non-transparent nature of David's grief, the potentially ambiguous character of the psalmist's complaint. Durant addresses the opacity of David's grief by asking: "*After what manner* ie., what kind of sorrow is this that fils thee? Is it the sorrow of faith, or of despaire?"[20] Unlike the Penitential Psalms, David's grief in Psalm 42 appears to be more explicitly occasioned by worldly concerns about status and political power than about his own sins. Durant's use of the psalm thus reflects the Geneva Bible's sense that David's grief in the psalm is incomplete and thus not without ambiguity, as implied by the gloss of the final verse which states that "David did not overcome at once, to teach us to be constant, for as much as God will certainly deliver his."[21] As a result of this incompleteness, Psalm 42 was interpreted as enacting how difficult it is sometimes to distinguish between modalities of grief that work salvation and those that do not.

Psalm 42 thus provided exegetes and poets with a way of addressing the kind of question posed in the anonymous Calvinist treatise *Compunction or the Pricking of Heart* (1648): "how shall I know whether my sorrow be for my sin, and fault, or for the punishment of it either felt or feared?" The distinction here is between a filial fear of offending God's majesty that signals election and a servile fear of being punished that denotes reprobation. The remarkable answer this treatise gives to the question demonstrates how godly sorrow mediates problems of sincerity as well as salvation, of subjectivity as well as soteriology. More precisely, the following anecdote discloses how in early modern England the discourse of godly sorrow renders ideas of sincerity, intention, and interiority more complex than the standard dichotomy of inward state and outward show can accommodate:

Many herein being like one *Polus* an Actor, who being to act a sorrowfull part on the stage, to move him thereunto, had secretly conveyed into a corner of the Stage, his fathers (or some dear friends) Urne, in which were the ashes of the deceased, on which whiles he looked, his sorrow was so much the more excited; only with this difference, he being to fain sorrow, came thus to act it truly, and truly to mourn: these while they pretend to sorrow truly for their sin, do it but in seeming for sin, but truly for the punishment of it, on which their eie is chiefly set.[22]

The object lesson here is a counter-intuitive one. The elect actor is led to a true mourning through a gift that is in excess of his intentions and which can thus come upon him without apparent cause, even when a cause appears visible; the reprobate sinner, on the other hand, may intend to mourn properly but cannot do so because the necessary gift is lacking. In other words, the actor's intention to give the appearance of sincerity for the sake of a theatrical performance has no causal relation to the authenticity of his grief in a soteriological sense, just as the reprobate's desire to properly mourn his sins has no determinative meaning for how such mourning will be received by God. In this scenario, a radical divide pertains not just between inward state and outward appearance, but between subjective intention and soteriological outcome – between what one means to say and what one is heard by God as actually saying.

In the Protestant context of this treatise, the author is working out the existential and interpretive implications of Luther's view of the *aliena vita*, the idea that the Christian lives a "double life: my own, which is natural or animate; and an alien life, that of Christ in me."[23] This distinction gives rise to the play of difference between intention and meaning that the Polus anecdote expresses. This difference, it is important to note, is far more radical than any dichotomy between inward state and outward show can accommodate because it is a difference that rests not simply on a gap between emotional reality and verbal expression, but on a more fundamental separation of conscious intention and the Word's immanent otherness. What is at issue here is not simply the failure of an outward language to express an inward reality, but the irrevocable difference between two forms of intentionality: one fleshly and one spiritual.

This gap between human life and Christ's alien life in the human soul accounts for the difference between intention and significance – between the desire for godly sorrow and its authentic realization – that underlies the confounding ending of George Herbert's "Affliction I": "Ah my dear God! though I am clean forgot, / Let me not love thee, if I love thee not" (65–66). However one makes precise sense of this paradoxical ending, the speaker's perception of a possible gap between his intent to love and the actual authenticity of his love is a function of the Protestant notion that Christ's "alien life" within the soul exceeds the speaker's agency as a worldly creature. If his love is authentic, it is because of the work performed by the Alien Word in his soul, not because of anything "his" soul does. To look at this another way, the speaker's confusion over the status of his love constitutes a somewhat bewildered response to the notion that the orthodox English Protestant is accounted or imputed righteous by God extrinsically, rather than having earned such righteousness intrinsically. As a result of this view, the Christian subject is, in Luther's words, "unknowingly righteous and knowingly unrighteous, sinners in fact but righteous in hope."[24] In this economy of justification, the soul is a signifier that appears one way when viewed from the point of view of the flesh and another way when viewed from the oblique angle of the spirit. If the soul is, as Augustine says, a *signum translatum* or thing acting as a sign, it signifies differently, according to Reformers, depending on whom it is acting as a sign for. By experiencing his love as a sign denoting the status of his soul, which is, in turn, a sign whose meaning is not intrinsic but is determined by God's extrinsic judgment, Herbert's speaker is caught in a play of signification not of his own authoring. Yet despite finding himself in a story not of his own making, Herbert's speaker wants to maintain a certain authorial intention over his love as a way of influencing his salvation.[25] This residual desire to make his soul say what he wants it to say leads to the slippage between the speaker's agency and God's agency at the end of "Affliction I": the speaker cannot conceptualize nor actuate the absence of agency implied by orthodox Protestant conceptions of justification. He clings to agency in the realm of justification even in the very gesture of acknowledging that he must relinquish it. As a result, it is not clear who is doing the forgetting and who is being forgotten; nor is it clear where his love ends and God's begins. Herbert's speaker is caught in the paradox of trying to intentionally renounce his claim to intention.

This tortured ambiguity results from the speaker's efforts to make sense of what his grief is saying to him exactly. This drama begins most clearly in stanza 5 when the speaker begins to echo the biblical psalmist: "My flesh began unto my soul in pain, / Sicknesses cleave my bones; / Consuming agues dwell in ev'ry vein, / And tune my breath to groans. / Sorrow was all my soul; I scarce believed, / Till grief did tell me roundly, that I lived" (25–30). The first thing to observe here is that his grief is an interlocutor, an other who reveals, despite his incredulity, that he "lived." The rest of the poem turns on what "lived" means here precisely. On one hand, it signifies bare earthly existence, as if the speaker were only aware of being alive through the presence of his afflictions. On the other hand, though, it intimates a life beyond life, as if he were in the midst of experiencing the dialectic of regeneration, where the force of his afflictions works to destroy the old man so as to reveal the presence of grace within the new man. Although the poem remains ambiguous on this point, it opens up the possibility that the meaning of "lived" exceeds the immediate context in which it is uttered and ultimately signifies in relation to an unfolding context of revelation. Like David's grief in Psalm 42, Herbert's afflictions remain opaque and incomplete. His sorrows only become fully legible when we take into account the possible gap between the speaker's intention and the full soteriological meaning of his words as they emerge retrospectively.

The play of difference between meaning and intention at work in the Polus anecdote and in Herbert's "Affliction I" informs the kind of voices often heard in the poetry of religious sorrow in early modern England – especially, though by no means exclusively, Protestant voices. For while such differences between intention and meaning are explicitly thematized and thus more discernible in poetry informed by Calvinist soteriology, such differences still pertain in Arminian or Catholic poems insofar as compunction always requires prevenient grace or the grace requisite to repentance. In Southwell's *St Peters Complaint*, for example, the grace offered to Peter by Christ has the effect of throwing Peter ahead of himself, of putting him into a state of wonder in ways that he does not fully understand and thus sometimes misinterprets. As I argue in Chapter 1, Southwell's poem works by drawing readers' attention to such moments, thereby demanding a critical as well as an empathic response. It is often this gap between intention and significance, between meaning and being, that gives the poetry of tears much of its power of fascination as literature: the poetry of religious sorrow consistently and dramatically draws attention to the way that the soul, which Augustine defines linguistically as an "aenigma" or non-literal sign, is subject to gaps between being and expression. By doing so, the poetry of godly sorrow works to differentiate the soul from God, who perfectly unifies intention and significance, expression and existence. Yet, at the same time that godly sorrow denotes the abyssal gap between the created soul and uncreated God, it simultaneously works to bridge this gap. We can further approach how early modern poetry grapples with the relationship between the soul and God at a time of great theological change by briefly considering a few of the major statements in the exegetical history of Psalm 42. For such a history not only informs the kinds of devotional work that the poetry of religious sorrow performed in early modern England, it also nourishes the literary power such poetry possesses.

St. Augustine offers one of the most philosophically sophisticated readings of Psalm 42 in the exegetical tradition, one that resonates with particular force in Herbert's exploration of godly sorrow in "The Search." For the Bishop of Hippo, as for many others after him, the Psalm articulates the counter-intuitive nature of desire for the uncreated God (in the form of *caritas*) as opposed to desire for created beings (in the form of *cupiditas*). In the experience of *caritas*, the devotee approaches God every time the soul's desire for God increases, every time its longing is enhanced rather than satisfied. Augustine sees this paradox expressed not only in the metaphor of the hart in the opening to the psalm, ("Like as the hart desireth the water-brooks, so longeth my soul after Thee, O God,") but even more revealingly in the image of repentant tears as food in verse 3. For Augustine, David's tears do not satiate his body in the sense that they provide physical relief, but rather they paradoxically nourish the psalmist's soul by reminding him of the enormous distance placed between himself and God by sin – a process requisite to repentance as such. In other words, David's tears are authentic expressions of repentance to the extent that they increase his hunger for God.

More remarkably, Augustine sees verse 3 as raising questions of signification, specifically the question of how one should predicate God. He sees the question at stake in Psalm 42 as being about the difference between the modes of predication proper to the Christian God and those proper to pagan gods. Thus just as Donne is led to a radical notion of identity through a meditation on godly sorrow, so Augustine's reading of David's weeping leads him to a philosophical analysis of how not to approach God:

if a Pagan should say this to me [where is thy God], I cannot retort it upon him, saying, "Where is thine?" inasmuch as he points with his finger to some stone, and says, "Lo, there is my God!" . . . He has found something to point out to the eyes of the flesh; whereas I, on my part, not that I have not a God to show to him, cannot show him what he has no eyes to see. For he indeed could point out to my bodily eyes his God, the Sun; but what eyes hath he to which I might point out the Creator of the Sun?[26]

Augustine here links the psalmist's increasing desire for God at the level of affect with the psalmist's longing to know God at the level of intellectual awareness, observing that both dimensions of Christian experience are paradoxical in ways that confound not only the pagan imagination, but the very idea of reference itself.

Augustine conveys the idea that the subjective attitude of the perceiver alters the appearance or non-appearance of God through a play of accumulating negatives: "ego autem non quasi non habeam quem ostendam, sed non habet ille oculos quibus ostendam" (whereas I, on my part, not that I have not a God to show to him, cannot expose to view what he has no eyes to see).[27] This play of negatives structures Augustine's interpretation of the psalm as a quest for God in the Hebrew sense of *darash*, "to seek" or "to search."[28] In his Christian reading of Psalm 42, Augustine sees David's search as involving not a desire to return to the

Tabernacle as a sanctified building (which is likely the historical meaning of the psalm)[29] but a desire for an ascending movement out of the soul through the act of weeping: "When would my soul attain to that object of its search, which is 'above my soul,' if my soul were not to 'pour itself out above itself'? For were it to rest in itself, it would not see anything beyond itself; and in seeing itself, would not, for all that, see God."[30] This ascending movement occurs through a kind of apophatic process of negation as Augustine paraphrases David's exclamation by remarking that "I seek my God in every corporeal nature, terrestrial or celestial, and find Him not: I seek His substance in my own soul, and I find it not, yet still I have thought on these things, and wishing to 'see the invisible things of my God, being understood by the things made,' I have poured forth my soul above myself, and there remains no longer any being for me to attain to, save my God."[31] In other words, the act of weeping involves a process of dilating the soul to a point at which the soul no longer perceives only its image reflected back to itself from worldly objects, but rather the soul's dilation clears the way for experiencing God. Such experience, Augustine maintains, is not a matter of "seeing," for God cannot be "seen." On the contrary, such experience is more on the order of allowing oneself to experience oneself being seen by God: "His dwelling-place is above my soul; from thence He beholds me; from thence He created me; from thence He directs me and provides for me; from thence he appeals to me, and calls me, and directs me; leads me in the way, and to the end of my way."[32] A peculiarly Christian form of passivity determines the modality of such contemplative perception. One approaches God by carefully delineating how not to approach him. This emptying of the soul is achieved, according to Augustine, by "pouring out my soul above myself" through weeping. The key paradox here is that the self is tricked out of its epistemological limitations through a process of becoming more deeply cognizant of such limitations. This process is kenotic or self-emptying in the sense that by becoming hypersensitive to one's cognitive inability to locate God at the level of created beings one becomes all the more attuned to his transcendent nature at the level of affect. Such a process clears the way for the Christian subject to experience the limited ways in which he participates in the divine nature. Devout sorrow, Augustine claims, allows one to acknowledge God's presence as "secretissime et praesentissime" – as deeply hidden and yet abundantly present.[33] By revealing the paradoxical nature of deity as concealed and yet overpresent, godly sorrow engenders meditation on the modes of predication proper to the divine. Like Hugo, Augustine views godly sorrow as a "mystic language" – a grammar that begins to signify the moment human speech fails to carve out a space adequate to God's alterity.

Calvin interprets Psalm 42 in similarly kenotic terms as Augustine, but he places less emphasis on the soul's role in the ascending or pleromic movement that follows the descending movement of kenosis. For Calvin, the psalm teaches that we "ought to remember in what manner it is that God allures us to himself, and by what means he raises our minds upwards. He does not enjoin us to ascend forthwith into heaven, but, consulting our weakness, he descends to us."[34] The psalm thus enacts the kenotic dynamics of the Incarnation, thereby revealing that this down-ward, humbling motion structures all proper forms of Christian know-ledge, be it self-knowledge or knowledge of God. Luther encapsulates the principle of kenotic knowledge that Calvin sees at work in Psalm 42 when the German Reformer, speaking in the voice of Christ within the context of a commentary on Psalm 32, asserts: "Things must go, not according to your understanding but above your understanding. Submerge yourself in a lack of understanding, and I will give you My understanding. Lack of understanding is real understanding; not knowing where you are going is really knowing where you are going. My understanding makes you without understanding."[35] For Calvin and Luther, as for Protestant culture more broadly, godly sorrow is the means by which this paradoxical knowledge-without-knowledge is revealed to the Christian soul. As Hayward remarks, when godly tears "seeme most pitifull, then they are most powerful: when they seem most forsaken, then they are most victorious."[36] For the young Luther, as for Augustine, Psalm 42 "is a sigh of human nature seeking to enter the Church of God."[37] It is an expression of *synteresis* or the law written on the flesh of the heart rather than on tablets of stone as expressed in Jeremiah 31:33 and Romans 2:15. But rather than expressing the issue in the philosophical terms Augustine employs, or in the systematic manner of Calvin, Luther adopts a more homely tone, writing that "tears refresh the soul above all things, for by them the soul is wonderfully graced and fattened."[38] In both Calvin's and Luther's accounts of the psalm, David's tears are interpreted as having epistemological as well as soteriological dimensions; tears are a paradoxical mode of contemplative knowing as well as an emotional expression of repentance.

George Herbert's poetic dilation of Psalm 42, "The Search," combines Augustine's philosophical sophistication with Luther's homely style. In the process, the poem explores the theological and devotional questions raised by the exegetical tradition's interpretation of Psalm 42 in the context of Pauline sorrow.

"The Search" begins by figuring the speaker in what appears to be an even more dire situation than the psalmist insofar as the "bread" from which Herbert's speaker derives sustenance never "proves," that is, never rises: "Whither, O, whither art thou fled, / My Lord, my Love? / My searches are my daily bread; / Yet never prove" (1–4).[39] The speaker thus begins by confessing that he remains stuck in the kenotic movement of descent, never rising through his tears and never successfully demonstrating his faithfulness. Because his sorrow is as sour as the dough of partially baked bread, it does not function sacramentally; it fails to forge the relationship between the soul and God that is promised by the Eucharistic dimensions of "bread." The speaker fails to locate God's presence at this point because, like Augustine, he begins his search in created things: "the earth ... the sky ... herbs ... stars ..." all of which "deny / That thou art there" (5–13). He even pursues God by means of sighs and groans: "I sent a sigh to seek thee out ... but my scout / Returns in vain" (17, 19–20). After exhausting both the external world of creatures and the internal world of sorrow, the speaker speculates that God has abandoned humanity in favor of some newly created world, only to leave off such a despairing thought and ask again: "Where is my God? what hidden place / Conceals thee still? / What covert dare eclipse thy face? / Is it thy will?" (29–32).

Up until this point, the speaker of "The Search" has pursued God according to the "pagan" modes of thought that Augustine insisted are anathema to Christian knowledge. Continuing to search for God through categories of time and space, the speaker turns to the question of God's will. In the process, he is led to realize the inappropriateness of spatial metaphors for understanding both his grief and the deity inspiring it: "Thy will such a strange distance is, / As that to it / East and West touch, the poles do kiss, / And parallels meet" (41–44). These empirical impossibilities allow a different form of knowing to emerge, the kind of knowing John Durant refers to as "soul-knowing" or "heart-knowing."[40] Such knowing emerges in the following stanza by means of an altered attitude towards the godly sorrow which failed the speaker earlier in the poem: "Since then my grief must be as large, / As is thy space, / Thy distance from me; see my charge, / Lord, see my case" (45–48). The notion that God is reducible to categories of space and time is beginning to break down at this point, and it is beginning to break down through an altered perspective on the meaning of grief. The process of coming to understand that God is "secretissime et praesentissime" occurs in tandem with coming to understand in what sense godly sorrow is a language.

Earlier in the poem, in stanzas 5 and 6, the speaker displayed an active, willful, relation to his grief: "I sent a sigh to seek thee out … I tun'd another (having store) / Into a groan" (17, 21–22). At this earlier point, he presumes that his grief signifies in basically the same way as normal human language, by a movement of intention from a speaker to an external interlocutor. Such an attitude, however, misunderstands both godly sorrow and its key interlocutor. The final stanzas of the poem admit and correct this misprision. In the final stages of the poem, the speaker's attitude changes as he re-interprets his sorrow in the wake of his meditations on God's will as "an entrenching" that "passeth thought" – a fortifying by trenches but also a wounding by means of cutting (37–38). Coming to recognize the paradoxes of strength in weakness, knowledge in non-knowledge, the speaker comes to learn that just as his grief is not be understood in the language of spatial reference, so God is not to be understood as giving himself to be seen as other objects in the world are given to be seen. In other words, the difference between his grief as lived experience and his grief as comprehended by the language of reference helps attune him to the difference between God and human modes of understanding: "my grief must be as large, / As is thy space, / Thy distance from me" (45–47). The speaker is rising above his everyday, empirical, modes of apprehension in the way Augustine speaks of David in Psalm 42. By this point in the poem, the speaker has gained an alternative perspective on his grief – seeing it not in the referential terms he did earlier, but in the oblique terms of faith.

By understanding his grief as a way of being oriented towards God, rather than as a purely subjective feeling-tone, he is now ready for the breakthrough expressed in the final stanza: "as thy absence doth excel / All distance known: / So doth thy nearness bear the bell, / Making two one" (57–60). Recognizing that God's "distance" from his creation is absolute in the sense that he remains totally unknowable through categories of space, the speaker is now able to experience God's "nearness" through faith in the Incarnation which made man and God, one. His godly grief opens him to recognizing both the spiritual proximity and the cognitive distance between himself and God. He thus comes to understand his relationship to God as characterized by distance and intimacy through a renewed perspective on his grief. What ultimately emerges in the process is not a spatial widening of his grief, but an understanding of the principle Donne expresses when he says that God "is absent when I doe not discerne his presence."[41] In other words, Herbert's speaker comes to appreciate the Lutheran idea that "God becomes God and changes in accordance with the change in our feeling toward Him."[42] Grief eventually helps Herbert's speaker discern God's presence as strangely dependent on his own attitude towards the divine, precisely because what appears "subjective" is not entirely his own, is not "proper" to him as a discrete being. Godly sorrow breaks down simple distinctions between subjective and objective, self and other, familiar and alien. By following the implications of this breakdown of distinctions, the speaker of "The Search" finds traces of the Word in his grief.

While these traces emerge for the speaker through a conceptually and temporally linear process – that is they emerge for the speaker *in time* – they were actually visible from the very start in the gap between the speaker's intended meaning and the implied soteriological meaning of the key word "prove." The initial failure of the speaker's searches to "prove" suggest that they are like unleavened bread, which in 1 Corinthians 5:7–8 is a symbol, following Exodus 12, of sincerity and truth. Warning the overly proud Corinthians that they are "puffed up, and have not ... mourned," St. Paul exhorts his auditors to "Purge out ... the old leaven, that ye may be a new lump, as ye are unleavened. For even Christ our passover is sacrificed for us." From the speaker's initial perspective, then, the verb "prove" indicates an absence of having been tried or tested. From another point of view – one opened up by the poem's unfolding of God's presence in time – "prove" indicates that the speaker's searches bear within them the very promise of success that he is initially unable to discern. In other words, the very absence of having been "puffed up" is a paradoxical sign of humility and thus of God's presence within him. In this way, the holy spirit becomes accessible within the very language of affliction – in the way its paradoxes signify in excess of the speaker's awareness and intention. Godly sorrow thus also breaks down distinctions between now and then, beginning and ending, up and down, as well as between what the speaker thinks he says and what, from the perspective of a fuller revelation, he is actually heard to say. The ostensible absence of Eucharistic promise in the speaker's searches in stanza 1 may also call attention, albeit implicitly, to the use of unleavened bread in the Anglican Communion, as advocated, against precisian critics, by Richard Hooker in *The Laws of Ecclesiastical Polity*.[43]

Herbert's speaker comes to recognize the paradoxical nature of God's presence by adopting a passive attitude towards his sorrow. Rather than sending his sighs and groans out like an arrow to a target, he begins listening to them as messages sent to him from somewhere other than himself. It is thus not accurate to say, as Arnold Stein does, that in "The

Search" "the expression of personal feeling is subordinate to the effort to express God's nature and the relation of God and man."[44] Rather, the process of searching out God's nature occasions, and is occasioned by, an alternative perspective on godly sorrow as something much more than "personal feeling." Godly sorrow emerges out of the *aliena vita* and as such it speaks in a voice more inward and more other than the speaker's own. As a result, "The Search" moves towards the view of godly sorrow explicitly articulated in the final stanza of "Affliction II" – the view that godly grief is really Christ's suffering meeting itself within the human soul: "Thou art my grief alone, / Thou Lord conceal it not; and as thou art / All my delight, so all my smart" (11–13). The proper search for God by means of godly sorrow does not entail moving out of the self in a directional or spatial sense, but rather it involves a shift of perspective on the very sorrow instigating the search itself. This shift in perspective allows the speaker to understand the lesson Herbert reaches in "Affliction III": "that thou wast in the grief, / To guide and govern it to my relief ... / making it to be / A point of honour now to grieve in me" (2–3, 14–15). The movement towards a better understanding of godly sorrow in "The Search" recapitulates the same general movement that takes place through the five Affliction poems which are essential to the overall design of *The Temple* – its basic spiritual motions from God's perceived absence to his realized, but paradoxical, presence.[45]

Through the experience of godly sorrow the speaker of "The Search" arrives at the Protestant thesis that God is understood not in his substance, not in his *being*, which would be far too overwhelming, but in what Luther identifies as "the category of relation." Indeed, the crucial point for understanding the place of godly sorrow in Protestant poetics that emerges in relation to "The Search" is that for Herbert, as for other Reformation poets such as Andrew Marvell, this "category of relation" pertains not just to the syntactic relations between spoken or written words but also between the relations of human and divine experiences of grief. Insofar as godly sorrow is a language, it is understood by Protestant poets as participating in the relational contexts by which God is experienced and predicated. By recognizing that his "grief must be as large, / As is thy space" and that "Christ is all my smart," Herbert's speaker acknowledges the radical gap between any grief that he can call "his" and the infinite grief that belongs to God. By acknowledging this profound difference, the speaker clears the way for understanding that he participates in Christ insofar as Christ's infinite grief continues in and through his own afflictions: "Thy life on earth was grief, and thou art still / Constant unto it, making it to be / A point of honour now to grieve in me, / And in thy members suffer ill" ("Affliction III"

13–16). As the pun on "members" implies, the speaker's grief exceeds purely personal or subjective experience; it forges a communal bond linking the soul to the mystical body of Christ. As Heather Asals has shown, the experience of affliction leads Herbert's speaker to the understanding Augustine articulates in his commentary on the Psalms when the Bishop of Hippo explains how "from the time that the body of Christ groans being in afflictions, until the end of the world, when afflictions pass away, that man groaneth and calleth upon God: and each one of us after his measure hath his part in the cry of the whole body."[46] Because God suffers and because he, the speaker, shares in this divine suffering, they are contiguously one – bonded together under the sign of sorrow. Just as God reveals and conceals himself in the image of the Christ on the cross, so he reveals and conceals himself in the afflictions of godly sorrow. As Herbert says in "Ephes. 4:30": "Almighty God doth grieve, he puts on sense" (16). Such afflictions not only are "sense" but they also make "sense."

The linguistic dimension of godly sorrow that the speaker of Herbert's "The Search" discovers is often overlooked in literary-critical accounts of Protestant poetics. I would thus add godly affect to the linguistic dimensions of Protestant thought that Georgia B. Christopher outlines when she observes that

Reformation rhetoric [is] almost impossible to label and fix in a doctrinal taxonomy, because often the same biblical phrase is used to describe the God who speaks, the language that conveys the divine word, the Spirit who underlines it, and the heart (or faith) that hears the word. This unity of deed makes the puritan esthetic, as it were, a "syntactical" esthetic. Spiritual mystery resided, not in *being*, but in grasping, via words, the *relation* between beings: Luther held that God was to be encountered, not in his substance, which was unknowable and terrifying, but "in the category of relation." In Milton's tradition, the Spirit clings, not to bodies, but to language itself and skips like Ariel along the tucks and gaps in the syntactical chain forming metaphor, metonymy, and other tropes.[47]

While the Spirit may not cling to bodies in Protestant thought, it does cling to affects. Or, more precisely, the Spirit resides in those alien affects that belong to the double-life of the reformed soul. What Herbert's "The Search" helps us see is that divine sorrow participates in the grammatical possibilities by which the Word is thought to be communicated. Moreover, these modes of divine communication are an important part of faith as lived and as literary experience in early modern English Protestantism, both its conformist and nonconformist strains.

When we look at Crashaw's "The Weeper" in Chapter 2 we will see that while godly sorrow is no less linguistic for the Arminian Crashaw than it is for the Calvinist Herbert, it signifies in an alternative way. Rather than expressing a relational context in which God is encountered through the differential "tucks and gaps" between metaphor and metonymy, Crashaw's divine sorrow speaks, in its most resounding voice, isomorphically or iconically. As we shall see, what is at issue in the differences between Crashaw and Herbert are two alternative "metaphysics of grief" and two related but theologically distinct poetic strategies for accommodating them.

Returning to exegeses of Psalm 42, it is worth observing that the fully mature perspective on grief that Herbert's speaker arrives at in the conclusion to "The Search" opens up the kind of double-vision Donne describes in relation to verse 3 of the psalm:

My tears have been my meat day and night, saies *David* ... It is a Grammaticall note of a Jesuit ... That when it is said *Tempus cantus, The time of singing is come,* it might as well be rendered out of the Hebrew, *Tempus plorationis, The time of weeping is come*; And when it is said, *Nomini tuo cantabo, Lord I will sing unto thy Name,* it might be as well rendered out of the Hebrew, *Plorabo, I will weepe, I will sacrifice my teares unto thy Name.* So equall, so indifferent a thing is it, when we come to godly sorrow, whether we call it sorrow or joy, weeping or singing. (*SD* 4.343).

What Donne explicitly sermonizes, Herbert's "The Search" presents as the product of an arduous pilgrimage. As in Augustine's homilies, this pilgrimage occurs through a certain movement of the negative – a movement away from worldly objects to that which lies before and beyond them, to that which is wholly alien and yet most oneself. Through this movement, the suppliant conforms to the image of Christ as the "man of sorrows" – the man who, in the litotes of Isaiah 53, is "acquainted with grief."

As this brief overview of Psalm 42's exegetical history suggests, the psalm form discloses the kinds of ambiguities and questions one encounters in the lived experience of godly sorrow as a determinative category of early modern Christian experience. Such ambiguities and questions are intensified in the post-Reformation context as individual writers negotiate the differences within and between varying devotional, literary, and soteriological regimes. Moreover, Psalm 42 discloses how the poem as medium both thematizes and enacts the question of how one predicates the experience of faith and the divine other grounding it. Along with the problem of signification, Psalm 42 also discloses how godly sorrow as a discourse raises epistemological questions such as how can one know oneself as a subject of faith? Or, how does the experience of holy mourning mediate one's relation to a God who is radically immanent and terrifyingly transcendent? While all of the questions believed to be raised by Psalm 42 in the exegetical tradition traced here are inherent to New Testament thought, they take on extraordinary weight in the context of Reformation debates over salvation, reason, grace, scriptural exegesis, and related issues. This book examines some of the most significant ways in which poets think through the questions thought to be raised by Psalm 42's expression of godly sorrow as a medium of communication between the human and the divine.

CRITICAL CONTEXTS

Given the predominant theological climate of the English Church from the 1590s through the 1620s, most critical studies of the poetry of religious grief have focused on the anxiety inspired by the Calvinist doctrine of predestination. The works of Peter I. Kaufman and John Stachniewski, for example, explain the perceived rise in religious melancholy as an inadvertent effect of Calvinist theories of grace, a thesis I shall develop in Chapters 5 and 6.[48] While such readings explain some of the negative effects of Calvinism on the lived experience of faith in England, they only account for a small part of a much larger literary and theological picture. To begin with, studies which focus on Calvinist despair leave out, by definition, the lugubrious body of Catholic and Laudian poetry in the period, particularly the large number of poems dealing with the sorrows of Mary Magdalene and the Virgin Mary that constitute part of the focus in Chapters 1, 2, and 4. By excluding Catholic and Laudian poetry this way, such studies generally overlook the conversations that take place within and between conformist and nonconformist, Catholic and Protestant, poems in early modern England. Thus one of the things that distinguishes my study from previous analyses of repentance and despair is that I consider the importance of intertextual relations between works by Shakespeare and Southwell, Crashaw and Herbert, Marvell and Crashaw, among others. And while there has been a recent resurgence of interest in English Catholic poetry, much of this criticism still remains descriptive rather than analytical – attempting to recover and celebrate rather than critically examine the literature. Recent exceptions to this include Debora Shuger's, *The Renaissance Bible*, Patricia Phillippy's *Women, Death and Literature in Post-Reformation England*, and Alison Shell's *Catholicism, Controversy, and the English Literary Imagination, 1558–1660*.[49] While each of these studies considers, to one extent or another, the relationship between literary depictions of religious grief and the shifting theological climate of early modern England, none offers a sustained analysis of poetic representations of the discourse of devout melancholy. Moreover, none of them proposes that the poetry of religious sorrow from Southwell to Milton constitutes a discrete discourse in which the experience of holy mourning serves as the medium for addressing the theological, philosophical, and literary problems which most vexed early modern culture.

And while Marjory E. Lange's, *Telling Tears in the English Renaissance*, surveys the different kinds of weeping one finds in Renaissance literature and the varying genres in which these depictions occur, she does not explain the conceptual power discourses of godly sorrow wielded in the period. In short, godly sorrow constitutes the one modality of Renaissance melancholy that remains largely unexplored in literary criticism. This, despite the fact that it is more ubiquitous and arguably more culturally significant than melancholy which is not explicitly religious in orientation.[50]

OUTLINE

Each of the following six chapters presents an analysis of at least one major tradition informing the predication of devout grief in English Renaissance verse, from the "poetry of penitential tears" tradition popularized by Robert Southwell (Chapters 1, 2, 3), to the iconography of the Virgin Mary's sorrow (Chapter 4), to the sacralization of Petrarchism in the religious lyric (Chapter 5), to the relations between despair and biblical typology (Chapter 6). The first three chapters explain the cultural work and poetic force of the poetry of tears tradition by tracing its development from Robert Southwell's introduction of the genre into England with *St Peters Complaint*, to Shakespeare's and Milton's henceforth unacknowledged parodies of the tradition in *Richard II*, *Venus and Adonis*, and *Paradise Lost*, to Crashaw's counter-reformation of it in "The Weeper," to Marvell's summation of the genre in the Protestant terms he inherits from Herbert's *The Temple*. Chapter 4 offers a deeper consideration of the gendered nature of the grammar of tears implicit in the first three chapters. I do this by analyzing Aemilia Lanyer's depiction of the Virgin Mary and her fashioning of herself as gifted with a "sad delight" – gifted, that is, with an intuitive understanding of the paradoxes of incarnation and kenosis. Chapters 5 and 6 then consider how John Donne fully realizes the modes of critical reading demanded by Southwell and the poetry of tears tradition more broadly.

In the final two chapters, I explain how Donne brings the gap between intention and meaning that is generated by the discourse of godly sorrow to its literary-historical apex. In Chapter 5 I demonstrate how Donne copes with the terrifying overpresence of *amor Dei* by applying lessons he learned about the psychic defensiveness inherent in Petrarchan grief while writing the *Songs and Sonets* to the devotional contexts of his religious verse. In this respect, I show how Donne offers the most psychologically perspicacious translation of Petrarchan tropes into a devotional register since Robert Southwell's challenge to English poets to turn from courtly to divine love in the early 1590s. Chapter 6 continues the analysis of Donne's depiction of the phenomenology of holy mourning as an experience in which there can be a radical distinction between meaning and intention, by analyzing the theme of spiritual death in *An Anatomy of the World. The First Anniversary.*

The last chapter draws together many of the major themes discussed throughout the book. In particular, it considers how religious grief can be dangerously excessive and how this excessiveness can offer a tempting, if perversely, pleasurable aesthetic and psychological experience. In *An Anatomy of the World*, as in many other poems I consider, the excessiveness of worldly grief consists of feeling belated – feeling as though one has become posthumous to oneself in a variety of senses. The strange power Donne's poem possesses lies in how it makes the dark attraction of despair vividly available to the reader in the very process of seeking a way out of its vortex. Among other things, the modalities of grief put into motion by Donne's poem further reveal how discourses of religious sorrow provide a language for expressing the experiential dimensions of desacralization, which I discuss in Chapters 1 and 3 in the context of Shakespeare's *Richard II* and *Venus and Adonis*. The final chapter also returns to the question of how the language of devout grief is gendered in the period, as evinced by virtually all of the poems considered in the book – especially and most thoughtfully in Lanyer's *Salve Deus*. To sum up, then, if early modern poets depict religious grief as a kind of language, this book is an attempt to understand what, exactly, can be said within the limits of its grammar and to what literary and religious ends.

NOTES

1 For a related thesis see Joan Hartwig, "Tears as Way of Seeing," in Claude J. Summers and Ted-Larry Pebworth (eds.), *On the Celebrated and Neglected Poems of Andrew Marvell* (Columbia: University of Missouri Press, 1992), pp. 70–85. See Chapter 3 for a discussion of Hartwig's essay.

2 For an authoritative discussion of the differences between Protestant and Catholic depictions of devout grief through readings of Herbert's poetry, see Richard Strier, "Herbert and Tears," *English Literary History* 46 (1979), 221–47. Among other things, Chapters 1 through 3 of this book develop Strier's general view that there are differences in form and theology between Protestant and Catholic tear literature.

3 Herman Hugo, *Pia Desideria*, trans. Edmund Arwaker (London, 1686), B2.

4 John Hayward, *Davids Tears* (London, 1623), pp. 65–66.

5 For a discussion of the scriptural passages exhorting believers to sorrow, see Sandra J. McEntire, *The Doctrine of Compunction in Medieval England: Holy Tears* (Lewiston, NY: Mellen Press, 1990), pp. 11–31.

6 St. Augustine, *The City of God*, trans. Henry Bettenson (New York: Penguin, 1984), p. 561 (book 14, chapter 8).

7 St. John Chrysostom, *Saint Chrysostom: Homilies on the Epistles of Paul to the Corinthians*, Nicene and Post-Nicene Fathers of the Christian Church, ed. Philip Schaff, vol. XII, ser. 1 (Grand Rapids, MI: Wm. B. Eerdmans, 1997), p. 350.

8 Ibid., p. 351.

9 For a discussion of Climacus' term see Bishop Kallistos Ware, "'An Obscure Matter': The Mystery of Tears in Orthodox Spirituality," in Kimberley Christine Patton and John Stratton Hawley (eds.), *Holy Tears: Religious Weeping in the Religious Traditions* (Princeton, NJ: Princeton University Press, 2006), p. 247.

10 Cited in McEntire, *Doctrine*, p. 54.

11 Irénée Hausherr, *Penthos: The Doctrine of Compunction in the Christian East* (Kalamazoo, MI: Cistercian Publications, 1982), p. 138.

12 *New Oxford Annotated Bible* (New York: Oxford University Press, 2001).

13 Thomas Aquinas, *Summa Theologiae*, trans. Eric D'Arcy (New York: Blackfriars and McGraw-Hill, 1975), vol. 20, q. 32, a. 4.

14 Cited in Hausherr, *Penthos*, pp. 145–46.

15 St. Augustine, *Confessions*, trans. Henry Chadwick (Oxford: Oxford University Press, 1998), book 3, section 6, paragraph 11.

16 Cited in Gérard Vallée, "Luther and Monastic Theology. Notes on Anfechtung and compunctio," *Archive for Reformation History* 75 (1985), 290–91.

17 Ibid., 296.

18 For studies of the influence of psalms on early modern English literary culture, see Rivkah Zim, *English Metrical Psalms: Poetry as Praise and Prayer 1535–1601* (Cambridge: Cambridge University Press, 1987) and Hannibal Hamlin, *Psalm Culture and Early Modern English Literature* (Cambridge: Cambridge University Press, 2004).

19 John Climacus, *The Ladder of Divine Ascent*, trans. Colm Luibheid and Norman Russell (New York: Paulist Press, 1982), p. 136: "Mourning which is according to God is a melancholy of the soul, a disposition of an anguished heart that passionately seeks what it thirsts for, and when it fails to attain it, pursues it diligently and follows behind it lamenting bitterly."

20 John Durant, *Comfort and Counsel for Dejected Souls or A Treatise Concerning Spiritual Dejection* (London, 1653), B3. See also, Christopher Love, *The Dejected Souls Cure* (London, 1657).

21 *Geneva Bible. A Facsimile of the 1560 Edition* (Madison: University of Wisconsin Press, 1969).

22 R. J. Doctor of Divinity, *Compunction or Pricking of Heart* (London, 1648), p. 193.

23 Cited in Georgia B. Christopher, *Milton and the Science of the Saints* (Princeton, NJ: Princeton University Press, 1982), p. 44.

24 Cited in Brian Cummings, *The Literary Culture of the Reformation: Grammar and Grace* (Oxford: Oxford University Press, 2002), p. 98. For an extended reading of Herbert in the context of this Reformation thesis see Richard Strier, *Love Known: Theology and Experience in George Herbert's Poetry* (Chicago: University of Chicago Press, 1983).

25 For Augustine's sign theory see St. Augustine, *On the Trinity: Books 8–15*, ed. Gareth B. Matthews and trans. Stephen McKenna (Cambridge: Cambridge University Press, 2002). My comments on Augustine's conception of the soul and his language theory are indebted to Marcia L. Colish, *The Mirror of Language: A Study in the Medieval Theory of Knowledge* (New Haven, CT: Yale University Press, 1968), chapter 1.

26 St. Augustine, *Expositions on the Book of Psalms*, Nicene and Post-Nicene Fathers of the Christian Church, ed. Philip Schaff, vol. VIII, ser. 1 (Grand Rapids, MI: Wm. B. Eerdmans, 1996), p. 133.

27 Sancti Augustini, "Enarrationes in Psalmos," in *Opera Omnia 42 vols.*, ed. D. A. B. Caillau (Paris: Paul Mellier, 1842), vol. 8, pp. 238–39. I have varied the previous translation.

28 For a discussion of this psalmic motif see Helmer Ringgren, *The Faith of the Psalmists* (Philadelphia, PA: Fortress Press, 1963), p. 3.

29 See ibid., pp. 1–19.

30 Augustine, *Expositions on the Book of Psalms*, p. 133.

31 Ibid., p. 134.

32 Ibid.

33 Augustine *Confessions*, book 1, section 4, paragraph 4. My translation.

34 Jean Calvin, *Commentary on the Book of Psalms*, trans. James Anderson, 5 vols. (Grand Rapids, MI: Wm. B. Eerdmans, 1949), vol. 2, p. 129.

35 Martin Luther, *Luther's Works*, ed. Jaroslav Pelikan, vol. 14, ed. Jaroslav Pelikan (Saint Louis, MO: Concordia, 1958), p. 152. Luther's emphasis on kenosis as a submerging of human knowledge, rather than an annihilation of it, is consistent with John L. Klause's, "George Herbert, *Kenosis*, and the Whole Truth," in Morton W. Bloomfield (ed.), *Allegory, Myth, and Symbol* (Cambridge, MA: Harvard University Press, 1981), pp. 209–26.

36 Hayward, *Davids Tears*, p. 66.

37 Martin Luther, *Luther's Works*, ed. Jaroslav Pelikan, vol. 10, ed. Hilton C. Oswald (Saint Louis, MO: Concordia, 1974), p. 197.

38 Ibid., p. 200.

39 Slater makes the observation about the word "prove" as a verb meaning "rise." See Slater's *Herbert*, pp. 471–72.

40 Durant, *Comfort and Counsel*, B3.

41 Cited in Gale H. Carrithers, Jr., *Donne at Sermons: A Christian Existential World* (Albany: State University of New York Press, 1972), p. 32.

42 Cited in Christopher, *Milton*, p. 115.

43 See Richard Hooker, *Of the Lawes of Ecclesiasticall Politie Eight Bookes* (London, 1604), book 4, chapter 10.

44 Arnold Stein, *George Herbert's Lyrics* (Baltimore, MD: Johns Hopkins Press, 1968), p. 93.

45 For a discussion of how the Affliction series organizes *The Temple* along these lines, see Daniel Rubey, "The Poet and the Christian Community: Herbert's Affliction Poems and the Structure of the Temple," *Studies in English Literature 1500–1900* 20.1 (Winter 1980), 105–23. See also, Heather A. R. Asals, *Equivocal Predication: George Herbert's Way to God* (Toronto: University of Toronto Press, 1981), p. 45 and Louis Martz, "The Action of Grief in Herbert's 'The Church,'" in Margo Swiss and David A. Kent (eds.), *Speaking Grief in English Literary Culture: Shakespeare to Milton* (Pittsburgh, PA: Duquesne University Press, 2002), pp. 119–35.

46 See Asals, *Equivocal Predication*, pp. 45–46. My account of Herbert's Reformation theology differs significantly from Asals' essentially Laudian view of him.

47 Christopher, *Milton*, p. 21.

48 See Peter Iver Kaufman, *Prayer, Despair, and Drama: Elizabethan Introspection* (Urbana, IL: University of Illinois Press, 1996) and John Stachniewski, *The Persecutory Imagination: English Puritanism and the Literature of Religious Despair* (Oxford: Clarendon Press, 1991). See Chapter 4 for a discussion of Stachniewski. See also, Martha Tuck Rozett, *The Doctrine of Election and the Emergence of Elizabethan Tragedy* (Princeton, NJ: Princeton University Press, 1984).

49 See Debora Shuger, *The Renaissance Bible: Scholarship, Sacrifice, and Subjectivity* (Berkeley: University of California Press, 1994); Patricia Phillippy, *Women, Death and Literature in Post-Reformation England* (Cambridge: Cambridge University Press, 2002) and Alison Shell, *Catholicism, Controversy, and the English Literary Imagination, 1558–1660* (Cambridge: Cambridge University Press, 1999). See Chapter 1 for discussions of Shell and Phillippy.

50 See Marjory E. Lange, *Telling Tears in the English Renaissance* (Leiden: Brill, 1996).

CHAPTER I

The poetry of tears and the ghost of Robert Southwell in Shakespeare's Richard II and Milton's Paradise Lost

With the support of the underground Catholic network operating between England and the Continent, the twenty-four-year-old Robert Southwell made his way back to England under the cover of night sometime in July of 1586. Having completed his training in the Jesuit Order at the English College in Rome, Southwell returned to England with his Jesuit superior, Henry Garnet, as part of the clandestine Catholic mission.[1] One of the things that Southwell brought with him from Italy as an important part of this mission was an accomplished ability to write in the "literature of tears" tradition – the Counter-Reformation practice of depicting the experience of repentance in varying prose and verse forms. Despite its Jesuit origins in England, this tradition would come to exercise a significant influence on English literary history, leading to the widespread popularity of "tear literature" in the 1590s and inspiring various "tear poems" throughout the seventeenth century.[2] While Southwell's influence on the popularity of tear poetry in England has been well documented, our understanding of the philosophical and theological work performed by the tradition is still lacking, particularly the work performed by parodies of the poetry of tears. Seeking to demonstrate the cultural work performed by the poetry of tears and aiming to account for its power of fascination as a genre, the following three chapters trace some of the revisionings of the tradition popularized by Southwell in works by Shakespeare, Milton, Herbert, Crashaw, Marvell, and others. In each of these three chapters, I demonstrate how the poetry of tears tradition constitutes a way of "thinking with tears" – how this genre becomes a medium for expressing the experience of sorrow within the theologically shifting contexts of Renaissance England.

In this chapter, I show how Shakespeare, Milton, and others enhance the possibilities for depicting despair by parodying the genre that Southwell introduced into England. More precisely, I show how

Shakespeare and Milton articulate what it feels like for the despairing soul to wrestle with questions about God, conscience, and finitude, by inverting some of the key conventions of the poetry of tears tradition. In *Richard II*, Shakespeare parodies the tradition popularized by Southwell in order to express the poet-king's experience of desacralization in the play's final act; while in *Paradise Lost*, Milton demonically inverts the penitential orientations that speakers in the literature of tears tradition often adopt as a way of articulating Satan's solipsism, specifically his failed repentance in Book 4 and his wondrous-terror before Eden in Book 9. *Richard II* and *Paradise Lost* are thus parodies of the Catholic literature of tears tradition in Gérard Genette's sense that they are hypertexts which rewrite hypotexts in more or less polemical ways.[3]

In the process of parodying Southwell, Shakespeare and Milton both represent the Catholic tradition of tear poetry as characterized by belatedness: while Shakespeare repositions the tradition of tear poetry within a desacralized world where it no longer appears meaningful, Milton performs a metaleptic reversal in which Southwell's Ignatian mode appears as a demonic expression of Satan's tyrannical imagination. Through these parodies of Southwell, both *Richard II* and *Paradise Lost* express what despair feels like as lived experience in post-Reformation England.

St. Peters Complaint

In order to demonstrate how Milton's characterization of Satan and Shakespeare's depiction of Richard II unfold by inverting the tropes and conventions of the Catholic literature of tears tradition, and in order to anticipate subsequent analyses of how this tradition gets reworked in Crashaw, Marvell, and Donne, we must first consider two influential features of Southwell's depiction of godly sorrow: the modes of critical reading demanded by his verse, particularly the mode demanded by the gap between intention and meaning, and his use of apostrophic poetics. By tracing these two features of Southwell's poetry, we will begin to see how poetic depictions of religious sorrow express the experiential dimensions of repentance and how these dimensions are complicated by confessional and doctrinal conflict.

Southwell's most popular and influential poem in the tradition is *St. Peters Complaint*, which circulated for years in manuscript form before going through fifteen editions between 1595 and 1640, with only two of them being published by underground Catholic presses.[4] In the prefatory address to the reader, Southwell sketches the modes of interpretation he expects from a reader:

> Dear eie that daynest to let fall a looke,
> On these sad memories of Peters plaintes:
> Muse not to see some mud in cleerest brooke,
> They once were brittle mould, that now are Saintes.
> Their weakenesse is no warrant to offend:
> Learne by their faultes, what in thine owne to mend. (1–6)

Warning his readers not to expect St. Peter, the "rock" (*petrus*) of the Catholic Church, to be preternaturally virtuous, Southwell informs his readers that Peter was even more sinful than they themselves are: "If equities even-hand the ballance held, / Where *Peters* sinnes and ours were made the weightes: / Ounce, for his Dramme: Pound, for his Ounce we yeeld" (7–9). By encouraging his readers to learn by the faults of saints, Southwell indicates that his devotional poems often require highly active, even critical, responses. Southwell is not advocating uncritical identification with Peter, as though the reader should become wholly absorbed by the penitential motions of the text – in the way one might in the case of a hymn or a liturgically oriented poem such as the conclusion to Crashaw's "The Flaming Heart." Although the text is designed to have readers participate in Peter's penitential experience, it is also asking its reader to interpret the saint's errors, those that are explicitly thematized as well as those expressed in gaps, suppressed allegories, inadvertent allusions, and in other oblique ways. In this respect, Peter's characterization conforms to Aristotelian peripety, not just in the sense of a recognition leading to a transformation from one mode of being to another, but also in the sense of a displacement from one form of meaning to another. Peripety can involve irony in the sense that a character may say something, the full meaning of which remains obscure to him. Such irony is crucial to Peter's characterization, to the way he says more than he intends. Such irony is also central to many subsequent depictions of godly sorrow in seventeenth-century English poetry, most significantly Herbert's and Donne's.[5]

Throughout the poem, Peter is figured as offering a model for analyzing the deceitful motions of the fallen soul. In the "anatomy of sin" sequence, for example (665–90), Peter both interprets and enacts the self-deceiving motions of transgression: "Bewitching evill, that hides death in deceites, / Still borrowing lying shapes to maske thy face, / Now know I the deciphring of thy sleightes" (667–69). Southwell is asking his reader to listen to his saintly speakers in much the same way that an exercitant listen to his sins in the Ignatian Meditations, especially in Colloquy I of The Third Exercise, where the exercitant is instructed to "feel an interior knowledge of sins and an abhorrence for them" so that he "may feel a sense of the disorder in [his] actions."[6] An "interior knowledge" of sins implies an awareness of the kinds of self-deceit implicit within sin; it indicates an awareness of how one suppresses one's sinful actions for narcissistic gain or what Peter calls "sugred poyson" (671). Southwell's poems train readers to listen for such internal "disorder" by having his saints enact such sin even as they analyze and confess it. By enacting as well as confessing sin, Southwell's poems possess a rhetorical dimension that is necessarily absent from both his and Ignatius' *Spiritual Exercises*. His poems demand an active, even critical, response from readers. Through characterization by peripety, readers are being attuned to the gap between intention and meaning; they are being encouraged to recognize how the Spirit signifies in excess of Peter's knowledge as the saint tarries with the double motions of compunction, its oscillations between sin and grace.

The mode of critically aware devotional reading which Southwell demands, along with the general Jesuit principle that poets should suppress their own idiosyncratically personal feelings in favor of generally shared spiritual experience,[7] helps explain why he chooses what is essentially a dramatic monologue form for many poems, especially those dealing with the godly sorrow of a saint. Such a form demands that one read "symptomatically," listening for absences or gaps that complete the meaning. For example, in the seventh stanza of *St Peters Complaint*, Peter depicts his state of near-despair as matter for "everlasting complaint," moaning that "My threnes an endlesse Alphabet do find, / Beyond the panges which *Jeremy* doth paint. / That eyes with errours may just measure keepe: / Most teares I wish that have most cause to weepe" (38–41). As Southwell's recent editors indicate, the reference to an alphabet of sorrow is an allusion to the practice in elegiac Hebrew poetry, such as the Lamentations of Jeremiah, to begin each stanza with one of the twenty-two letters of the Hebrew alphabet.[8] What they do not mention and what Peter himself is overlooking at this moment of near-total grief, however, is the typological truth lurking in his own figure. For Southwell's audience(s), the "sad subject" of Peter's sin is greater than Jeremiah's in its capacity to inspire grief, but it is also greater in its capacity to inspire joy as implied by the submerged *figural* sense of Peter's allusion to Hebrew lamentation. What Peter alludes to, without recognizing, is Jesus' role as the anti-type of all anti-types: the Name of Jesus is believed to announce God's grace beyond the limits of the Law – beyond the limits of Jeremiah's Old Testament "Alphabet." The Hebrew equivalent of "Jesus" – Joshua – contains all the letters of the pronounceable form of the Tetragrammaton and is thus thought to speak beyond a purely Old Testament language, just as Christ is the anti-type speaking beyond all Old Testament types promising his arrival. While this focus on typology belies the thesis that *figural* interpretation is somehow distinctly Protestant, it also shows Peter in the process of learning to speak in the language of tears.

Peter comes to recognize the typological legibility of his sorrow later in the poem once he is caught in the gaze of Christ – a gaze that is initially self-shattering but eventually self-constituting: "In time, O Lord, thine eyes with mine did meet, / In them I read the ruines of my fall" (325–26). Captured by the transformative gaze of Jesus, Peter interprets his sorrow within the typological pattern that remained latent at the beginning of the poem:

> O Bethelem cisternes, *Davids* most desire,
> From which my sinnes like fierce Philistims [*sic*] keepe,
> To fetch your drops what champion should I hire,
> That I therein my withered heart may steepe.
> I would not shed them like that holy king,
> His were but tipes, these are the figured thing. (427–32)

Peter experiences his repentance in and through the signifying force of his tears; they disclose the typological structure of revelation to him, allowing him to make explicit the *figural* dimensions of his grief that remained latent in his initial complaint: "Twice *Moyses* wand did strike the Horebb rocke, / Ere stony veynes would yeeld their christall blood: / Thy eyes, one looke servd as an onely knocke, / To make my heart gush out a weeping floode" (439–42). At this crucial juncture in the poem, the moment right at which the apostrophe to Christ's eyes ends, Peter begins to recognize himself as a figure within the story of Christ. He implicitly identifies himself as the rock upon which Christ will build his Church (Matthew 16:18) and as the stone that will weep out in tears in Jesus' Name (Luke 19:40). In other words, Peter begins to recognize himself as the typological fulfillment of the rock that Moses strikes in Exodus 17:6 in order to feed the Israelites. He is coming to know how he is *in* the universal story of salvation that he is personally living out. Through this process, Peter undergoes the second baptism of repentance as his name positions him within the story of all things. He experiences himself as the object of

Christ's desire and as a subject within the Christian narrative of salvation that he has been living without fully knowing it. Like the speaker of Herbert's "Affliction I," Peter's grief plays a significant role in his coming to understand himself as a *signum translatum*, whose meaning can only be known in relation to the Word. But unlike Herbert's speaker, Peter must do more than recognize Christ in his grief; he must willingly assume this sign as denoting his true destiny.

By interpreting the implicit and explicit typological allusions working themselves out in the poem, readers are being encouraged to recognize their own place in the story of Peter's compunction. As Peter is in the process of being made subject to Christ, so Southwell's readers are being encouraged to become subject to Christ through Peter. This is where the communal dimension of Peter's grief as participating in Christ's grief emerges. By recognizing Peter as the first apostolic model of true compunction before Christ, a reader testifies to the authority of the communion of saints – thereby activating the poem's distinctly Catholic features.[9] Read this way, Southwell's Peter becomes more than an individual sinner, he emerges as the first Apostle of the Church and thus a symbol of the Catholic Communion as such. We can thus see that Southwell chooses to write extensively on Peter (as well as Magdalene) not only because the Apostle provides a way of embodying Counter-Reformation models of repentance, but also because he provides a way of expressing the terror and self-sacrifice inherent in bearing witness to Christ, thus offering recusants a realistic model of the type of suffering expected of them in the context of Protestant England. The painful drama of Peter's witnessing of Christ at a moment of personal danger unfolds through an active and critical mode of interpretation that is alert to the significance of suppressed allusions and contexts.

Southwell demands the same kind of critical reading in the conclusion to "Marie Magdalens Complaint at Christs Death," a dramatic monologue on Mary's experience at the empty tomb in John 20. The poem opens with Magdalene in a state of living death, what the Petrarchists would call a *viva morte*: "my life from life is parted" (1). By the second stanza, she insists that her personal feeling of posthumous existence should extend to the universe itself: "Seely starres must needes leave shining" (7). What most startlingly characterizes the poem is that this state of near-despair, what Southwell calls in his prose treatise on the same theme "fatal oblivion," is never resolved.[10] The poem ends with Magdalene affirming her love but failing to arrive at the kind of knowledge of faith that Peter expresses in the final stanzas through his prayer for

Christ's mercy. In other words, Magdalene does not undergo peripety in the sense of a radical change in existential comportment. She stays at the tomb not out of faith, but out of the exemplary love she displays – a love whose power is all the more impressive because it is not predicated on a knowledge of the Resurrection and the faith that flows from it: "Spitefull speare, that breakst this prison, / Seate of all felicitie, / Working thus, with double treason, / Loves and lifes deliverie: / Though my life thou drav'st away, / Maugre thee my love shall stay" (37–42). The poem ends without an account of the Resurrection, leaving out the consolation offered by the *Noli me tangere* scene that one would expect, as in the case of Southwell's *Marie Magdalens Funeral Teares*. The unresolved structure of the poem demands further meditation by the reader, rather than a full identification with Magdalene.

Following Counter-Reformation traditions of representing Magdalene as the *Beata Dilectrix Christi*, Southwell's reader is being encouraged to recognize in her an exemplary love of Christ, but an incompletely realized faith. In this respect, Southwell's Magdalene is prone to what the Anglican minister William Annand calls Mary's tendency for "religious error" – her penchant for making interpretive mistakes predicated on openness and love rather than selfishness.[11] Because Mary commits such errors, readers are being encouraged to "Learne by [her] faultes": they must supply the homiletic dimension missing from the poem. In the case of Magdalene's and Peter's complaints, then, devotional reading consists of a form of critical reading – one attentive to gaps, silences, and inadvertent meanings.

Some of the most important "silences" one must listen for in Southwell's poems are the suppressed allegories and oblique references to the experience of Catholics in England – a rhetorical practice Milton will put to work for opposite confessional ends in *Paradise Lost*.[12] The importance of listening for suppressed allegories in Southwell's poetry is thematized in the title of "A Vale of Teares." As Heather Arvidson has observed, the title of Southwell's poem refers reflexively to its own strategies of "veiling" its topical references. But where Arvidson interprets the title's play of "veils/vales" in the context of Jesuit equivocation, I think it's clear that Southwell is alluding to the poem's allegorical status. While equivocation presumes discontinuous levels of reference expressed through dissembling acts of mental reservation, allegory presumes varying but continuous levels of signification.[13]

First of all, the poem's title derives from the Vulgate's Psalm 83:7: "in valle lacrimarum in loco quem posuit," which the Douai-Rheims translates as "in the vale of tears, in the place which he hath set." The King James translation of this verse actually gives a clearer sense of its overall relevance to Southwell's poem: "Blessed is the man whose strength is in thee: in whose heart are the wayes of them: Who passing through the valley of Baca [tears], make it a well: the raine also filleth the pooles" (84:5–6). This verse encapsulates the poem's penitential motions: the alienated pilgrim confronts a terrifying landscape that is of "arte untoucht" (25) and rather than falling into despair he turns the scene into an occasion of penitential weeping: "Let teares to tunes, and paines to plaints be prest, / And let this be the burdon of thy song" (73–74). What Southwell adds to the psalmic intertext is that the conversion is of a distinctly poetic nature: Southwell's speaker is able to work through his anguish by alchemizing it through verse. In this respect, Southwell's poem is a unique example of the movement from the *valle lacrymarum ad montem Dei* that the Jesuit theologian Robert Bellarmine would later describe in his treatise on holy weeping *De Gemitu Columbae* (The Mourning of the Dove) – the first book of which begins with an analysis of Psalm 83 as exemplifying the necessity of contrition for salvation and which ends with an explanation of the call for weeping in the "Salve Regina": "Ad te clamamus, exsules, filii Evae: ad te suspiramus, gementes et flentes, in hac lacrimarum valle" (To you [Mary], we exiled children of Eve, cry out: to you we sigh, groaning and weeping, in this valley of tears).[14] Given that Protestant texts tend to use the phrase "valley of Baca," rather than "vale of tears," and given the use of the phrase in the "Salve Regina" which is a distinctly Catholic form of prayer, the title of Southwell's poem intimates its devotional allegiances without being overly explicit or polemical.

Southwell's conversion to the poetry of tears takes place in the *valle lacrimarum*, which is depicted in the poem as being of a twofold nature. First, it is a general allegory of the soul alienated in the fallen world of sin. In this respect, the poem is a creative response to the Ignatian *Spiritual Exercises*, specifically the practice of imagining "my whole composite self as if exiled in this valley among brute beasts" in Preamble One of the First Exercise.[15] Secondly, the valley of tears is an allegory of England under oppressive Protestant rule. While this dimension of the poem is oblique, it can be heard when Southwell vaguely alludes to the Jesuit Mission and the clandestine life its priests were forced to lead, specifically the infamous practice of hiding in "priest-holes": "Here christall springs crept out of secret vaine, / Strait finde some envious hole that hides their grace. / Here seared tufts lament the want of raine, / There thunder wracke gives terror

to the place" (49–52). Though the allusions are buried, the reference to
the Jesuits bringing the grace of the Church's sacraments to those in
"want of rain," and thus risking the terror of the "wracke" in the process,
is audible. The association of rain with grace is a common biblical figure,
appearing throughout Southwell's verse as in "Times Goe by Turnes"
which is more clearly about the heretical state of the English Church than
"A Vale of Teares": "THE lopped tree in time may grow againe ... / The
soriest wight may find release of paine, / The dryest soyle sucke in some
moystning shower" (1, 3–4). The conclusion and Alpine setting of "A Vale
of Teares" further suggest that it dramatizes Southwell's own commitment to use poetry as part of his missionary project – a commitment
made within the fiction of the poem during his passage through the Alps
on his return to England from Rome.

The term "vale" in the poem's title refers to not only the "valley" of
tears in Psalm 83, but also reflexively to the "veil" of allegory theorized in
2 Corinthians 3:12–18 – an epistle about pastoral care that is of particular
relevance to much of Southwell's work, especially *Epistle of Comfort* and
St Peters Complaint. In this passage from 2 Corinthians, Paul praises the
"boldness" and courage of the early Christian apostles who derive their
hope from the unveiling of the Word in the person of Christ:

Having therefore such hope, we use much confidence: And not as Moses put a
veil upon his face, that the children of Israel might not steadfastly look on the
face of that which is made void ... But we all beholding the glory of the Lord
with open face, are transformed into the same image from glory to glory, as by
the Spirit of the Lord.[16]

In St. Chrysostom's reading of this passage, the veil obscuring the Hebrews from the Gospel truth lies in the act of reading, not in the Mosaic act
of writing: "[Paul] said not, 'The veil remaineth on the writing,' but 'in
the reading'," implying that "The veil lieth upon their heart."[17] By
evoking the common idea of allegory as a "veil" that is lifted by those with
understanding, Southwell draws attention to the allegorical status of his
own poem. He implicitly distinguishes between those (Catholic) readers
who will unveil the full allegorical meaning of his text from those who will
not, something he also does in "At Home in Heaven," where the alienation of the soul in the body similarly figures the suppression of Catholic
modes of expression in England: "FAIRE soule, how long shall veyles thy
graces shroud? / How long shall this exile with-hold thy right? / When
will thy sunne disperse this mortall cloud, / And give thy gloryes scope to
blaze their light?" (1–4). Moreover, he obliquely identifies the bold men

participating in the Jesuit Mission with the bold apostles Paul celebrates and encourages in 2 Corinthians 3.

The modes of characterization at work in Southwell's lachrymal poetics and the forms of critical reading demanded by them will be fully realized in subsequent devotional writing, especially Donne's *Holy Sonnets* (Chapter 5). Before turning to later instances of tear poetry, though, it is necessary to consider the importance of apostrophe to Southwell's penitential verse, for this figure structures the longest, most influential, and in my estimation, most stunning sequence in *St Peters Complaint*, namely the nineteen-stanza apostrophe to Christ's eyes.

O LIVING MIRRORS: SOUTHWELL'S APOSTROPHE

Given the highly stylized and hyper-conventional nature of the apostrophe to Christ's eyes, it has tended to resist close analysis – tempting us to equate what is common with what is inconsequential. Yet the popularity of this type of scene begs the question of where its power of fascination lies. Nancy Pollard Brown offers something of an answer to this question when she observes that the apostrophe to Christ's eyes is an expression of wonder in the sense expressed in "the fifth point of the Ignatian exercise."[18] Such a meditation calls for

Exclamations of wonder, with intense feeling, as I reflect on the whole range of created beings, how ever have they let me live and kept me alive! ... the heavens, the sun, the moon, the stars and the elements, the fruits, the birds, the fishes, and the animals, how have they kept me alive till now! As for the earth, how has it not opened to engulf me, creating new hells where I might suffer for ever.[19]

While the Ignatian context is certainly at work in Peter's apostrophe, the experience of wonder depicted in the sequence is of a more specific kind than that which Ignatius describes. The specific form of wonder that Southwell expresses derives from the experience of looking at another face and being looked at by it in return – the experience, as St. Paul expresses it, "of seeing face to face."

The experiential dynamics of looking at a human face and being looked at by it in return have been analyzed by the Catholic phenomenologist Jean-Luc Marion. Marion situates this common but potentially wondrous experience in the context of saturated phenomena, or experiences that are not fully absorbed by an intentional consciousness. In such experiences, the beholder does not assimilate the perceived phenomenon into an object given-to-perception but remains subject to it in some respect. By situating Peter's apostrophe in relation to Marion's account of saturated phenomena we can do more than say that Southwell uses an address to a saintly face as a way of expressing repentance as an experience of wonder that opens Peter to the divine otherness of Christ as well as an experience of shame that leads him to conversion; we can describe how the formal properties of this sequence enact the experiential dimensions involved in the specific kind of wonder felt when looking at another human face and being looked at by it in return. Indeed, by situating Southwell in relation to Marion, we will gain significant leverage into the way the poem expresses aspects of Peter's repentance that are irreducible to, if nonetheless consistent with, the Tridentine doctrine of penance. In the final analysis, then, such a contextualization of Southwell's poem will help us understand how *St Peters Complaint* is a rather remarkable account of compunction as an experience of radical finitude – an experience that is articulated through the feelings that scriptural traditions and contemporary phenomenology insist are characteristic of "beholding ... with open face" the face of an other.

The moment that St. Peter experiences *metanoia* – the turning towards Christ and away from worldly attachments – occurs when he is caught in the absolute singularity of "the sight of the Lord": "The matchles eies matchd onely each by other, / Were pleasd on my ill matched eyes to glaunce: / The eye of liquid pearle, the purest mother, / Brochte tears in mine to weepe for my mischaunce" (355–58). The scriptural basis for this type of apostrophe to Christ's eyes is explained in Donne's sermon on Psalm 6: "the *Eye*, is ordinarily taken in the Scriptures, *Pro aspectu*, for the whole face, the looks, the countenance, the ayre of a man; and this ayre, and looks, and countenance, declares the whole habitude, and constitution of the man; As he looks, so he is: So that the *Eye* here, is the whole person" (*SD* 8.204). The apostrophe to Christ's eyes is thus an encounter with Christ's person as manifested through his face. In this respect, Peter's experience of feeling himself being seen by Christ intimates the anagogic experience Paul speaks of in I Corinthians 13:12 when he says that in life "we see through a glass, darkly" but in heaven we shall see "face to face," as well as the experience of full revelation which Paul defines in 2 Corinthians 3:12 as "beholding ... with open face."

Along with this scriptural practice of depicting the entire face as expressed through the eyes, and of envisioning heaven as an experience of seeing God face to face, Southwell's apostrophe also sacralizes the Petrarchan tradition of depicting the lover's gaze as emanating a captivating beam of light as in Donne's "The Ecstasy": "Our eye-beames twisted, and did thred / Our eyes, upon one double string" (7–8). What is notable about Southwell's sacralization of this trope, though, is that Peter's eyes do all the receiving and Christ's all the giving: "In [Christ's eyes] I read the ruines of my fall: / Their chearing raies that made misfortune sweet / Into my guilty thoughts powrde flouds of gall" (326–28). This opening to the apostrophe is a perfect example of the modes of reading and characterization outlined in the prefatory address as Peter feels the "ruines of his fall" in the double sense of the catastrophic effects of his sin as well as the residue or end of the fall itself. This passage thus intimates that in the very moment of compunction lies the promise of satisfaction and grace, as indicated in the paradoxical phrase "misfortune sweet." The oscillations between guilt and comfort, despair and relief, suggest that Peter is at the initial stage of receiving the gift of compunction. Before Peter can actively accept the *donum lacrimarum*, he must first receive it as indicated by the verb "broached," which signifies that Christ's eyes pierce Peter's so as to draw forth liquid. The word "broached" evokes the etymological meaning of *compunctio* as "sting" or "puncture," indicating the prevenient grace that must be accepted before repentance becomes salvific according to post-Tridentine thought. At the moment Christ's eyes "brochte tears" in Peter's, the distinction between Peter and Christ becomes blurred through a chiastic crossing of their eyes and tears: "The matchles eies matchd onely each by other, / Were pleasd on my ill matched eyes to glaunce: / The eye of liquid pearle, the purest mother, / Brochte tears in mine to weepe for my mischaunce" (355–58). This figure complicates any clear sense of whether Peter is crying or whether Christ is crying in Peter. The act of weeping becomes as sacramental as the act of confession itself: Peter comes to know himself as witness by recognizing Christ as the author of his tears.

Having been looked at by Christ, Peter is in the process of being authorized as his witness. Such authorization occurs by having Christ weep in Peter and by having Peter accept this weeping as a divine imprimatur that now identifies him as witness. This sacramental conjoining of Peter and Christ in the act of weeping is theorized two stanzas later through a kind of mirror scene in which Peter comes to know himself as the ideal image reflected back to him in Christ's gaze: "O living mirrours, seeing whom you shew, / Which equall shaddows worthes with shadowed things: / Ye make things nobler then in native hew, / By being shap'd in those life giving springs. / Much more my image in those eyes was grac'd, / Then in my selfe whom sinne and shame defac'd" (367–72). Caught in the interminable gaze of Christ, Peter experiences himself not as an expression of his own intention, but as an ideal image reflected back to him from the point of view afforded by the grace and judgment of

Christ. This mirror scene thus re-envisions Paul's account of the trans-formative nature of beholding Christ with open face in 2 Corinthians 3:18, which in the Vulgate appears as "nos vero omnes revelata facie gloriam Domini speculantes in eandem imaginem transformamur a claritate in claritatem" and which the King James Bible translates as "But we all, with open face beholding as in a glass the glory of the Lord, are changed into the same image from glory to glory." Southwell's depiction of Peter as knowing Christ through his grief is thus an elaborate poeticization of the idea expressed in William Allen's 1582 martyrology that "Jesus ... onely seeth through our miseries."[20] Here again, grief and affliction are the windows through which one knows and is known as a true witness of Christian faith.

The Christ who sends Peter's redeemed image back to the Apostle is not the kenotic, self-emptying divinity of Philippians 2:6–7, but rather this is the self-sufficient Logos of the opening of the Gospel of John; it is the God of the metaphysicians, not the God of the prophets who inter-pellates Peter into the story of salvation: "*All seeing eyes* more worth then all you see, / ... By seeing things, you make things worth the sight. / You seeing, salve, and being seene, delight" (373, 377–78, my emphasis). This mutual gazing makes Peter and Christ appear as Christian counterparts to Ovid's Narcissus and Echo, who are being contrasted throughout this sequence as part of an opposition between Christian inter-mutuality and classical egoism. Such contrasting of Pauline and Ovidian narratives is evinced in Peter's apostrophe of Christ's eyes as "Pooles of *Hesebon* ... / Where Saints rejoyce to glasse their glorious face, / Whose banks make Eccho to the Angels quires" (379, 380–81). While Narcissus looks into the mirror, sees himself, and drowns, Peter looks into Christ, sees his own true image, and is given eternal life. Peter's profound indebtedness to Christ, whose image he echoes, is figured in this sequence by having Christ's eyes continually glorify the things they gaze upon: "Ye make thinges nobler then in native hew, / By being shap'd in those life giving springs" (369–70). This same idea is expressed in the subtle shift from many "Saints" to gloriously singular "face" in the previously cited lines. This shift indicates how Christ unifies the many into the One – changing everything into an image of himself: *transformamur a claritate in clar-itatem*. Southwell is careful, though, not to reproduce the passive voice of 2 Corinthians 3:18, where the beholders are changed rather than helping perform the change (*transformamur*), for such a grammatical shift emphasizes the active role saints play in compunction. This active role of assuming the gift of tears is indicated in Peter's petition for tears which is figured as a paying of debts: "Come sorrowing teares, the ofspring of my griefe, / . . . By you my sinfull debts must be defraide" (463, 466).

The specular dynamics of Southwell's Pauline mirror scene take on a synaesthetic quality as the perspective shifts from a visual to an auditory register with Christ's eyes, which are figured as baths, becoming banks that "Eccho . . . the Angles quires: / An Eccho sweeter in the sole rebound, / Then Angels musick in the fullest sound" (382–84). We get lost in the semantic and synaesthetic complexity of these lines in the same way that Peter loses himself in the excessive and overwhelming richness of Christ's gaze. By accumulating and blending metaphors of vision and hearing, Southwell reproduces in a reader something like the saturated experience of feeling overwhelmed by Christ that Peter himself is undergoing. Mixed metaphor thus works here to create a mimesis of compunction; such figures recreate the penitential experience of wonder that Peter is undergoing so that the text engages us in the saturated experience being described.

In the process of feeling himself being seen by Christ, Peter oscillates between compunction, or the alienating feeling of guilt for his sins, and the awe-full enjoyment of sacramental communion with Christ in and through his tears. His tears continually speak to him of this dialectic, embodying both the alienation of sin and the union with Christ's self-presence promised by absolution. In this way, the highly stylized imagery conveys the phenomenological dimensions of repentance as a dialectical experience characterized by self-division through sin and self-recognition through the absolute self-presence of Christ. But at the heart of Peter's repentance is the specific way he encounters Christ's face as a site of wonder – as disclosing more phenomena than he can process or assimilate. As a poetic topos in this and other works, the apostrophe to Christ's eyes enacts the experiential dimensions involved in the encounter of the other's face as described in Marion's development of Emmanuel Levinas' discussion of the topic. For Marion, a human face shows itself differently than other objects in the world. Faces, he insists, appear as one of the most common forms of saturated phenomena – phenomena in which intuition exceeds intention, in which the sheer abundance of sensory data exceeds the mind's ability to assimilate the experience being given. According to Marion, faces appear differently than almost all other objects in the world because the face can return a gaze and thus can always-already anticipate one's look. Because the face of the other can see one seeing it, the face remains constitutively in excess of interpretation and understanding; a human being's face remains beyond any attempt to constitute it as an object of perception or intention precisely insofar as it can return our gaze, thereby refusing to be taken in the terms imposed on it. According to this analysis, a human face is not experienced as an "object" in the same way as most other objects are.[21]

Taking Magdalene's experience of Christ's face in John 20 as exemplifying this phenomenological principle, Marion offers an account of what it feels like to see "with open face," which reads like a philosophical paraphrase of Peter's apostrophe to Christ in Southwell's poem. For both Southwell and Marion, the experience of seeing and being seen by a human face is characterized by a certain dimension of excess, a sense that such experiences take one to the limit of one's intentional hold over the world:

I do not approach [the face] following my intention, but following its intentionality, because it is the face that asks me ... to renounce any mastery over it, and to distance myself from it – "*noli me tangere!*" ... Thus it is I who submit myself to its point of view and must situate myself in the exact, precise, and unique place where it intends to appear as pure face. An anamorphosis *par excellence* is substituted for the centrifugal intentionality coming from me – a point of view come from another place, which imposes on me its angle of vision.[22]

According to Marion, the other's face remains resistant to interpretation and intention, not because it expresses lack or is poor in phenomena, but because it saturates one's perception, giving more to see in its infinite complexity of expression, history, suffering, love, etc., than can be processed. The other's face evokes wonder or amazement because it produces a saturation of intuition over concept, because it appears in a bedazzling array of signifying forms that resist any effort to constitute it as an object. The dilations on Christ's eyes in the apostrophe convey exactly this experience of oversaturation: "But those unspotted eyes encountered mine, / As spotlesse Sunne doth on the dounghill shine. / Sweet volumes stoarde with learning fit for Saints, / ... Wherein eternall studie never faints, / Still finding all, yet seeking all it findes / How endlesse is your labyrinth of blisse?" (335–37, 339–41). Peter's experience of becoming captured by Christ's eyes is wondrous precisely insofar as the point of view from which Christ sees him remains unapproachable in its oversaturating radiance, as implied when Peter addresses Christ's eyes as "Sunnes, all but your selves in light excelling" (397).

The ever expanding descriptions of Christ's eyes, whose "glaunces are a silent speech, / In cyphred words," seek to enact the inexhaustibility of the experience Peter is undergoing (385–86). Such images conform to the experience of the other's face Marion describes when he says that during such a moment a "counter-look rises up; it escapes my look and envisages me in return – in fact, it sees me first, because it takes the initiative. The look of the other person, precisely because it cannot be looked at, irrupts in the visible."[23] In both Southwell's apostrophe and Marion's phenomenology, the face of the other is experienced as an injunction – a call that cannot ever be fully answered because it appears in excess of any ability to constitute or bind the perceptions themselves. The saturation of Christ's face over and against Peter's ability to assimilate it as an object of intention helps express repentance as an experience in which one is made subject to a power that both precedes and exceeds one's self.

What is ultimately conveyed by the apostrophe to Christ's eyes is the experience of compunction as an experience of finitude in a very specific sense: Peter's experience of compunction entails feeling his limits in the primordial sense given through the structure of the visual field as it takes shape in an encounter with Christ's face as irreducible to objectification. Repentance, then, is not simply figured in the poem as a dialectic between alienation and communion, between guilt and forgiveness; nor does it simply unfold according to the Tridentine sacrament of penance – contrition, confession, satisfaction, absolution; it is also envisioned as a very specific form of wonder – one in which Peter is made hypersensitive to his mortal delimitations through an experience of feeling himself being seen by an other whose look remains unable to be looked at. This hypersensitivity to finitude is what the poem means by compunction as an *experience* of grace.[24]

REWRITING SOUTHWELL

The significant influence of *St Peters Complaint* on later poetry, both sacred and secular, was enhanced by the enormous popularity of Southwell's devotional prose treatise *Marie Magdalens Funeral Teares* – which circulated widely in manuscript form before being published in 1591 and then republished in England nine times and twice abroad before 1634.[25] Both of these texts were praised, imitated, and satirized throughout Elizabethan and Jacobean England. Southwell's depictions of Magdalene before the empty tomb and Peter after his third betrayal of Christ inspired works by fellow Catholics, such as Thomas Lodge and William Alabaster, as well as conforming Protestants, such as Gervase Markham, Giles Fletcher, and William Lithgow. Southwell's work also informs poems by writers whose confessional identity is not easy to identify, such as

Nicholas Breton and John Davies of Hereford. While Southwell was satirized by some English writers for an indecorous mixing of Parnassus' secular muse with the divine muse of Sion, as in the case of Joseph Hall,[26] he was praised by others with avowed envy, as in the case of Ben Jonson.[27] More important for our purposes is the way that Protestant revisionings of Southwell's work tend to efface or occlude the cultural memory of Southwell, thereby deepening the ideological work the state performed by hanging and quartering the young Jesuit in 1594 for treason.

Alison Shell explains this phenomenon when she demonstrates how the preface to Markham's 1601 poem *Marie Magdalens Lamentations* substitutes Spenser in place of the more obviously relevant Southwell. Although Markham's poem is essentially a versification of Southwell's prose homily, Shell explains how its preface positions the poem within the pastoral tradition popularized by Spenser rather than the penitential tradition popularized by Southwell. Alluding to "Collin" Clout, Spenser's poetic *alter ego*, Markham's text "claims the best-respected English writer of religious verse as a character within the fiction ... and in doing so, it erases another pastor, the poet who was primarily responsible for bringing lamentation back into fashion."[28]

What Shell might have gone on to say but didn't, is that Markham rewrites key moments in Southwell's text in order to account for Magdalene's experience at the empty tomb in a more discernibly Protestant manner, further annulling the recusant subtext of Southwell's prose homily.[29] By doing so, Markham's poem exemplifies the kind of theologically invested re-appropriations of Southwell's work that occur in seventeenth-century England. For example, Markham follows both Southwell and Southwell's medieval source text, the pseudo-Origenist, *An Homilie on Mary Magdalene*, in having Magdalene berate herself at the empty tomb for misinterpreting the relation between letter and spirit:

> being too precise to keepe the Law,
> The lawes sweet maker I have thereby lost,
> And bearing to his ceremonies too much awe,
> I misse his sweetest selfe, of far more cost,
>   Sith rather with the Truth I should have beene,
>   Than working that, which but Tipe was seene.[30]

According to Patricia Phillippy, Markham's Magdalene "condemns the dead letter of the law ... according to Protestantism's censure of the 'merely outward signs' of Catholic ceremony." This condemning of Catholic idolatry is communicated through Magdalene's reference to typology that echoes the 1559 *Book of Common Prayer* which "explains the abolishment of Catholic ceremonies by affirming 'Christ's gospel is not a ceremonial law, as much as Moses' law was, but it is a religion to serve God, not in bondage of the figure or shadow, but in the freedom of the spirit.'"[31] Although Phillippy's reading is accurate, she does not recognize that Markham is rewriting Southwell's Counter-Reformation depiction of this scene as well as the medieval version Southwell himself rewrote. In the pseudo-Origenist dilation of John 20, Magdalene is depicted as confusedly grappling with the paradox that by following the law of Jewish mourning rites she has lost "him to whom the lawe it selfe is obediente."[32] Faced with the counter-intuitive reality of Christ's apparent resurrection, Magdalene awkwardly adjusts her understanding of and devotion to Jesus; she begins to mourn the man's physical absence in order to embrace the God's spiritual presence. Magdalene thus functions in the medieval homily as a means of acknowledging the virtue in devotion to Christ's humanity, while privileging worship of his divinity. Southwell's Magdalene forwards a rhetorically similar, though theologically distinct, complaint that "through too much precisenesse in keeping the lawe, I have lost the lawmaker, and by being too scrupulous in observing his ceremonies, I am proved irreligious in loosing himselfe."[33] Southwell's Magdalene thus discovers Counter-Reformation critiques of Protestant literalism, even obliquely referring to the epithet "precisian" in her efforts to understand how Christ transforms the relation between letter and spirit.[34] The godly sorrow of this recusant Magdalene serves as an example of the Ignatian principle that temperance applies even in acts of virtue and devotion. It should be clear then that while Markham closely follows Southwell's text, which closely follows a medieval source, his ostensibly minor emendations to Magdalene's misapprehensions, along with the different reading community to which the work is primarily addressed, have the effect of reversing the theological polemic of Southwell's homily. In this passage and in the work as a whole, Southwell is everywhere and nowhere; he has become more of a ghost than a clearly avowed intertextual presence within the work. This invoking and effacing of the tradition associated with Southwell also occurs in Shakespeare's *Richard II*.

RICHARD II AND THE METAPHYSICS OF GRIEF

While numerous reworkings of Southwell's *Marie Magdalens Funeral Teares* have been documented by literary historians, no one, to my knowledge, has suggested that such a revisioning takes place in the Tower of London scene in Shakespeare's *Richard II* as well as its most likely source text, Samuel Daniel's *The Civil Wars*. Moreover, no one has offered a sustained demonstration of how Shakespeare's *Richard II* informs subsequent forays into the poetry of tears tradition, especially the way in which this tradition constitutes a practice of "thinking with tears." Because Richard's meditations on grief constitute one of the most complex depictions of worldly sorrow in the English Renaissance, later poets, particularly Marvell, develop some of the strategies Shakespeare uses in the play.[35] Given the influence that Shakespeare's play has on the poetry of tears in the early seventeenth century, no analysis of the tradition would be adequate without recognizing the place of *Richard II* within it.

While Shakespeare's interest in Southwell has been documented since the nineteenth century,[36] his place within the poetry of tears tradition is only beginning to come to light. Richard Wilson, for example, has recently developed Christopher Devlin's thesis that Southwell's assertion that *St Peters Complaint* was inspired by a "pagan" poem circulating in England may be a reference to the very popular *Venus and Adonis*. This claim is based on the view that Southwell appears to be berating Shakespeare when the Jesuit complains: "Still finest wits are stilling Venus' rose. / In Paynim toys the sweetest veines are spent : / To Christian works few have their talents lent." Wilson also follows Devlin in asserting that Southwell addressed Shakespeare again in a letter prefacing the 1616 version of *S. Peters Complaint and Mary Magdalens Funerall Tears*. In this letter, Southwell confesses that it was "Master W. S." who "importuned" the publication of *S. Peters Plaint*.[37] More compellingly for my purposes is Devlin's argument that Shakespeare's *Rape of Lucrece*, written in 1593–94 – which is probably a good two years before *Richard II* was composed – echoes *St Peters Complaint* numerous times.[38] These contexts support my thesis that the poet-king's despair in Act 5 of *Richard II* is expressed through a parodic inversion of the literature of tears, particularly the metaphysical variety popularized by Southwell's *Marie Magdalens Funeral Teares* and *St Peters Complaint*.

Shakespeare's tragical history of Richard II offers an account of what it might feel like to undergo an experience of desacralization. In the course of the play Richard moves from an experience of the world as *anima mundi* – a world in which nature responds to human desire, where language is isomorphic with reality, and where his position atop the social order is as natural as the rising of the sun – to an experience of the world as *vanitas mundi* – a world in which nature and language are alienating, where the social order is contingent, and where his predominant mood is one of *taedium vitae* – a weary sense of having overlived himself. One of the more striking features of this desacralizing process involves the shift in Richard's use of language. At moments of despair and desacralization Richard does not, as we might expect, shift from an animating language of analogy, metaphor, and apostrophe to a de-animated language emptied of such personifying figures. In other words, he does not begin to sound more like Bolingbroke or Northumberland. On the contrary, at moments of intense grief Richard's language becomes hyperbolically sacral in nature; his poetry becomes overstrewn with animating figures of personification and scriptural allusion. The result of this hyperbolization of sacral language is that Richard's conceits become so strained that he is made subject to his own discourse; he gets caught up, so to speak, in his own conceits. As a result, Richard's hyperbolized use of animating figures, such as prosopopeia, have the paradoxical effect of de-animating him, just as his misuse of biblical typologies betrays his experience of desacralization.[39] In short, the experience of desacralization in the play gets depicted through a parodic use of the rhetorical terms central to the poetry of tears tradition as practiced by Southwell. Shakespeare, in effect, expresses Richard's despair by turning inside out, as it were, the rhetorical conventions that are used to express godly sorrow in the literature of tears tradition. The inversion of the conventions and tropes characteristic of the poetry of tears are deployed in many of the poet-king's complaints, but they are particularly evident when Richard tries to offer solace to Isabel before being put in the Tower, by depicting himself as Christ and her as Magdalene. The result is a parody of a Gospel scene made popular by Southwell several years before the play was composed.

When Queen Isabel first sees her deposed husband Richard in the opening to Act 5, she plays on the theme of misperception or "religious error" that was generally associated with the character of Mary Magdalene in the Renaissance: "But soft, but see, or rather do not see / My fair rose wither. Yet look up, behold, / That you in pity may dissolve to dew / And wash him fresh again with true-love tears" (5.1.7–10). If Isabel found herself confronted with an image of what she perceived as "Old Adam's likeness" in the gardener scene (3.4.71), she now finds herself gazing at an image she wants to perceive as a likeness of Christ. She thus speaks as though she were the kind of well-intentioned but exegetically naive Magdalene-figure found in works such as the pseudo-Origenist, *A Homily of Mary Magdalene* and Southwell's *Marie Magdalens Funeral Teares*. By implicitly, and presumably self-consciously, figuring herself as Magdalene to Richard's Christ, Isabel engages in an act of sacred parody as she seeks to "wash ... fresh again" her husband-king. Isabel's echoing of Magdalene's anointing of Christ with her tears in Luke 7 and the saint's desire to anoint the body of Christ in John 20 develops Richard's attempt to fashion himself as Christ-like in the previous scene when he engages in a quasi-blasphemous example of the outbidding topos: "[Christ] in twelve / Found truth in all but one; I, in twelve thousand, none" (4.1.171–72).[40] Picking up Richard's scriptural allusions, Isabel gazes at Richard as though he were Christ and she his *Beata Dilectrix*: "look up, behold, / That you in pity may dissolve to dew."

Samuel Daniel's account of this scene makes the connections between Isabel and Magdalene no less clear than Shakespeare's does. Daniel has Isabel respond to the sight of the deposed Richard in basically the same way that Southwell has Magdalene respond to the empty tomb and then to Christ, whom she mistakes as the gardener; she presumes that her physical sight is somehow mistaken and that an alternative order of perception must be applied in order to understand what she is misperceiving. Daniel's depiction of this scene thus unfolds by relying on the reader's awareness of the parallels and differences between Isabel's misperception of Richard and Magdalene's misperception of Christ as the gardener:

> But stay, ist not my Lord himselfe I see
> In truth, if 'twere not for his base array,
> I verily should thinke that it were hee;
> And yet his basenes doth a grace bewray:
> Yet God forbid; let me deceiued be,
> And be it not my Lord, although it may:
> Let my desire make vowes against desire;
> And let my sight approue my sight a lier. [41]

Just as Southwell's Magdalene must undergo a transformation from reading at the letter to reading by means of the spirit, so Isabel asks that her physical sight be effaced and thus overcome by her spiritual sight. Yet the tragic force of Isabel's speech lies in the knowledge that Richard is not Christ and she is not Magdalene and thus the transcending movement of *lectio spiritualis* is out of place within this political context.

The parallel between Magdalene's near-despair at the empty tomb in Southwell's prose homily and Isabel's first encounter with the deposed king in both Daniel's and Shakespeare's texts lies in the way that these scenes depict feelings associated with the loss of legible access to divinity or quasi-divinity. Shakespeare makes this connection between Isabel's feeling of desacralization and Magdalene's near-despair in prose dilations of John 20 by having her perceive Richard as a walking tomb: "Ah, thou, the model where old Troy did stand, / Thou map of honour, thou King Richard's tomb, / And not King Richard! Thou most beauteous inn, / Why should hard-favoured Grief be lodged in thee" (5.1.11–14). In the course of this brief speech, Isabel manages to cram together allusions to Magdalene's tearful anointing of Christ in Luke 7 and John 20, the pitiful beholding of the crucified Christ (often symbolized as a rose) and the encounter at the tomb. There may also be a vague reference to the nativity in the inn – though in this case it's a death and not a life that is being anticipated. There is something manic in this flood of allusions to the birth, life, and death of Christ. Isabel wants desperately to see Richard as Christ and herself as Magdalene but the scriptural narrative fails to map onto her own lived experience. The result is a breakdown in allusive coherence. In fact, the allusions end up calling attention to the difference between Richard and Christ rather than substantiating their likeness: while Richard is in the process of losing his spiritual-body and is thus[42] being reduced from divinely anointed king to a mere man, the resurrected Christ before the tomb is in the process of shedding his humanity as implied in the "noli me tangere" scene, which Shakespeare would evoke again in *Twelfth Night, Antony and Cleopatra*, and *The Winter's Tale*.[43] Despite Isabel's best efforts, Richard appears as an exact inversion of Christ throughout this scene. Isabel will later make this disjunction between the deposed Richard and the resurrected Christ more obvious when she inquires if "Richard both in shape and mind is / Transformed and weakened" (5.1.26–27). Making explicit what was implicit in her initial allusions, Isabel calls attention to the way that Richard's degeneration appears as the reverse of Christ's transfiguration.

The contradictory nature of Isabel's and Richard's scriptural allusions continue to express the experience of desacralization in the scene as Richard picks up his cue from Isabel and takes a stab at playing the role of Christ before the empty tomb. Richard instructs Isabel not to weep as Christ does in John 20 and its Elizabethan prose dilations. Only rather than introducing Isabel to a deeper sense of reality through divine revelation, Richard encourages Isabel to wake up from her dream and perceive that she is in an historical tragedy, not a divine comedy: "Join not with grief, fair woman, do not so, / To make my end too sudden. Learn, good soul, / To think our former state a happy dream, / From which awaked, the truth of what we are / Shows us but this. I am sworn brother, sweet, / To grim Necessity, and he and I, / Will keep a league till death" (5.1.16–22). The deposed and degenerated Richard tells Isabel a story of alienation and death while the resurrected Christ relays the promise of future salvation. Deepening the connections between Isabel and Magdalene, Richard tells his Queen to return to France and "cloister thee in some religious house," recalling the apocryphal tradition that Magdalene spent the last years of her life in Marseilles, but contradicting Magdalene's active rather than purely contemplative life there (5.1.23).

Probably the most significant contradiction in Richard's speech occurs in the last line of this exchange, where Richard tells Isabel that "Our holy lives must win a new world's crown, / Which our profane hours here have thrown down" (5.1.24–25). As is often observed, this is an explicit reference to Paul's second letter to Timothy: "Henceforth there is laid up for me a crowne of righteousness, which the Lord the righteous judge shall give mee at that day" (4:8).[44] Richard thus puts another scriptural subtext into circulation, one in which he plays Paul to Isabel's Timothy. The similarities between Paul and Richard make the allusion superficially appropriate. In the letter to Timothy, Paul is dying and has been forsaken by even his close friends. Speaking with the authority of someone near death, Paul exhorts Timothy to suffer with him by forgoing the temptation to comfort in this world. An audience intimately familiar with these New Testament narratives would likely recognize, however, that the depiction of Richard as being simultaneously like Paul in 2 Timothy and Christ in John 20 conflict with one another. While Christ offers comfort to Magdalene through his resurrection and its promise of grace, Paul insists that Timothy not be seduced by comfort, but suffer as he and Christ suffered.

This contradiction in Richard's message to Isabel is confirmed when Richard asks his Queen to be his apostle and to go tell the "lamentable tale of me" so that hearers will be sent "weeping to their beds" (5.1.44–45). The scene's parody of John 20 is thus further contradicted by Richard's allusion to 2 Timothy, which has the effect of sending very mixed messages to Isabel. He is instructing her not to weep and yet is telling her to narrate a story that will send its hearers "weeping to their beds"; he is telling her to experience the world as a vale of tears and yet is asking her to relate the tragic force of his life to others. Thus even as the scriptural allusions enhance the tragic pathos of the scene – situating Richard's story within a metanarrative of cosmological proportions – they simultaneously qualify this pathos by calling attention to the incongruent relation between Richard's tragical history and Christ's divine comedy. Any sympathy one might feel for Richard as suffering like Christ is complicated by the inverse relation between his self-indulgent sorrow and Christ's self-sacrificial actions.

If I sense a disjunction between Paul's situation in 2 Timothy and Christ's in John 20 being played out in Richard's strained attempt to console Isabel, then Isabel senses a contradiction between Richard's cowardice and Paul's courage. She challenges Richard, asking him "Hath Bolingbroke / Deposed thine intellect? Hath he been in thy heart? / The lion, dying, thrusteth forth his paw / And wounds the earth, if nothing else, with rage / To be o'erpowered" (5.1.27–31). Isabel thus hears Richard's allusion to Paul and retorts by reminding him that the pastoral letter is an instruction to courage, not despair. As Paul says: "God did not give us a spirit of cowardice, but rather a spirit of power and of love and of self-discipline" (2 Timothy 3:7). Here again though, Richard's story does not map onto Paul's. While Paul concludes his letter by deriving hope from his having been "rescued from the lion's mouth" (4:17), Isabel reminds Richard that he is a lion and should thus rage in the manner of the king of beasts. At each moment a scriptural allusion is made, its relevance to the situation is undermined. The result is a desacralizing of biblical typology as it applies to Richard and his Queen and, perhaps, to English history as a whole. As J. A. Bryant observes, biblical exegetes in Shakespeare's culture tended to view typology as "genuinely sacramental; that is, [they] insisted upon the sign as something participating *in* Christ, not merely standing for him."[45] This sacramental power gets drained in *Richard II* as virtually each and every allusion becomes an instance of Richard's subsequent realization that it is all too easy "to set the word itself / Against the word" (5.5.12–13).

A crucial part of this process of desacralization is the play's parody of a Gospel scene that would have been familiar to many Elizabethans through Southwell's popular prose dilation of it. In the opening to Act 5 and in the play as a whole, Richard repeatedly deploys and parodies the rhetorical features of Southwell's tear literature and the complaint mode Southwell sought to sacralize. Such parody is crucial to the psychological and philosophical involutions of Richard's final and most "metaphysical" soliloquy.

Alone in prison and facing almost certain death, Richard meditates on the question of finitude by spinning a conceit that is tortured enough to be worthy of the kind of criticism often leveled at Southwell and the metaphysical vogue he initiated in England well before John Donne. As John W. Hales complains, thinking perhaps of Peter's apostrophe to Christ's eyes, Southwell "heaps up metaphor on metaphor," producing a verse that is defective "not from poverty but from imperfectly managed wealth."[46] Sounding both like and unlike one of Southwell's saintly heroes, Richard heaps up metaphor upon metaphor as he depicts the experience of finitude and desacralization through figures of de-animation. Imagining himself metamorphosing into a clock, Richard reveals how the animating force of prosopopeia can betray an uncanny power of de-animation. The result is an inversion of the modality of grief we saw in St. Peter's apostrophe to Christ's eyes: where Southwell's apostrophe to Christ's eyes generates a scene in which Peter gains access to being through submission to Christ, Richard's prosopopeia signals the moment where Richard loses all sense of being and identity at the thought of having become subject to Bolingbroke. Thus if Peter exemplifies a sacralizing poetics of godly sorrow, then Richard articulates a desacralizing rhetoric of worldly grief:

> For now hath Time made me his numb'ring clock.
> My thoughts are minutes, and with sighs they jar
> Their watches on unto mine eyes, the outward watch,
> Whereto my finger, like a dial's point,
> Is pointing still, in cleansing them from tears.
> Now, sir, the sound that tells what hour it is
> Are clamorous groans which strike upon my heart,
> Which is the bell. So sighs, and tears, and groans
> Show minutes, times, and hours. But my time
> Runs posting on in Bolingbroke's proud joy,
> While I stand fooling here, his jack o' the clock. (5.5.50–60)

Echoing the common image of saints telling time by tears, this speech develops Richard's earlier attempt to fashion himself as a pious monk: "I'll give my jewels for a set of beads, / My gorgeous palace for a hermitage, / My gay apparel for an almsman's gown, / My figured goblets for a dish of wood, / My sceptre for a palmer's walking staff, / My subjects for a pair of carved saints" (3.3.147–52).

Richard's fantasy of becoming a clock is organized by the animating figure of prosopopeia, or the practice of conferring a mask or face on an inanimate object or abstraction (*prosopon poiein*). What is curious about Richard's speech, though, is that the personification of Time coincides with the de-personification of his own subjectivity. He imagines Time making him into a "numb'ring" clock, where the prefix "numb" accentuates that Richard is being "deprived of physical sensation or of the power of movement" as he imagines himself metamorphosing from man to mechanical object (*OED*). The sense of paralysis expressed here is psychologically sophisticated. To begin with, it conveys the psychodynamic consequences of having lost the political potency sustained by the idea of the king's two bodies. The sense that Richard has given up the claim to complete self-sufficiency to which absolutist kings and obsessive-neurotics aspire is expressed in the image of being Bolingbroke's "jack o' the clock." This image, which concludes the overall conceit, encapsulates the self-alienating and desacralizing movement of the figure as a whole. According to the Arden Edition, a "jack o' the clock" is a "small mechanical figure on certain old clocks of a man who struck the bell with his mallet to mark the hours."[47] This concluding image thus introduces a second kind of timepiece into the speech, reducing Richard from the "numb'ring clock" of the opening lines to a more subordinate part of a yet larger clock. In this respect, the conceit concludes with a conceptually unexpected but thematically coherent turn as Richard is reduced from being an inanimate signifier of time, to being a signifier of a signifier of time. By accumulating metaphors this way, the speech creates the effect that Richard's fall into the full consciousness of mortality coincides with a deepened sense of the alienating capacities of language. In the course of this increasingly complicated conceit, Richard loses control of his rhetoric as he becomes emptied of substance by the de-animating qualities latent within prosopopeia. It is as though Richard experiences his own words as belonging to someone else, as though they emanate not from the private world of his thoughts but from the shared social field which Bolingbroke now dominates. By getting literally caught up in his own metaphysical conceit, Richard fades as a subject, becoming absorbed by the forces of language inhabiting him.

The de-personifying movement of Richard's speech is predicated on a feature of prosopopeia that both fascinated and disturbed Paul de Man. As Jonathan Culler explains in an essay inspired by de Man's work on this trope, there is "an intimate relation between apostrophes addressed to the dead or the inanimate and prosopopeia that give the dead or inanimate a voice and make them speak."[48] Culler is referring here to de Man's thesis that "the latent threat that inhabits prosopopoeia, namely that by making the dead speak, the symmetrical structure of the trope implies, by the same token, that the living are struck dumb, frozen in their own death."[49] Viewed this way, prosopopeia can betray not only one's own mortality, "but our actual entry into the frozen world of the dead."[50] It is precisely this sense of being frozen by the deathly powers inherent in language that is enacted in Richard's prosopopeia of Time. His use of the sacralizing language of personification has the uncanny effect of expressing his experience of desacralization. Becoming subject to his own conceit, Richard conveys the experience of having felt his mortality in a way that has nothing do with an act of will and which is thus profoundly disturbing to his narcissism. And in the face of that terror he recoils so profoundly as to actually fade as a subject, losing himself in one of the deepest forms of worldly grief imaginable.

Richard's experience of being frozen in place is enacted metrically through the onomatopoeic alexandrine of line 51: "My thoughts are minutes, and with sighs they jar, / Their watches on unto mine eyes, the outward watch" (5.5.50–51).[51] While the word "sigh" is such a conventional feature of dramatic complaint as to appear almost meaningless, Shakespeare gives it an extraordinary density of ontotheological significance in this speech. By the end of this play, the term "sigh" signifies in exactly the opposite way than the word "breath" signified at the outset. As M. M. Mahood notes, at the beginning of the play Richard speaks with what Bolingbroke describes with awe as the "breath of kings" (1.3.215). In such usage, the word "breath" works by "Elizabethan analogy [in which] the 'breath' of the king should be a life-giving force, a human imitation of the Divine Spirit."[52] In other words, when the political theology of the king's two bodies is ideologically operative, the breath of the king should be perceived in the terms of visionary mimesis: to breathe is to engage in a creative act of will. The king's breath is thus an instance of *ruah* or *spiritus* – the life-giving force of divine creation. By the second scene of Act 5, though, Richard is out of "breath." As a result, his breaths have become sighs, his forceful *spiritus* reduced to the involuntary spasms of an exhausted, de-animated sigh. Where "breath" incarnates the intention of the quasi-divine will, "sighs, and tears, and groans / Show minutes, times, and hours" (5.5.57–58). Thus if the word "breath" connotes a sense of self-presence and willful sufficiency, then the word "sigh" signifies a lack of effective will, a vaporous absence of power within the most intimate recesses of his own person. In this way, Richard's sighs emanate the *vanitas* or *hebhel* that the psalmist speaks of when he says that "Man [is] like a breath [*hebhel*], his days, like a shadow that dissipates" (144:4). Confronted with an experience of radical nothingness, Richard's "sighs" signal the loss of existential orientation that phenomenologist Erwin W. Straus speaks of when he asserts that a "sigh occurs when the equilibrium between the individual and the world is disturbed, when pressure and resistance are increased ... A sigh does not have the character of a reflex, but it is not intentional either."[53] Richard's "sighs" are symptoms of exactly such disequilibrium and loss of intention.

The desacralizing experience registered in Richard's last prison speech is first evoked when Richard confesses that "My thoughts are minutes, and with sighs they jar." The use of the verb "jar" in this play of mixed metaphors brings together several of the word's meanings, all of which indicate that Richard's grief is existentially and ontologically opposite to St. Peter's compunction in Southwell's poem. Richard uses the word "jar" in the multiple senses of "to strike with discordant or painful effect upon the nerves, feelings, or conscience"; "to make a musical discord"; "to tick, as of a clock's minutes" (*OED*). Richard's claim to autonomy and self-sufficiency is thus completely breaking down as his sighs "jar" with his thoughts even as they conflict with his eyes, bringing them to tears. Richard's "jar" is the inverse of Peter's "broached," precisely insofar as it takes him deeper into the nothingness of his own self, rather than towards the substance of Christ within him.

While St. Peter's sacred weeping emerges when Christ "broaches" his eyes, thereby enabling him to receive the image of his redeemed self reflected back to him in Christ's eyes, Richard's desacralized grief begins with a discordant "jarring" that follows on Richard losing the image of his ideal self in the deposition scene when he asks, while looking into a mirror: "Was this the face / That like the sun did make beholders wink?" (4.1.283–84). In other words, Richard's and Peter's respective mirror scenes are reverse images of one another. In Peter's mirror scene, the saint's compunction speaks to him of Christ's grace operating within him, thereby signifying his transformation into the Logos' image: "O living mirrours, seeing whom you shew, / Which equall shaddows worthes with shadowed things: / Ye make thinges nobler then in native hew, / By being shap'd in those life giving springs" (367–70). Richard, on the other hand, loses all claim to substance in his mirror scene. In the deposition scene, Richard wakes up from his dream-like misrecognition of himself as having the self-presence that Southwell attributes to Christ. Having cracked his image, the deposed Richard thus declaims: "Mark, silent King, the moral of this sport, / How soon my sorrow hath destroyed my face," to which Bolingbroke replies, perhaps echoing St. Peter's "Which equall shaddows worthes with shadowed things": "The shadow of your sorrow hath destroyed, / The shadow of your face" (4.1.290–91, 292–93). Refusing to submit to Bolingbroke, Richard responds by trying to relocate his substance in his grief. By doing so, the poet-king further figures himself as an inverse image of St. Peter and other such penitent saints in the poetry of tears tradition: "Say that again! / The shadow of my sorrow? Ha let's see. / 'Tis very true, my grief lies all within; / And these external manners of laments / Are merely shadows to the unseen grief / That swells with silence in the tortured soul. / There lies the substance" (4.1.293–99).

While St. Peter's grief unifies his outward expression with his contrite state which is grounded in Christ's reflecting back to him his real image, Richard's "unseen grief" demarcates a radical difference between emotion and expression – a difference that emerges through the very lack of an ontological guarantee of meaning.

Like the actor Polus in the Calvinist treatise on compunction I discuss in the introduction, Richard identifies a radical gap between his grief and his outward countenance. But unlike a Calvinist saint, Richard locates this grief within himself as a means of grounding his claim to being, rather than locating his sorrow within the *aliena vita* of Christ within him. Moreover, Richard's act of self-definition occurs within the context of an obstinate refusal to submit to Bolingbroke rather than as part of a passive submission to a divine authority. Thus where St. Peter's godly weeping instigates and signals his submission to eternal life through Christ, Richard's worldly weeping signifies the dissolution of his world and the pain of being subjected, against his will, to Bolingbroke. So if Richard begins the play presuming a continuity between word and thing, intention and substance, he ends it by recognizing an irremediable gap between them.

This desacralizing process unfolds through the play's parodying of the kind of poetics of sorrow operative in *St Peters Complaint* – a parody that is further evinced in Richard's use of mixed metaphors. For example, the catachresis in which Richard's thoughts are figured as minutes jarring with his sighs involves a complex play of synaesthesia reminiscent of Peter's apostrophe to Christ. The immaterial movement of Richard's thoughts conflict with the audible emission of his sighs which have "watches" in the sense of vigils, guards, wakes, or clock faces, all of which must be in some sense internal because his eyes are said to be the "outward watch." Needless to say, the conflict here is not simply between inward grief and its outward show, as it was in the deposition scene, but within and between all aspects of Richard's thoughts, emotions, and their various emissions. In this way, Richard's desacralizing use of prosopopeia conveys a disassociation of sensibility, a growing dissension within and between thought as felt-experience and emotion as consciously registered affect. Richard is suffering from despair in the Pauline sense of worldly grief precisely insofar as he is alienated from his own emotions as well as his thoughts. Rather than undergoing the compunctive pangs of a remorseful conscience, in which godly sorrow proclaims the immanent presence of God within him through a dissolution of defensive postures, Richard's grief leads him to recoil further into himself. Moreover, the confusing play of synaesthesia in *Richard II* creates the effect that the poet-king is losing himself into nothingness, while such play expresses Peter's experience of wonder before the substance of Christ. In short, Richard's grief is metaphysically and existentially the inverse of Peter's.

In the final analysis, Richard's imaginary metamorphosis into a "jack o' the clock" is a symptom of the way he has begun to experience himself not as a self-present king but as a sign for another sign, as something to be used rather than as a subject enjoying and using things. Rather than feeling himself as a self-present subject, Richard experiences himself as a sign in the Augustinian sense as a thing (*res*) used to signify something else (*aliquid*). If, as Augustine says in the context of his analysis of the relationship between language and reality, "Some things are to be enjoyed, others to be used," then Richard feels himself to have become the signifying thing Bolingbroke now uses.[54] In other words, Richard's loss of self-possession is represented as a deepening of the loss of ontological immediacy inherent in the Augustinian idea that the soul is a signifier for God. At the moment when Richard experiences himself as subject to a field of meaning centered by Bolingbroke, Richard disappears into his own conceit, becoming not just divided from himself, but paralyzed and inanimate. Incapable of tolerating the self-division Shakespeare presents as attendant upon such subjection, Richard becomes enraged – dying in the kind of homicidal spasm that Isabel expected of him in the opening to Act 5.

In the course of the final act, then, Richard loses more than the onto-logical immediacy that all Christians renounce when they assert that "Christ 'is' while we and all else 'signify'." He finds himself a sign for a man who is no closer to God than he is himself.[55] For by the time we reach *1 Henry IV*, the desacralizing process initiated by Richard's parody of peni-tential literature will itself become the subject of parody as Prince Hal will mock Falstaff's pseudo-puritanical fascination with time: "Unless hours were cups of sack, and minutes capons, and clocks the tongues of bawds, and dials the signs of leaping-houses, and the blessed sun himself a fair hot wench in flame-coloured taffeta, I see no reason why thou shouldst be so superfluous to demand the time of day."[56] By this point in the Henriad, Richard's earnest, but failed, effort to live life sacramentally has given way to Falstaffian irony and Hal's imaginative pragmatism.

Throughout *Richard II*, but especially in the final act, Shakespeare empties the language of sighs and tears of the metaphysical substance grounding Southwell's depiction of it in *St Peters Complaint*. This desa-cralization of the poetry of tears is an important part of the larger nar-rative of decline operating in the play. However much Shakespeare parodies such religious traditions, though, he maintains the view that weeping is a complex form of signification. By focusing not just on the affective, but also on the existential and theological meanings of Richard's grief, Shakespeare expands the conceptual and literary possibilities of complaint as a rhetorical mode. In particular, Shakespeare inverts and parodies the sacralizing language of Southwellian complaint to convey the experience of desacralization – the dividing asunder of divine narrative from lived history. By representing despair through an inversion of tear poetry as practiced by Southwell, Shakespeare helps make possible, among other figures, Milton's Satan.

TEARS SUCH AS ANGELS WEEP

Paradise Lost

In Book 4 of *Paradise Lost* Satan enters Eden for the first time. This entry into Paradise is generally recognized as an essential part of the poem's anti-Catholic, and more precisely for our purposes, anti-Jesuit, satire:

> As when a prowling wolf,
> Whom hunger drives to seek new haunt for prey,
> Watching where shepherds pen their flocks at eve
> In hurdled cotes amid the field secure,
> Leaps o'er the fence with ease into the fold:
> Or as a thief bent to unhoard the cash
> Of some rich burgher, whose substantial doors,
> Cross-barred and bolted fast, fear no assault,
>   In at the window climbs, or o'er the tiles;
>   So clomb this first grand thief into God's fold:
>   So since into his church lewd hirelings climb. (4.183–93)

As John King observes, Milton's depiction of Satan as a "prowling wolf" who sneaks into "God's fold" just as "lewd hirelings" have snuck into his Church alludes not only to Milton's familiar anti-Laudian critique, but also to the anti-Jesuit polemic that runs intermittently through the poem. This polemic arose from fears "concerning Romanist plots organized by a fifth column of Jesuit missionaries or crypto-Catholic bishops [which] were pervasive throughout the seventeenth century."[57] Arthur Marotti summarizes this aspect of Milton's religious satire when he notes that Satan's "seduction of Eve takes place in the context of anti-Catholic and anti-Jesuit polemic. A diabolical disguiser who is a skillful rhetorical seducer succeeds in enticing his female victim into idolatrous, superstitious practice and alienating her from both her husband and the faith in which they have grounded their marital relationship."[58] Though Marotti appears to be referring primarily to Book 9, his reference to Robert Sibthorpe's very typical warning about Jesuits in a 1618 sermon applies just as well to Satan's original entry into Eden. According to Sibthorpe, one must be on guard against "Romanists who creep into great houses to lead captive 'simple women laden with sinnes.'"[59]

While Satan's initial entry into (and then his exile out of) Eden works by drawing on anti-Jesuit paranoia, especially the view that Jesuits use disguise, lie, steal, and abuse women, so too does his reappearance in Eden in Book 9: "When Satan who late fled before the threats / Of Gabriel out of Eden, now improved / In meditated fraud and malice ... / fearless returned" (9.53–55, 57). This account of Satan's improvement in the dark arts of deceit echoes Phineas Fletcher's description of the arch-Jesuit, "Once Proteus, now Equivocus ... hight," in his anti-Jesuit poem, *The Locusts, or Apollyonists*, which has long been recognized as a source of *Paradise Lost*.[60] Describing Proteus' transformation into Equivocus, Fletcher figures the arch-Jesuit's return from abroad by remarking that he is "now more practike growne with use and art, / [and] Oft times in heavenly shapes he fooles the sight."[61] Fletcher's and Milton's description of this Jesuitical return from foreign places relies on the anxiety that English Protestants felt towards those young Catholic men who fled England only to return after having been trained at the colleges in Douai, Paris, and Rome. Anti-Jesuit polemicists referred to such men as having been "Jesuitized" or "Jesuited" – as having been trained in the arts of equivocation and other methods of deceit.[62]

By depicting Satan in the language of such anti-Jesuit polemic, Milton develops the anti-Catholic allegory of Spenser's *The Faerie Queene*, especially the figure of Malengine, whose destruction in Book 5 is symbolic of Elizabeth's capture of missionary priests such as Edmund Campion in 1581 and the widely known Southwell in 1592.[63] Though Milton's Satan is not a direct allegory of Jesuit priests, any more than he is of Laudian prelates, royalist generals, Charles I, or Cromwell, he is, nonetheless, often depicted in the kind of anti-Catholic polemic visible in Milton's Latin poem on the Gunpowder Plot, *In Quintum Novembris*. As John King puts the issue: "Neither consistent nor ever-present, Milton's polemicism constitutes an allusive network of intimations, hints, echoes, and innuendoes within a polysemous interplay of narrative and dramatic voices."[64] I would like to pursue one thread of "intimations, hints, [and] echoes" by demonstrating how Satan's Niphates speech in Book 4 and his return to Eden speech in Book 9 unfold as parodies of the poetry of tears – a tradition inevitably associated in England with Robert Southwell, whose Collegio Romano Milton most likely visited during his time in Italy[65] and whose poetry he certainly would have known. While the speech in Book 4 loosely parodies general conventions found throughout Catholic and Protestant traditions of poetic repentance as a way of articulating Satan's despair, the speech in Book 9 appears to pervert the Ignatian poetics of wonder associated with Southwell's *St Peters Complaint* and "A Vale of Teares." One of the results of this demonic parody of the poetry of tears tradition is a metaleptic reversal in which Milton creates the effect that Satan precedes, and thus originates, the Jesuit poetics that he parodies.

Like Richard II, the predominant genre through which Milton communicates Satan's involvement in his own grief is the mode of complaint, often one tinged with the nostalgia of elegy.[66] In the Niphates speech of Book 4, this complaint begins with an apostrophe to the sun, in which Satan initiates but ultimately thwarts a desire for repentance. The speech plays on a reader's expectations of repentance by recalling some of the key tropes of penitential poetry, only to betray such expectations by inverting the existential orientations normally delineated through them. This parody is first signaled in the narrator's lead-up to the soliloquy, when he evokes the common penitential idea that human grief is fundamentally determined by the experience of time: "now conscience wakes despair / That slumbered, wakes the bitter memory / Of what he was, what is, and what must be" (4.23–25). The narrator's depiction of the temporally mediated nature of Satan's despair echoes, among many other penitential treatises, William Cowper's 1613 *The Anatomy of a Christian Man* in which the "causes of grief in a Christian man" are said to be "threefold": "the first is the consideration of that which we have been: the second is the consideration of that which we are: the third, the consideration of what we would be, and are not."[67] Cowper's analysis of repentance in temporal terms would have been familiar to most early moderns through the account of repentance in the *Homily on the Misery of Mankind* included in *Certaine Sermons Or Homilies Appointed to be Read in Churches, In the Time of the Late Queene Elizabeth*. Exhorting readers to repentance, this homily "warne[s] vs all to consider what wee bee, whereof wee bee, from whence we came, and whither we shall."[68] The slight difference between Satan's grief and penitential sorrow articulated in these two accounts is an essential one: while a Christian man experiences grief over what he would like to be but is not, Satan experiences grief over what he "must be." In other words, Satan occludes the possibility for *metanoia* by refusing to admit his creatureliness, part of which now entails the mediations of time and an undying death. The narrator's contextualization of Satan's speech should thus lead us to expect the Niphates soliloquy to be a demonic inversion of godly sorrow, a soliloquy hopelessly "revolving … in sighs" (4.31) rather than, as in the case of Southwell's St. Peter, one "resolve[d] in tears" (13).

The opening of Satan's speech recalls the apostrophic nature of many of the psalms, including Psalm 51, which it later echoes in order to pervert: "O thou that with surpassing glory crowned, / … to thee I call" (4.32, 35). As we saw in relation to *St Peters Complaint*, penitential apostrophes conventionally declare a speaker's constitutive dependence on God's mercies. This dependence is inherent to the *anima mea* tradition's dialogical structure, the way that a psalmic address to the soul is designed to admit God's presence into the *anima*. Satan's invocation to the sun, however, does the reverse. It is an oxymoronic refusal of subjection and ontological dependence: "to thee I call, / But with no friendly voice" (4.35–36). Thus while St. Peter's apostrophe to Christ's eyes initiates a recognition of his true self as reflected back to him in Christ's constituting gaze, Satan's apostrophe to the sun does the reverse. As Victoria Silver explains:

In the egoistic allegory of the sun's diminishing the stars, apostrophe and personification at once betoken and illustrate Satan's estrangement from his creator as well as creation itself. These figures betray his already habitual projection of self onto everything he sees, his urgent impulse to make the whole world conform to his private experience of it.[69]

While Satan finds in apostrophe an idolatrous temptation to mistake the poetic gesture for the thing in and of itself, St. Peter finds in this figure a way of moving out of himself as worldly being and into the image of Christ. The gap between intention and meaning thus tends to be exactly opposite with these two figures: while Peter does not recognize the full typological meaning of his grief due to his extreme experience of abasement and awareness of mortality, Satan resists hearing the very creatureliness implied by the dialogical structure of his sighs. In other words, while Peter opens himself to the excessive abundance of God's overpresence within the soul by listening for the dialogical dimensions of his own grief, Satan continually recoils from the overpresence of the divine by insisting upon the monological nature of his despair. Peter opens himself to the experience of wonder before Christ, while Satan resists being saturated by the experience of Eden's sublimity.

The gap between intention and meaning in Satan's pseudo-penitential apostrophe is audible in the way he personifies key words in the speech. At the very moment he inquires into the possibility of repentance, he swerves away from the eventful decision he is making by placing agency not in his own self-conscious action but in a word: "is there no place / Left for repentance, none for pardon left? / None left but by submission; and that word / Disdain forbids me" (4.79–82). By placing agency in the word "Disdain" rather than directly in his own will, Satan betrays a lack of confidence – admitting, in effect, that he is in over his head: "Ay me, they little know / How dearly I abide that boast so vain" to "subdue / The omnipotent" (4.86–87, 86). By slightly disowning his own intention, Satan generates a meaning other than the one he is explicitly articulating: he is opening up, even as he is closing down, a desire for redemptive submission. Satan thus experiences the kind of Kierkegaardian anxiety that John S. Tanner demonstrates is so crucial to the spiritual psychology of Milton's epic. As Kierkegaard writes: "Anxiety is a desire for what one fears, a sympathetic antipathy; anxiety is an alien power which grips the individual, and yet one cannot tear himself free from it and does not want to, for one fears, but what he fears he desires."[70] In the course of the Niphates speech, Satan tries to renounce one mode of "sympathetic antipathy" for another: he performs a disavowal of his ambivalence over grace in favor of the ambivalent joy-in-misery he experiences as king of hell. In other words, he rejects the joyful-miseries of godly sorrow, which Adam and Eve will experience, in favor of the miserable-joys of reigning in hell: "They little know ... / Under what torments inwardly I groan; / While they adore me on the throne of hell, / With diadem and sceptre high advanced / The lower still I fall, only supreme / In misery; such joy ambition finds" (4.86–92). Despite Satan's exasperation with this feeling of miserable-joy, it is exactly this affective modality that will "ground" his experience of himself: Satan is Satan precisely because he bases his identity on a disavowal of godly sorrow as the affect that initiates the spiritual "clearing" of Pauline *apologia*.

Within the terms of Milton's spiritual psychology, the act of deciding to fully assume such a disavowal of joyful-sorrow comes at the cost of psychological coherence because it rests on a denial of God. It is the purest act of negation possible at an affective level. This is why Satan becomes abstracted from himself in the course of the Niphates speech, opening up an even wider abyss between will and being, intention and expression. This self-difference continues to be expressed through the personification of words as agents of action, such as when Satan displaces his will to rebellion in the following metonymy: "But say I could repent and could obtain / By act of grace my former state; how soon / Would *height* recall high thoughts, how soon unsay / What unfeigned submission swore" (4.93–96, my emphasis). As with the word "Disdain," Satan's use of the word "height" displaces the will to rebel from himself to the situation in which he envisions himself, thereby reducing sin from a heroic act of rebellion to a symptom of his repeated misinterpretations of his relation to God. Words do more than describe in the Niphates speech; they become beings who take on a life of their own. Satan's words function like his offspring, Sin and Death, speaking in excess of their progenitor's will. This relation to language is symptomatic of Satan's idolatry – his tendency to invest everything, worst of all his grief, with his own image. Thus in the very gesture of trying to choose divine subjection or infernal rule he reiterates the terms of the choice, ceaselessly "revolving in sighs."

While this devolution takes place at every stage of the Niphates speech, it is most clearly performed when Satan parodies the Vulgate version of Psalm 51: "Me Miserable! Which way shall I fly? / Infinite wrath and infinite despair" (4.73–74).[71] Satan ends up turning the open-ended supplication, "misere mei deus secundum misericordiam" ("Have mercy on me, O God, according to thy great mercy"), into a close-ended act of self-definition. By employing "and" rather than "or" in line 74, Satan implicitly "fixes" his own feelings about repentance. The grammatical structure of his question has the effect of predetermining his response, indicating that the question is posed in bad faith. Such grammatical subtleties pave the way for Satan's fully thematized attempt to define himself in and through despair: "So farewell hope, and with hope farewell fear, / Farewell remorse: all good to me is lost" (4.108–9).

One of the more remarkable features of this speech is that it does not simply perform a reprobate's experience of sin – as theorized in Protestant or Catholic penitential discourse – but rather it presents the narrative conditions of possibility for such an experience. Through this performative gesture, Satan establishes the original conditions for a reprobate's experience of sin rather than just dramatizing reprobation as presented in Protestant theory. William Cowper explains the typical experience of reprobation when he says that "so long as a man and his sinne are one he neyther feels the weight of it, nor the wrath that followeth it, but rejoyceth in that which should be the matter of his grief."[72] Unlike this typical reprobate, Satan senses the weight of his sin at certain moments, but he elects to foreclose such feelings. Satan thus emerges here as the "Artificer of fraud" not just in the Machiavellian sense of purposeful guile, but also in the Calvinist sense that Daniel Dyke intends in his treatise titled *The Mystery of Self-Deceiving*. The conditions of possibility for self-deceit and thus worldly sorrow more generally begin with Satan's active repression of acknowledging the emotional effects of sin. It is the very impossibility of successfully foreclosing such knowledge that makes Satan demonic. We continue to hear the potentially dialogical nature of Satan's grief, even when he does not.

The Niphates speech establishes some of the generic expectations and rhetorical strategies operative in Satan's apostrophe to the earth in Book 9. In particular, the Niphates soliloquy initiates some of the ways Satan rejects the experience of wonder and the encounter with genuine otherness that is the focus of his return to Eden. In this way, Book 4 puts us on guard against the way Satan appears to parody the Ignatian poetics of wonder throughout his long soliloquy in this book. Satan's parody of this Jesuit poetics is first established through his re-entry into Eden which, as I have already suggested, furthers the poem's anti-Jesuit satire. When Satan first returns to Eden he remains "cautious of day," concerned that his presence will be detected because "Uriel regent of the sun descried / His entrance, and forewarned the cherubim / That kept their watch" (9.59, 60–62). This clandestine return to Eden is likely designed to bring to mind the secret entry of Jesuits into England whose arrivals were sometimes anticipated by the spies placed at French ports, as in the case of Southwell and his superior, Henry Garnet, whose entry into England became known by Elizabethan officials.[73] If so, Satan's entry into Eden echoes anti-Catholic accounts of Jesuit entries into England, in which Catholic missionaries are often figured as arriving in order to "perturb the quiet of the Realme ... sow sedition ... practice revolts, and alienate the minde of the subjects."[74]

The moment Satan arrives "involved in rising mist" he "sought / Where to lie hid," perhaps evoking Protestant anxiety about the tendency of Jesuits to hide and use disguise (9.75–76). If we recall that Satan's first disguise in the poem is as a cormorant – which emblematizes "greedy exploitation of the weak, in particular by 'hireling' clergy"[75] – then we are more likely to see his desire to conceal himself in the serpent within the anti-Jesuit subtext: "of these [angels] the vigilance / I dread, and to elude, thus wrapped in mist / Of midnight vapour glide obscure, and pry / In every bush and brake, where hap may find / The serpent sleeping, in whose mazy folds / To hide me, and the dark intent I bring" (9.157–62). Given that Satan is re-entering Eden as part of a missionary project, the discourse of concealment would likely evoke Protestant anxiety about Jesuit hiding places which feature in the Malengine episode of *The Faerie Queene*, as well as in anti-Jesuit polemic like John Baxter's *A Toile for Two-Legged Foxes*. Baxter warns that Catholics "make their burrows strong, they have so many streight passages, so many muses, so many winding corners, so many turnings, so many interturnings, and starting holes, that it is a matter full of difficultie to find the couch of a Catholicke, especially of a Priest or Iesuite."[76] Like Malengine, Satan shares exactly this capacity for concealment – a capacity to which Southwell alludes in "A Vale of Teares" when he describes how "springs crept out of secret vaine, / Strait finde some envious hole that hides their grace" (49–50).

Satan also shares with English Jesuits a sense of being exiled and alone within the very place that should be comforting. This theme of exile is central to many of Southwell's poems, but none more successfully than "A Vale of Teares," which, as A. Lytton Sells observes, was occasioned by Southwell's crossing of the Alps on his way back into England in 1586.[77] This is also a journey Milton took on his way from Milan to Geneva. This journey clearly left its traces on the Puritan's account of chaos, just as it left its imprint on the Jesuit's most unique and remarkable lyric. Southwell's penitential poem has a number of intriguing affinities with Satan's apostrophe to earth in Book 9, enough to entertain the possibility that Milton may be echoing it as part of the anti-Jesuit parody in the epic. To begin with, both Southwell's poem and Satan's plaint involve an exclamation of wonder before the awesome force of nature experienced while returning for a missionary project. While Satan experiences the overwhelming vitality of Paradise as an alienating world and thus the occasion for making Adam and Eve experience such alienation, South-well's speaker experiences an alienating world as an occasion for penance and the pursuit of the Jesuit mission. Southwell's "A Vale of Teares" thus appears to be an even clearer example of the Ignatian exclamation of wonder than *St Peters Complaint*: "Exclamations of wonder, with intense feeling, as I reflect on [how] the earth ... has ... not opened to engulf me, creating new hells where I might suffer for ever."[78] In Southwell's poem the world is on the brink of engulfing the speaker but, in the end, does not. Resisting despair, the speaker slowly finds signs of his sinfulness in the landscape and is thus able to turn it into a scene of repentance and poetic sublimation: "Let teares to tunes, and paines to plaints be prest, / And let this be the burdon of thy song" (73–74). Satan, on the other hand, suffers exactly what the Ignatian meditation is designed to avoid. He appears to initiate Point 5 of the Ignatian meditation on sin, but is unable to derive either the gratitude or the penance it is designed to offer. Instead, his isolation is furthered and he experiences resentment rather than gratitude over creation. The result is a speech that looks like a parody of the Ignatian method informing the only poem published in early modern England that does anything like depict a Jesuit's return to England from a Jesuit point of view.

When Satan returns to Eden, "The Sun was sunk, and after him the star / Of Hesperus, whose office is to bring / Twilight upon the earth, short arbiter / Twixt day and night, and now from end to end / Night's hemisphere had veiled the horizon round" (9.48–52). Southwell's poem opens with similar, if more explicitly threatening, imagery as the speaker confronts a "Vale" that is "enwrapt with dreadfull shades, / Which thicke of mourning pines shrouds from the sunne" (1–2). Like the speaker of Southwell's poem, Satan is unable to find any refuge within the landscape surrounding him. Speaking as though he is elegizing himself, Satan mourns never having experienced Eden in an un-fallen state: "With what delight could I have walked thee round, / If I could joy in aught, sweet interchange / Of hill and valley, rivers, woods and plains, / Now land, now sea, and shores with forest crowned, / Rocks, dens, and caves; But I in none of these / Find place or refuge" (9.114–19). The motion of Paradise inspires in Satan a sense of awesome vitality, a sense of amazement that momentarily interrupts his solipsism. Shocked into a kind of wondrous stupor, much as he is moments later when he sees Eve again, Satan has a momentary intimation of genuine otherness. But because of his narcissistic sensitivity to what he diagnoses as the "terror in love / And beauty" (9.490–91), Satan experiences the sublime beauty of creation as a threat to his identity. So rather than following the inclinations of wonder to move out of the familiar world of the self and into the unexpected world of Eden, Satan recoils further into his grief – which he finds comforting so long as he resists the dialogical potential within it. Satan must deny the effects of "wonder" (the emotion we feel when confronted with something that cannot be interpreted within the horizon of our experience) because doing so would demand a re-ordering of self different than the "reassembling of ... afflicted powers" that occurs in Book 1 (1.186). Satan thus complains that "the more I see / Pleasures about me, so much more I feel / Torment within me, as from the hateful siege / Of contraries" (9.119–22). Rather than allowing himself to be constituted by the awe-inspiring landscape around him – rather than allowing its infinite excess of experience to reveal to him his own delimitations as a creature – Satan resists amazement by turning back into himself. Recoiling back to his defensive posture, Satan tries to constitute himself as an object of perception and interpretation rather than recognizing himself as having been constituted by God as a part of creation.

Satan's feeling of alienation, occasioned by an overwhelming landscape that he experiences as a "hateful siege Of contraries," recalls Southwell's anti-pastoral description of the landscape alienated from human desire:

> Resort there is of none but pilgrim wights,
> That passe with trembling foot and panting heart,
> With terror cast in cold and shivering frights,
> They judge the place to terror framde by art:
>
> Yet natures worke it is of arte untoucht,
> So strait indeed, so vast unto the eie,
> With such disordered order strangely coucht,
> And so with pleasing horror low and hie,
>
> That who it viewes must needs remaine agast,
> Much at the worke, more at the makers might,
> And must how Nature such a plot could cast,
> Where nothing seemed wrong, yet nothing right. (21–32)

If one hears in Satan's "siege Of contraries" echoes of Southwell's "disordered order ... / horror low and hie," a strange effect takes place, one that Harold Bloom defines as characteristically Miltonic: we experience Satan's soliloquy as chronologically prior to Southwell's plaint, so that Southwell's depiction of the natural world as a horrific "place for mated minds" where "the wind weepes," "sighes," and "cries aloude" (33, 36) appears as an effect of Satan's misapprehension of Eden as a place that inspires the "relentless thoughts" of a "mazy" mind (9.130, 161).[79] In other words, if such echoes are heard, one experiences Southwell as being one of those persons Satan speaks of proleptically when he declares "only in destroying I find ease / To my relentless thoughts; and him destroyed, / Or won to what may work his utter loss, / For whom all this was made, all this will soon / Follow, as to him linked in weal or woe; / In woe then" (9.129–34). It is as though Southwell's anti-pastoral nightmare inspired by the Alps were now an effect of Satan's refusal to experience wonder before Eden. If such echoes are heard, the Jesuit poetics associated with Southwell come to feel belated – metaleptically subsequent to their Satanic predecessor. Thus if Southwell's "A Vale of Teares" stages the entry of the Catholic literature of tears tradition into England, then Satan's soliloquy in Book 9 of *Paradise Lost* works to annul the authority of this Catholic tradition by re-inscribing its origins as satanic rather than saintly.

CONCLUSION

Throughout *Paradise Lost*, Satan remains eternally trapped within the kind of "anatomy of sin" that St. Peter carries out in *St Peters Complaint*, when the saint analyzes the motions of his fallen soul and finds himself caught in a vicious hermeneutic circle: "My eye, reades mournefull lessons to my hart, / My hart, doth to my thought the griefes expound, / My thought, the same doth to my tounge impart, / My tounge, the message in the eares doth sound. / My eares, backe to my hart their sorrowes send: / Thus circkling griefes runne round without an end" (673–78). Peter's solipsistic anatomy gets reworked in Herbert's "Sin's Round," which offers a vision of sin similar to *Paradise Lost*. Like Milton's Satan, the speaker of "Sin's Round" offers up an unfeeling repentance – a confession of sin that does not rise to contrition: "Sorry I am, my God, sorry I am, / That my offences course it in a ring ... / My words take fire from my inflamed thoughts, / Which spit it forth like the Sicilian hill. / They vent the wares, and pass them with their faults / And by their breathing ventilate the ill. / But words suffice not, where are lewd intentions: / My hands do join to finish the inventions" (1–2, 7–12). In all of these examples, ungodly sorrow is depicted as a failure to meet the otherness of God, a failure not so much to cope with the apparent absence of God but an inability to bear his overpresence. As a result, despair is figured as a narcissistic state of infinitely repeating regression into ever deepening self-division. Like Shakespeare before him, Milton expresses such a state by both drawing on and parodying the literature of tears tradition.

The density of existential, ontological, and theological meaning inhering in the sighs and tears of Richard and Satan is testament to the literary promise of the poetry of tears tradition popularized by Southwell. The internally conflicted, endlessly self-dividing rhetoric characteristic of these two figures is achieved by, among other things, deepening the experiential dimensions of the poetry of repentance. In the case of *Paradise Lost* and *Richard II*, this deepening of the tradition's capacity to express self-difference occurs largely through a parodic appropriation of penitential complaint. In particular, the despairing solipsism Richard II and Satan experience is expressed by the way they resist the intersubjective dimensions of the poetry of tears as a mode. Richard and Satan sound alike insofar as they repeatedly deny the dialogical nature of Christian sorrow. This denial of the intersubjective nature of the sighs and tears is also accompanied in both Richard and Satan by a particular experience of time. Both Richard and Satan experience time as infinitely dilated, as a numbing and claustrophobia-inducing force. In Crashaw's "The Weeper" and Marvell's

"Eyes and Tears" this dilation of time takes on entirely different dimensions, revealing the otherness of God rather than the alienations of despair.

NOTES

1 Philip Caraman, *Henry Garnet 1555–1606 and the Gunpowder Plot* (London: Longmans, 1964), pp. 20–25.
2 See Herbert Thurston, "Catholic Writers and Elizabethan Readers, II: Father Southwell, the Euphuist," and "Catholic Writers and Elizabethan Readers, III: Father Southwell, the Popular Poet," *Month*, LXXX III(Jan.–April 1895), 231–45 and 383–99; Louis Martz, *The Poetry of Meditation: A Study in English Religious Literature of the Seventeenth Century*, rev. edn. (New Haven, CT: Yale University Press, 1969), pp. 179–210; Alison Shell, *Catholicism, Controversy and the English Literary Imagination, 1558–1660* (Cambridge: Cambridge University Press, 1999), pp. 58–96; and Scott R. Pilarz, *Robert Southwell and the Mission of Literature, 1561–1595: Writing Reconciliation* (Aldershot and Burlington, VT: Ashgate, 2004), pp. xi–xxxi.
3 See Gérard Genette, *Palimpsests Literature in the Second Degree*, trans. Channa Newman and Claude Doubinsky (Lincoln and London: University of Nebraska Press, 1997), especially chapters 3–8.
4 Shell, *Catholicism*, p. 60. For a discussion of the manuscript forms of Southwell's poems and conclusions about their pre-publication history, see James H. McDonald and Nancy Pollard Brown (eds.), *The Poems of Robert Southwell, S.J.* (Oxford: Clarendon Press, 1967), pp. xxxv–xcix.
5 For discussions of peripety, see Lodovico Castelvetro, "The Poetics of Aristotle Translated and Annotated," in *Literary Criticism, Plato to Dryden*, ed. Allan H. Gilbert (New York: American Book Co., 1940), pp. 342–48 and Geoffrey H. Hartman, "On Traumatic Knowledge and Literary Studies," *New Literary History* 26.3 (1995), 539.
6 St. Ignatius of Loyola, *Personal Writings*, ed. and trans. Joseph A. Munitiz and Philip Endean (London: Penguin Books, 1996), p. 297. For a balanced reassessment of the place of Ignatius' Exercises in Southwell's work, see Pilarz, *Robert Southwell*, pp. 100–3, pp. 109–10.
7 For a discussion of this Jesuit principle in the context of Southwell's writing, see Pierre Janelle, *Robert Southwell the Writer: A Study in Religious Inspiration* (London: Sheed and Ward, 1935), p. 122.
8 McDonald and Brown (eds.), *Poems of Robert Southwell*, p. 156.
9 Karen Bruhn, "Reforming Saint Peter: Protestant Constructions of Saint Peter the Apostle in Early Modern England," *Sixteenth-Century Journal* 33.1 (2002), 33–49, makes much the same point in the context of early modern English Catholic representations of Peter, 37.
10 Robert Southwell, *Marie Magdalens Funeral Teares* (London: 1594), p. 6.
11 See William Annand, *Mysterium Pietatis* (London, 1671), p. 199.
12 The active mode of reading that Southwell demands in "Marie Magdalens Complaint at Christs Death," for example, is occasioned by the fact that many

of his Catholic readers would not have had a priest readily available for confession. Thus just as Magdalene must sustain faith in the absence of the resurrected Christ, so recusant readers have to sustain sacramental traditions in the absence of a functioning Church. For studies of suppressed religious polemic and commentary in Southwell's poems, see Gary Kuchar, *Divine Subjection: The Rhetoric Sacramental Devotion in Early Modern England*, Medieval and Renaissance Literary Studies (Pittsburgh, PA: Duquesne University Press, 2005), chapter 1; Nancy Pollard Brown, "Robert Southwell: The Mission of the Written Word," in Thomas M. McCoog (ed.), *The Reckoned Expense: Edmund Campion and the Early English Jesuits: Essays in Celebration of the First Centenary of Campion Hall, Oxford (1896–1996)* (Woodbridge and Rochester, NY: Boydell, 1996), pp. 193–213; Sadia Abbas, "Polemic and Paradox in Robert Southwell's Lyric Poems," *Criticism* 45.4 (2003), 453–82. Ann Sweeney's *Robert Southwell: Snow in Arcadia: Redrawing the English Lyric Landscape, 1586–95* (Manchester: Manchester University Press, 2006), came to my attention just as this book was going to press and thus could not be integrated into the argument.

13 Heather Arvidson, "Equivocating Veils/Vales: The Poetics of Equivocation in Robert Southwell's 'A Vale of Tears,'" paper presented to the Pacific Northwest Renaissance Society Conference, Banff, AB, 2005. While I think allegory and not equivocation is the context informing Southwell's poem, the following three paragraphs owe a clear debt to Arvidson's reading of the poem's title as reflexive. For discussions of Southwell's use of allegory, see F. W. Brownlow, *Robert Southwell* (New York: Twayne, 1996), p. 55.

14 Roberto Bellarmino, "De Gemitu Combrae," in *Opera Omnia*, 12 vol. (Paris: Ludovicum Vivés, 1874), vol. 8, pp. 397–484.

15 Ignatius, *Personal Writings*, p. 295. For a discussion of "A Vale of Tears" in relation to the Ignatian Exercises, see Martz, *Poetry of Meditation*, pp. 207–10.

16 Douai-Rheims, 1582.

17 St. John Chrysostom, *Saint Chrysostom: Homilies on the Epistles of Paul to the Corinthians*, Nicene and Post-Nicene Fathers of the Christian Church, ed. Philip Schaff, vol. XII, ser. 1 (Grand Rapids, MI: Wm. B. Eerdmans, 1997), p. 312.

18 Nancy Brown, "The Structure of Southwell's 'Saint Peter's Complaint,'" *Modern Language Review* 51 (1966), 3–11, 8.

19 Ignatius, *Personal Writings*, p. 297.

20 William Allen, *A Briefe Historie of the Glorious Martyrdom of XII Reverend Priests* (1582), biiii.

21 Jean-Luc Marion, *In Excess: Studies of Saturated Phenomena*, trans. Robyn Horner and Vincent Berraud (New York: Fordham University Press, 2002), pp. 113–19.

22 Ibid., p. 117.

23 Ibid., p. 116.

24 For Lévinas' discussion of the phenomenology of the face, see "Philosophy and the Idea of Infinity," in *Collected Philosophical Papers*, trans. Alphonso

Lingis (Pittsburgh: Duquesne University Press, 1987), pp. 47–60. For a
reading of Southwell's poem as expressing the Tridentine view of penance, see
Brown, "The Structure of Southwell's 'Saint Peter's Complaint'," 3–11.

25 Pilarz, *Southwell*, p. xvi.

26 See ibid., pp. xix–xx, and Shell, *Catholicism*, pp. 84–85.

27 Pilarz cites Drummond's remark that "Southwell was hanged, yet so he had
written that piece of his, the Burning Babe, [Jonson] would have been
content to destroy many of his," in *Southwell*, p. xxi.

28 Shell, *Catholicism*, p. 77. For a description of a parallel phenomenon in
the context of William Broxup's *Saint Peters Path*, see Bruhn, "Reforming
St. Peter."

29 For an account of Southwell's treatise as a commentary on recusant
experience in England, see Kuchar, *Divine Subjection*, chapter 1. Lisa
McClain, "'They have taken away my Lord': Mary Magdalene, Christ's
Missing Body, and the Mass in Reformation England," *Sixteenth Century
Journal* 38.1 (2007), 77–78, discusses Markham's text as Catholic but without
any justification as to why.

30 Gervase Markham, *Marie Magdalens Lamentations for the Losse of her Master
Jesus* (London, 1601), Biii.

31 Patricia Phillippy, *Women, Death and Literature in Post-Reformation England*
(Cambridge: Cambridge University Press, 2002) p. 67.

32 Pseudo-Origenist, *An Homilie of Marye Magdalene* (London, 1565), B6.

33 Robert Southwell, *Marie Magdalens Funeral Teares* (London, 1591), p. 19.

34 For a more developed reading of Southwell's anti-Protestant critique in this
poem, see Kuchar, *Divine Subjection*, chapter 1.

35 See Chapter 3.

36 That Shakespeare alludes to Southwell several times in his work was first
suspected by A. B. Grosart, in his nineteenth-century edition of Southwell's
work, *The Complete Poems of Robert Southwell, S. J.* (London, 1872). For two
recent discussions of Southwell's influence on Shakespeare, see John Klause,
"New Sources for Shakespeare's *King John*: The Writings of Robert
Southwell," *Studies in Philology* 98.4 (2001), 401–27, and Richard Wilson,
"A Bloody Question: The Politics of *Venus and Adonis*," *Religion and the Arts*
5.3 (2001), 297–316. For discussions of Shakespeare's allusions to Magdalene,
see Laura Severt King, "Blessed when they were Riggish: Shakespeare's
Cleopatra and Christianity's Penitent Prostitutes," *Journal of Medieval and
Renaissance Studies* 22.3 (1992), 429–49, and Cynthia Lewis, "Soft Touch: On
the Renaissance Staging and Meaning of the 'Noli me Tangere' Icon,"
Comparative Drama 36.1–2 (2002), 53–73.

37 See Richard Wilson, "A Bloody Question," 298, 297, 298.

38 Christopher Devlin, *The Life of Robert Southwell: Poet and Martyr* (New York:
Longmans, Green and Co, 1956), pp. 261–73.

39 For a related reading of the role of metaphor in Richard's loss of a sacramental
experience of the world, see James L. Calderwood, "*Richard II* to *Henry IV*:
Variations of the Fall," in Harold Bloom (ed.), *William Shakespeare's Richard*

II (New York: Chelsea House, 1988), pp. 67–78. For essays that treat the depiction of grief in the play in different, but for the most part not incompatible, ways than I do, see Dorothy Kehler, "King of Tears: Mortality in *Richard II*," *Rocky Mountain Review of Language and Literature* 39.1 (1985), 7–18; Charles R. Forker, "Unstable Identity in Shakespeare's *Richard II*," *Renascence* 54.1 (Fall 2001), 3–22; and Stanley Wells, "The Lamentable Tale of *Richard II*," *Shakespeare Studies* 17 (1978–79), 1–23.

40 It was conventional in the Renaissance to follow the patristic tradition of identifying Magdalene as the woman who anointed Christ with her tears in Luke 7. See, for example, George Herbert's "Mary Magdalene."

41 Samuel Daniel, *The Civil Wars*, ed. with introd. and notes by Laurence Michel (New Haven, CT: Yale University Press, 1958), p. 119.

42 I refer here to the idea of the king's two bodies studied in E. H. Kantorowicz, *The King's Two Bodies: A Study in Medieval Political Theology* (Princeton, NJ: Princeton University Press, 1957).

43 See Lewis, "Soft Touch."

44 Cited in *King Richard II*, ed. Forker, p. 418 fn. 24.

45 J. A. Bryant, Jr., *Hippolyta's View: Some Christian Aspects of Shakespeare's Plays* (Lexington: University of Kentucky Press, 1961), p. 13.

46 Cited in Pilarz, *Southwell*, p. xxii.

47 *King Richard II*, ed. Forker, p. 467 fn. 60.

48 Jonathan D. Culler, *The Pursuit of Signs: Semiotics, Literature, Deconstruction* (Ithaca, NY: Cornell University Press, 1981), p. 153.

49 Cited in ibid.

50 Ibid.

51 Forker's Arden edition notes the onomatopoeic nature of this line, p. 466 fn. 52.

52 M. M. Mahood, "Wordplay in *Richard II*," in Nicholas Brooke (ed.), *Shakespeare: Richard II: A Casebook*: (London: Macmillan Press, 1973), p. 202.

53 Erwin W. Straus, *Phenomenological Psychology*, trans. Erling Eng (London: Tavistock, 1966), pp. 244, 246.

54 St. Augustine, *De Doctrina Christiana*, ed. and trans. R. P. H. Green (Oxford: Clarendon Press, 1995), p. 15 (book 1 section 3).

55 For a discussion of how Protestant thought results in a loss of ontological immediacy, see Thomas H. Luxon, *Literal Figures: Puritan Allegory and the Reformation Crisis in Representation* (Chicago: University of Chicago Press, 1995), p. 67.

56 *The Norton Shakespeare*, ed. Stephen Greenblatt (New York: Norton, 1997), 1.2.5–10.

57 John N. King, *Milton and Religious Controversy: Satire and Polemic in Paradise Lost* (Cambridge: Cambridge University Press, 2000), p. 37, p. 5.

58 See Arthur Marotti, *Religious Ideology and Cultural Fantasy: Catholic and Anti-Catholic Discourses in Early Modern England* (Notre Dame, IN: University of Notre Dame Press, 2005), p. 65 and Catherine Canino, "The Discourse of Hell and the Irish Rebellion," *Milton Quarterly* 32.1 (1998), 15–23.

59 Cited in Marotti, *Religious Ideology*, p. 53.

60 Marotti notes the influence of Phineas Fletcher on Milton in *Religious Ideology*, p. 242 fn. 137.

61 Giles and Phineas Fletcher, *Poetical Works*, ed. Frederick S. Boas (Cambridge: Cambridge University Press, 1908–9), Canto 2 Stanza 7.

62 See Julian Yates, "Parasitic Geographies: Manifesting Catholic Identity in Early Modern England," in Arthur Marotti (ed.), *Catholicism and Anti-Catholicism in Early Modern English Texts* (New York: St. Martin's Press, 1999), p. 67.

63 See Elizabeth Heale, "Spenser's Malengine, Missionary Priests, And The Means of Justice," *Review of English Studies* 41.162 (1990), 171–84.

64 King, *Milton and Religious Controversy*, p. 22.

65 See Shell, *Catholicism*, p. 172.

66 Barbara Lewalski makes this observation in *Paradise Lost and the Rhetoric of Literary Forms* (Princeton, NJ: Princeton University Press, 1985), pp. 97–98. Her focus is primarily on the tragic elements of Satan's speeches, while mine is on the way Satan offers a demonic-inversion of penitential verse and the poetry of tears.

67 William Cowper, *The Anatomy of Christian Man* (London: 1613), p. 155.

68 *Homily on the Misery of Mankind*, 1997, Renaissance Electronic Texts 1.2. 15–16 http://www.library.utoronto.ca/utel/ret/homilies/bk1hom2.html (accessed August 23, 2006).

69 Victoria Silver, *Imperfect Sense: The Predicament of Milton's Irony* (Princeton, NJ: Princeton University Press, 2001), p. 245.

70 Cited in John S. Tanner, *Anxiety in Eden: A Kierkegaardian Reading of Paradise Lost* (Oxford: Oxford University Press, 1992), p. 30.

71 This allusion is observed by Lewalski, *Paradise Lost*, p. 100, and in Fowler's Longman Edition, p. 219.

72 Cowper, *The Anatomy*, p. 155.

73 Caraman, *Henry Garnet 1555–1606*, p. 24.

74 Cited in Yates, "Parasitic Geographies," 67.

75 *Paradise Lost*, ed. Fowler, p. 228.

76 Cited in Heale, "Spenser's Malengine," 176.

77 A. Lytton Sells, *The Italian Influence in English Poetry: From Chaucer to Southwell* (London: George Allen and Unwin, 1955), p. 330.

78 Ignatius, *Personal Writings*, p. 297.

79 See Harold Bloom, *A Map of Misreading* (Oxford: Oxford University Press, 2003), p. 84 and *The Anxiety of Influence* (Oxford: Oxford University Press, 1997), pp. 77–92.

CHAPTER 2

The poetry of tears and the metaphysics of grief: Richard Crashaw's "The Weeper"

While Milton and Shakespeare participated in the desacralization of Catholic tear poetry, Richard Crashaw sought to further its Counter-Reformation. His 1648 work, "The Weeper," has long been recognized as developing the poetic conventions of Southwell's *St Peters Complaint*, Giambattista Marino's "La Maddalena di Tiziano," and other poems in the Catholic tradition that were popular in both Laudian and Tridentine Counter-Reformations. What critics have not recognized, however, is that "The Weeper" participates in a literary agon over the theology of poetic tears: just as Milton's *Paradise Lost* inverts the conventions of the Ignatian "Exclamation of wonder," so George Herbert's Calvinist poem "Grief" – to which "The Weeper" is a kind of Counter-Reformation response – parodies the Southwellian tradition by refuting its ability to express a genuinely contrite experience of godly sorrow. In "Grief," Herbert disavows the formality of Catholic tear poetry as a means of conveying the authenticity of devout sorrow, thereby offering a Protestant critique of the genre. Crashaw responds to Herbert's Calvinist poem by translating "Grief" from the private, meditative context of solitary prayer and into the public, liturgical space of Eucharistic worship. In the process, "The Weeper" turns away from Herbert's Calvinist poetics, in which the medium is not the message, developing, in its place, a more deeply sacramental poetic predicated on the ideal of linguistic isomorphism – the Eucharistic conjoining of word and thing.

Crashaw's "The Weeper" also differs from Herbert's "Marie Magdalene" in revealing ways. While Herbert's poem is a meditation upon Magdalene as an exemplary convert encountering the mysteries of the Gospel, Crashaw's poem is an apostrophe to her as an embodiment of grace. And given that Crashaw has Magdalene's tears speak in the poem's final stanzas, "The Weeper" pushes to breaking point the distinction between apostrophe and invocation that the Laudian writer Anthony Stafford uses in his celebration of the Virgin Mary – *Femall Glory* (1635) – to defend the reformed

77

status of his work against anticipated accusations that it is Catholic in orientation.[1] Thus by coming very close to transgressing, if not outright flouting, the Protestant thesis that prayers to saints are idolatrous, "The Weeper" stands at the highest reaches of the "High Church" Laudianism of the Caroline establishment, if not actually within the Tridentine Counter-Reformation.[2] More importantly for my purposes, the prayerful orientation of "The Weeper" is a central part of the way it rewrites Herbert's self-consciously Protestant poem "Grief" in a distinctly non-Calvinist way. In this respect, "The Weeper" bears within it the conflicted, if highly fluid, relations between poetry and theology in seventeenth-century England. This chapter attempts to tell the story of these relations through a close reading of Crashaw's poem.

While "The Weeper" rewrites Herbert's "Grief," it also develops the phenomenology of encountering the other's face that Southwell depicts in *St Peters Complaint* – an experience in which the saturation of intuition over concept "so exceed[s] the Kantian categories of quality, relation, or modality, that [it] interrupt[s] or even blind[s] the intentional aim."[3] In this type of encounter, intention is exceeded by intuition in such a way that the subject cannot fix the horizon of interpretation so as to bring the revelation of meanings to a close. As Southwell says in *St Peters Complaint*, Christ's eyes are "Sweet volumes stoarde with learning fit for Saints, / ... Wherein eternall studie never faints, / Still finding all, yet seeking all it findes" (337, 339–40). In "The Weeper," the entire poem takes place within this phenomenal mode of wonder. Each stanza depicts Mary Magdalene's face, and more precisely her eyes and tears, as a site of phenomenal saturation – as a site of infinite meaning overflowing into and beyond the speaker's field of perception. By recognizing how the poem expresses a very specific modality of wonder – one involving the experience of seeing and being seen by a face – we can explain how "The Weeper" is a patient exploration of the kind of saturated phenomenon that Southwell's St. Peter experiences before Christ.

If there is one key difference between Southwell's Peter and Crashaw's Magdalene it is that the female penitent is more idealized and thus more other-worldly. Magdalene embodies the kenotic or self-emptying modality of God's love of man in Philippians to an even greater extent than Peter. Such kenotic love, "The Weeper" insists, makes possible the promise of God's communication of himself as the self-present Logos of John. This promise is formally and thematically expressed in the poem's opening invocation: "Hail, sister springs! ... Still spending, never spent! I mean / Thy fair eyes, sweet MAGDALENE!" (1). The poem unfolds by deepening the animating force inherent in its opening trope, prosopopeia, or the giving of face or voice to a faceless or voiceless object. By trying to create the effect that the poem is bringing Magdalene's tears into being, "The Weeper" not only expresses but seeks to convey the Eucharistic mystery of Real Presence – a conjoining of sign and signed, of what is said and the position of enunciation from which it is said. The overall result of this deepening of the animating force of prosopopeia is a poem that asks us to perceive Magdalene's tears from every conceivable angle until finally we, as readers, are called into the text itself – until we are constituted by it as a face that we not only look at but whose imperceptible look returns our gaze. Through this structure, the poem articulates a theologically specific understanding of three interrelated incarnational mysteries: the agapic mystery of kenosis, or the self-emptying of God into man; the mystery of transcendence through immanence – the mystery that one approaches the unapproachable infiniteness of God by deepening rather than trying to escape from the experience of finitude; and the mystery of Real Presence (probably best understood in the Laudian sense of a spiritual embodiment of Christ that is somehow more immediate than if the host is viewed as a mere sign of Christ's Presence, as in Calvinism, but in which the exact modality of such presence is not specified as it is in Catholicism or Lutheranism).[4] In other words, there is a remarkable and thus far unappreciated congruence of form and theme in the poem: "The Weeper's" baroque strategy of bringing its objects of representation to life, giving them the effect of proceeding out of the text itself, is part of its celebration of Eucharistic worship; similarly, its baroque expression of wonder before the penitent Magdalene, in which there is a kenotic emphasis on movement, dynamism, and tension, helps convey the normally Catholic idea that the female saint embodies compunction in a way that makes it accessible to others. By recognizing this congruence of apostrophic form and kenotic/Eucharistic theme, we can see that the poem does not "lack focus" such that it is little more than a "necklace of epigrams."[5] On the contrary, "The Weeper" consciously develops a poetics of Real Presence in response to Herbert's Calvinist parody of the Counter-Reformation poetry of tears in "Grief."[6]

PROSOPOPEIA

The epigram to "The Weeper" expresses the incarnational paradoxes explored in the poem as a whole, thus condensing the kenotic and penitential themes central to the work: "Loe where a WOUNDED

HEART with Bleeding EYES conspire. / Is she a FLAMING Fountain, or a Weeping fire?"[7] The conjunction of opposites voiced here function as a preparative meditation, as a way of getting the reader to step into the state of mind appropriate to the experience of a sacramental mystery. The epigraph thus functions in relation to the poem the way that St. Ambrose's Prayer for the Preparation of Mass functions in relation to Communion: it moves one from the distracted state of everyday consciousness into the focused, humbled, meditative state of prayer. The prayerful state of mind encouraged by the epigraph is constitutively interrogative, as the Christ-event being celebrated through Magdalene's exemplary contrition exceeds comprehension; such excess works to constitute us within its ever-receding horizon rather than being constituted by us as readers. In this way, the conjoining of opposites prepares us for the incarnationist poetics to follow – a poetics that is embodied by Magdalene's affective state of joy-in-sorrow. Throughout the poem, her tears index this affective state. By imitating Christ's "joyful" suffering, Magdalene comes to embody the mystery of kenosis described in Philippians 2:6–7, in which "God emptied [*ekenosen*] himself, taking the form of a servant."[8] Like Christ, Magdalene is superlatively prodigal in giving of herself completely: "O pretious Prodigall! / Fair spend-thrift of thy self! thy measure / (Mercilesse love!) is all" (22). The poem's apparently unruly structure, its seeming capacity to flow from stanza to stanza without logical succession, is a function of its kenotic theme – its emphasis on Magdalene's contrition and love as without limit.[9]

Following the epigraph that introduces the key paradoxes and imagistic patterns at work in "The Weeper," the poem begins with a salutation to Mary Magdalene: "Hail, sister springs! / Parents of sylver-footed rills!" (1). The poem thus opens in the same way that it will conclude, with prosopopeia. While prosopopeia is often conflated with apostrophe, which is also a form of address, the two figures are, strictly speaking, distinct, and have been treated as such since at least Quintilian.[10] While prosopopeia refers to the giving of voice or face to a voiceless or faceless entity (as in Crashaw's animation of Mary's tears in the final stanza), apostrophe implies a turning of voice from one addressee to another (as in stanza 3's *aversio* from Magdalene's eyes to the royal "we" who perceive them: "But we'are deceived all.").[11] The speaker's initial invocatory "hail" in "The Weeper" is thus prosopopeiac to the extent that it addresses Magdalene by means of a synecdoche: her eyes are lent a figurative ear so that they can come to stand for Magdalene as an emblem of ideally realized godly sorrow. Like apostrophe, this form of prosopopeia is not descriptive but optative, not referential but ritualistic. The mood of the poem's vocatives is liturgical in the broadest sense; what is at issue in them, as Jonathan Culler says of invocative modes in general, "is not a predicable relation between a signifier and a signified, a form and its meaning, but the uncalculable force of an event. Apostrophe is not the representation of an event; if it works, it produces a fictive, discursive event."[12] The particular "event" enacted in "The Weeper" is sacramental in nature: Magdalene's tears are presented not only as signs of godly sorrow but as powers participating in the divine immanence from which godly sorrow emerges.

The poem's invocative and prosopopeiac structure asks that we not only meditate on Mary's tears, but that we experience them as powers revealing to us the Real Presence of Christ. The poem's prosopopeiac structure, especially its ending, encourages us to experience Magdalene's eyes as being able to return our gaze. By doing so, the poem invites us to experience her face not as an object that can be seized but as a subject who constitutes us within its horizon. This phenomenological dimension of the poem is expressed in the initial image of Mary's tears as active agents, as "sylver-footed rills," who will lead us not, as the final stanzas say, to "Auroras bed" but to "our lord's FEET" (1, 30, 31). This movement from the footed-streams of Mary's tears to the Feet of God unfolds by a deepening of the logic inherent to prosopopeia and its related trope, apostrophe. This deepening of the animating force of prosopopeia tries to express the presence of Christ in time as the poem moves from an implicit to an explicit animation of tears. Moreover, this formal structure complements the poem's soteriology, its anti-Augustinian emphasis on Magdalene's passive acceptance of Christ's grace in a way that makes her compunction accessible to those who call upon her in imitation of the speaker's invocation of the saint. Crashaw thus positions the reader in relation to Magdalene as Southwell depicts his reader in relation to Peter: by following her saintly example the reader-penitent participates in the saint's mediation of Christ's grace. Magdalene's acceptance and embodiment of *agape* is figured through images of sacred marriage in stanza 11 and in related figures of tearful reciprocity in stanza 14: "Such the maiden gemme / By the purpling vine put on, / Peeps from her parent stemme / And blushes at the bridegroome sun" (11); "Well does the May that lyes / Smiling in thy cheeks, confesse / The April in thine eyes. Mutuall sweetnesse they expresse" (14). Magdalene's active role in accepting God's love is then thematized in stanza 21 when she is figured as a "A voluntary mint." As Marc F. Bertonasco observes, this emphasis on Magdalene's role in her own repentance soon gives way to a focus on how her weeping makes compunction more readily available for others, as indicated in the image of her eyes as a "FOUNTAIN [that] weeps for all" (23).[13] Crashaw thus uses the tendency within apostrophic modes of utterance to position readers within the circle of address as a way of communicating the sacramental or participatory dimension of Magdalene's tears: the poem's apostrophe creates a liturgical sense of active participation between speaker, saint, and reader, leading readers of "The Weeper" to share in the salvific power of Magdalene's tears rather than merely to interpret them as signs.

"The Weeper" leads readers to experience Magdalene's tears as powers rather than as signs by literalizing, in effect, what the invocative figure of prosopopeia does. As Paul de Man reminds us, the etymology of prosopopeia means "to confer a mask or a face" (*prosopon poiein*).[14] Crashaw's opening thus gives, as it were, face to a face. More precisely, the invocation gives presence to what is conventionally configured as being the phenomenal ground of presence – the face and with it the voice. This proximity between face and voice, de Man insists, is intrinsic to prosopopeia as a rhetorical figure. As he puts it, "voice assumes mouth, eye, and finally face, a chain that is manifest in the etymology of the trope's name."[15] In "The Weeper," this intimacy between face and voice is literalized or made explicit, not only here at the beginning but also, and much more strikingly, through the projecting of voice onto Magdalene's tears in the poem's final two stanzas. By addressing Magdalene's eyes and then making her tears literally speak, the poem's trajectory from beginning to end follows the logic inherent to prosopopeia as the figure of voice *par excellence*. In this way, Crashaw's invoking of Magdalene works not only by employing prosopopeia but by rendering thematic the associations between face and voice inherent in it.

The invocatory structure of "The Weeper" also initiates a chiastic movement which expresses the kenotic paradoxes of godly sorrow, such as when Mary's eyes are figured as "Still spending, never spent," and where she experiences a "sweetness so sad, sadness so sweet" (1, 10). In this way, the poem continually reinforces and extends, rather than resolves, Mary's exquisite sorrow. The cross-coupling figures so central to this process continuously sharpen rather than alleviate the sense of lack initiated in the "hail" that opens the poem; they express the counter-intuitive experience of joy-in-sorrow that Herman Hugo calls the "strange delight" of penitent weeping,[16] and which Crashaw conveys in the image of Mary being in a state of constant "seed-time." The poem's invocatory structure thus articulates the infinite nature of Magdalene's weeping that Cristóbal de Fonseca describes in a sermon "Englished" in 1629: "We know the beginning of these teares, but not the end; for that fountaine of teares which had its Well-head and spring at the feet of our Sauiour Christ, did neuer grow emptie or drie in the eyes of *Marie Magdalen*."[17] The infinite openness of Magdalene's weeping is the penitential correlative to the phenomenology of the face expressed in the poem; her unreserved prodigality in matters of spiritual love is the soteriological basis for a poetics that expresses an infinite generosity of meaning: the faith, hope, and love embodied by Magdalene's tears saturates the speaker and reader with an abundance of signification that is presented as being impossible to fully absorb. In this respect, the metaphysics of grief in Crashaw's poem is predicated on the paradox that in godly sorrow lack turns over into excess, suffering sublates into pleasure, and alienation becomes communion. The relation between the polarities expressed in the poem is not that of a binary but more like two sides of a Möbius strip; by experiencing sorrow profoundly and authentically, the emptying form of kenosis reveals itself in the fulfilling form of pleroma.

The economy of desire expressed through Crashaw's apostrophe to Magdalene exemplifies the difference between Renaissance and baroque approaches to form. While Renaissance form tends towards balanced harmony, completeness, and order, the baroque is characterized by incompleteness, tension, and irregularity. As Heinrich Wölfflin explains, the baroque "never offers us perfection and fulfilment, or the static calm of 'being,' only the unrest of change and the tension of transience ... a sense of movement." While "The Weeper's" baroque qualities have often been noted, critics have yet to recognize how these qualities emerge through and are largely controlled by its handling of prosopopeia. Similarly, critics have not noted how the poem's kenotic movement – its attempt to enact the infinite prodigality of Magdalene's tears as embodiments of infinite grace "still spending never spent" – finds its formal correlative in the baroque practice of giving a viewer more forms and figures than can be visually apprehended at once. Wölfflin describes such baroque excess when he explains that in "the baroque the number of figures became ever greater [than in Renaissance form] ... the spectator, not minded to follow up individual elements, is content with a general effect. Since he cannot possibly absorb every single thing in the picture he is left with the impression that it has unlimited potentialities, and his imagination is kept constantly in action."[18] "The Weeper" produces this effect of unlimited dynamism by flooding the reader with images of Magdalene's infinite prodigality, thereby enacting the wonder one should feel in the experience of accepting Christ's gift of compunction.

This flood of images exemplifies the pseudo-Augustinian idea quoted in Aquinas' interrogation of contrition that a "penitent should always be sorrowing, and always rejoicing in his sorrow."[19] This capacity for ceaseless weeping is the central motif of Bellarmine's 1617 treatise on holy mourning which includes a chapter on tears of divine love which extend from three sources: the glory of God, the state of blessedness, and the grace inspiring them.[20] Developing Magdalene along these lines, Crashaw figures her as iconic not in the sense that she directly transcends temporality, but in the more radically incarnational sense that she is so entirely within time that she cannot be said to be of it. Rather than transcending temporality altogether, Crashaw's Magdalene dilates time, as in stanza 16 of the 1646 version: "Thus dost thou melt the yeare / Into a weeping motion / Each minute waiteth heere." The same process occurs in the revised 1648 version of this stanza, which concludes, "Each winged moment waits, / Takes his TEAR, and gets him gone" (25). Following the model set by Christ, Magdalene is depicted as transcending time by remaining superlatively immanent within it. She thus exemplifies the kenotic paradox that one can approach God through the experience of finitude rather than despite it. In this way, the poem seeks to convey the counter-intuitive temporality of such a state – a temporal mode characterized not by an escaping of the flux of time through ascension, but by a descending movement into it. By dilating time, Magdalene clears the space for an experience of transcendence. This phenomenology of time characterizes the experience of a godly sorrow, rather than the despairing experience of dilated time suffered by Shakespeare's Richard and Milton's Satan.

Crashaw's phenomenology of kenotic time, of time slowed down, of time deepened, and felt in the fullest sense, is the theme of stanza 24:

> Does thy song lull the air?
> Thy falling teares keep faithfull time.
> Does thy sweet-breath'd praire
> Up in clouds of incense climb?
> Still at each sigh, that is, each stop,
> A bead, that is, A TEAR does drop.

In this stanza, Crashaw links the temporality of meditative weeping with the experience of time characteristic of rosary prayers. The "time" of weeping is identified with the "time" of praying the rosary as each tear becomes a bead focusing attention on the "now" of every passing moment. It is as though Crashaw seeks to enact the experiential dimensions informing Herbert's description of prayer as "Angels' age" in "Prayer I." This experience of time is accompanied by an intense focus on the "now" of weeping, a "now" marked not by "minutes, times, and hours," but the fall of each tear. Such focus prevents the type of "distraction" so often bemoaned in seventeenth-century religious lyrics,[21] leading to the kind of elevation of mind that John Bucke writes of when he characterizes the goal of the rosary in his 1589 treatise as an effort

to set before the eyes of the Soule some conceit or Imaginacion of one or other matter conteined in the lyfe of our Savior, or of the blessed virgin Marie. And this conceit well imprinted in the ... thoughtes ... will make it more attentiue and hedefull: werby devocion is soner kindled: without which prayer yeeldeth small fruit.[22]

In stanza 24, the idea of focusing one's attention on the time of weeping as a way of elevating oneself out of the very temporality that makes such focus possible, is depicted in kenotic terms, as part of the immanence of the divine within time.

This paradox is communicated through the onomatopoeic term "lull," which modulates "air," both in the sense of the medium in which all physical experience occurs and in the sense of "a light and spritely tune" (*OED*). The latter meaning calls for an immediate reconfiguration of perspective through an expansion of context: Magdalene's "song" is "spritely" only insofar as it is really a mourning song that sings the promise of grace. Such a conflation of opposites within a single moment and a single word reminds us that it is not a "song" in any literal sense, but something like the perfect silence of godly sorrow. More importantly, this conflation of opposites implies that Magdalene's weeping reveals how the "now" of a particular moment is non-coincident with itself, how it is "out of joint" as the tragedians say. Only from Magdalene's transcendent perspective, this "out of jointness" of time is not viewed from the perspective of tragedy, but from the anagogic perspective of Christian comedy. What is thus seen is the redemptive movement upwards, rather than just the kenotic movement downwards. As George W. Williams observes, the poem figures the paradoxical mode of vision enabled by godly silence through an allusion to the way that lutenists viewed the silence of a "rest" as the expression of a "breath" or "sigh."[23] Like Shakespeare's *Richard II*, this figure seeks to convey the metaphysics of a "sigh." Magdalene's "sighs" are depicted as powers rather than as figures. Yet such powers do not give themselves to be seen as other objects in the world; they appear only as the gap or silence within the "now" of consecutive moments – as the hinge disjointing flesh from spirit, human from divine. Magdalene's "sighs" signify this very gap as a way of petitioning for its dissolution in and through Christ. Her sighs are to time what a rest is to the sounded notes of a musical score. In this silence, the poem paradoxically insists, we catch a glimpse of what it feels like to move out of the Aristotelian "now" of diachronic succession and into the *Nunc-stans* of contemplative perception – the eternal "now" of an indivisible presence.

Taking us through the strange temporality of kenotic prayer, Crashaw brings us to the desire for transcendence implied by the very idea of immanence at work in the meaning of her sighs:

> At these thy weeping gates,
> (Watching their watry motion)
> Each winged moment waits,
> Takes his TEAR, and gets him gone.
> By thine Ey's tinct enobled thus
> Time layes him up; he's pretious. (25)

The Eye's "tincture" ennobles "Time" in the sense of submitting it to a transmuting elixir (the tear), but also in the sense of imbuing it with a new moral and intellectual quality (*OED*). Rather than being constituted by time, Magdalene's profound sensitivity to the experience of finitude has the alchemical effect of constituting time in relation to her as an image of Christ. Thus, instead of representing Magdalene's conversion, the poem depicts how Magdalene's weeping converts time by slowing it down, breaking it into its constitutive parts, so as to effect a paradoxical transcendence of it. The personification of time as a subject rather than a medium of experience expresses this transcendence, preparing us for the poem's ending where Magdalene is not only depicted as having power over time but also over the limits of representation itself.

The kenotic process being depicted in the poem unfolds by taking literally the rhetorical possibilities latent within prosopopeia. The poem's depiction of Magdalene's weeping as a song thematizes, in effect, the way that prosopopeia strives to turn mimesis into music, to move from referentiality and temporality to non-referentiality and iconicity. While this formal feature is evident at virtually every step in the poem, it is encapsulated in the reflexive pun on the deictic indicator "here" in stanza 6: "Not in the evening's eyes / When they Red with weeping are ... / Sitts sorrow with a face so fair, / No where but here did ever meet / Sweetnesse so sad, sadnesse so sweet." The deictic term "here" refers both to Magdalene's face and to the poem itself.[24] By referring to itself this way, the poem strives to identify itself with the powers it is describing. Culler's account of the iconicity of apostrophe helps explain this pursuit of linguistic isomorphism:

Apostrophe resists narrative because its *now* is not a moment in a temporal sequence but a *now* of discourse, of writing. This temporality of writing is scarcely understood, difficult to think, but it seems to be that toward which the lyric strives. Proverbial definition calls the lyric a monument to immediacy, which presumably means a detemporalized immediacy ... or in Keats's phrase ... "one eternal pant."[25]

While Culler's assessment of apostrophe helps account for the poem's basic rhetorical structure, it lumps all forms of iconicity together and thus precludes a precise understanding of Crashaw's kenotic poetics. In "The Weeper" the discursive "here" that is foregrounded is presented not as a "detemporalized" iconicity as such, but a strangely hyper-temporalized one.

The poem's depiction of Magdalene's tears as powers rather than signs reaches its climax in the final stanzas. In what is quite possibly the strangest moment in the English history of the literature of tears tradition, the poem's final two stanzas present Magdalene's tears as literally responding to the poem's interrogative structure:

> ... ô say
> Why you trip so fast away?
>
>   We goe not to seek,
>   The darlings of Auroras bed,
>   The rose's modest Cheek
>   Nor the violet's humble head.
> Though the Feild's eyes too WEEPERS be
> Because they want such TEARES as we.
>
>   Much lesse mean we to trace
>   The Fortune of inferior gemmes,
>   Preferr'd to some proud face
>   Or pertch't upon fear'd Diadems.
> Crown'd Heads are toyes. We goe to meet
> A worthy object, our lord's FEET.

"The Weeper" thus ends by literalizing the Renaissance commonplace of making tears "mighty orators" as Southwell says in *Marie Magdalens Funeral Teares*.[26]

Crashaw's theology of tears comes into full view when we recognize that its final two stanzas rewrite the meditative conclusion of Herbert's "Grief" in more sacramental, liturgical terms. To the best of my knowledge, no Crashaw scholar has observed that the end of "The Weeper" echoes Herbert's "Grief," which concludes by poetically disavowing poetry as inadequate to the expression of devout sorrow.[27] After praying for the grace that is requisite for godly weeping, Herbert's speaker disavows poetry as being capable of accommodating the violence of his desired grief: "Verses, ye are too fine a thing, too wise / For my rough sorrows: cease, be dumb and mute, / Give up your feet and running to mine eyes, / And keep your measures for some lover's lute, / Whose grief allows him music and a rhyme: / For mine excludes both measure, tune, and time / Alas, my God!" (13–19). As Elizabeth Clarke argues, "Grief" is a parody of the Counter-Reformation tradition of tear poetry as "the outrageous and elaborate puns on the 'feet,' 'running' in his verse and to his eyes, and the smooth-'running' line which supports the witticism, gives the lie to the sincerity of the 'rough sorrows'. Only the final inarticulate gasp – the more powerful because of its contrast with the urbane poetry that precedes it – has any sense of authenticity."[28] "Grief" thus ends by reinforcing the Calvinist aesthetic that the medium is not the message. "Grief" insists that the outward form of representation has an accidental rather than essential relation to the spiritual meaning conveyed through it. In "Grief," poetry is figured as too "wise," in the pejorative sense of self-aware and cultivated, to express the unmediated violence of godly sorrow. For the speaker of Herbert's poem, poetry's courtliness renders it inadequate to the raw sincerity of penitent grief.

Though Crashaw's "Weeper" depicts godly sorrow in the same incarnationist terms as Herbert's "Grief" – as a sign of Christian mystery revealing itself at the level of affect – it aims at a sacramental meaning that Herbert's poem does not. As a result, Crashaw's "Weeper" expresses a different theology of language than Herbert's "Grief." In the closing lines of "The Weeper" the poem turns from invocation to incarnation, from an apostrophe of Mary's tears to an "actual" presencing of the tears themselves. Crashaw seeks to harness the animating force within prosopopeia as a way of realizing what we might call a Eucharist effect, a stepping out from representation to reality. In Plotinian terms, Crashaw tries to turn from imagery that is fantastic to imagery that is icastic; from imagery that is a shadow of the truth to imagery that embodies and realizes the truth immediately or hieroglyphically. Crashaw attempts this by trying to harness the tendency in prosopopeia to generate surprise, even shock, in readers. Culler explains this feature of prosopopeia in an essay responding to Paul de Man's reading of the trope when he asserts that "there is an intimate relation between apostrophes addressed to the dead or the inanimate and prosopopeia that give the dead or inanimate a voice and make them speak."[29] This relation reveals, according to de Man, a certain threat latent within the figure: "the latent threat that inhabits prosopo-poeia, namely that by making the dead speak, the symmetrical structure of the trope implies, by the same token, that the living are struck dumb, frozen in their own death."[30] Crashaw draws on this aspect of prosopopeia for sacramental rather than uncanny ends, seeking to create the effect that Magdalene's eyes and tears are looking back at us, constituting us rather than being constituted by us. In this way, Crashaw's poem breaks down its own frame, so to speak, in the way that Counter-Reformation painters sought to break down the frame of a painting as a way of allowing viewers the sensation of entering into the picture's depiction of a devotional scene.[31] In the case of "The Weeper," though, this strategy is not only designed to enhance the emotional effect of the poem by drawing the reader into the scene but is also intended to recreate the effect of Real Presence.

By signaling a shift from the metrical "feet" of a verbal commemor-ation to the Real Feet of a sacramentally present God, Crashaw offers a highly figural disavowal of figurality, an attempt to poetically recreate the incarnating force of Christ's Real Presence within the Eucharist. Crashaw's poem does not call for a giving-up of poetic feet, as does "Grief," but rather it seeks to enact the sacramental moment at which figure becomes reality, where metrical foot becomes flesh. The ending of Crashaw's poem is not so much about the gap between poetry and affect, between medium and message, but rather it is an effort to close this gap, to make present in language that to which language refers. Crashaw tries to turn the grammar of poetry into the grammar of tears – making word and affect fully coincident with one another. In Herbert's "Grief," on the other hand, poetry works to convey the difference between mental state and rhetorical form – between Christian mystery and its predication in human gram-mars. "The Weeper" offers a more deeply sacramental metaphysic of tears than "Grief," to the extent that it tries to express the Eucharistic moment of Real Presence through the animating impetus of prosopopeia. Where "Grief" gestures at the ineffability of Christ's *aliena vita* in the soul, "The Weeper" offers a poetic gesture that aspires to realize a sacramental mystery. In short, Herbert articulates a poetics of difference whereas Crashaw aspires towards a poetics of similitude.

By revising Herbert's poem in this manner, Crashaw appears to be engaging in an agon *with* Herbert as a way of participating in a cultural debate *over* Herbert. On the one hand, Crashaw rewrites Herbert's poem in such a way as to frame "Grief" more closely within the Catholic tradition from which it seeks to differentiate itself. By doing so, Crashaw is also participating in an agon over Herbert in the sense that he is trying to rescue *The Temple* from more puritanical appropriations – appropriations that take various forms, from poetic imitations to different book bindings.[32] By repositioning *The Temple* within the continental tradition that Southwell brought to England, Crashaw seeks to soften the extent to which "Grief" is in sympathy with the idea expressed in "The Quiddity," when Herbert asserts that true poetry "never was *France* or *Spain*" (6). As a reading of Herbert's "Grief," then, Crashaw's "The Weeper" positions Herbert's poem as being continuous with the Catholic traditions from which it disassociates itself. In this way, "The Weeper" anticipates the kinds of debates that continue to this day in Herbert studies.

Despite the theological and formal differences between "Grief" and "The Weeper," both poems exemplify the way that seventeenth-century devotional poets depict the metaphysics of grief. Godly sorrow is not just an emotional state but it is a medium of thought; the discourse of devout grief constitutes a way of thinking with tears about the theological and metaphysical questions at issue in post-Reformation England – be they the soteriological questions of salvation or the sacramental questions about the modality of God's presence. In the case of "The Weeper" tears are literally made to speak and what they try to reveal is both the theological mystery of Real Presence and the phenomenological experience of encountering such a mystery. In this respect, the conclusion to Crashaw's poem is consistent with the "painterly" style of the baroque – a style that often works by giving "an illusion of physical relief," where "the different objects seem to project or recede in space," generating an effect of *elusiveness* or lack of definition in which "some parts of the composition remain hidden and one object overlaps another, [such that] the beholder is stimulated to imagine what he cannot see."[33] In "The Weeper" it is the miraculous presencing of Christ's body that is enacted but not represented: consistent with the mystery of Real Presence, the body is made present, but it is not made visible.

By trying to enact a shift from representation to presentation, from verbal commemoration to iconic reality, "The Weeper" anticipates a pictorial strategy that Johannes Vermeer uses in his 1671 painting, *An Allegory of Faith*, in which a figure identified as Mary Magdalene appears to have stepped out of a picture of the Passion while she participates in a clandestinely domestic Catholic Mass. As Valerie Lind Hedquist has demonstrated, Vermeer's painting is a presentation of the Catholic doctrine of transubstantiation. Hedquist explains that the doctrine is figured in the parallelisms between the painting-within-the-painting and the altar upon which the objects of the Catholic Mass rest:

In both the painting-within-the-picture and on the crucifix, Christ's knees are bent and twisted to the viewer's right. The figural positions of the painted and sculpted Christ tie the historical Crucifixion with the sacrifice at the altar. Furthermore, Christ's body within the painting leads directly to the figure of faith, who turns toward the altar while looking heavenward. Again, Vermeer's composition connects the depicted scene in the painting on the back wall to the events in the sacred domestic interior.[34]

Most important for my reading of Crashaw's sacramental use of prosopopeia is Hedquist's observation that "Vermeer's figure of faith assumes the position of the seated Mary Magdalen in the background painting and comes to life as the penitent saint within Vermeer's domestic church interior."[35] In Vermeer's painting as well as in Crashaw's poem, the Real Presence of Christ is announced through a highly figural dissolution of figurality, a breaking down of rhetorical and pictorial frames.

"The Weeper" thus ends by completing the breakdown of itself as an object being "looked at" so as to emerge as a process involving the reader *in* it – of including the reader within its frame as Magdalene's tears are figured as returning our gaze. In this respect, the poem's final two stanzas complete a process that begins with the visual image accompanying the poem. The poem's exploitation of the tendency within prosopopeia to generate a chiasmic structure in which the reader is hailed by the apostrophized object, serves as the verbal equivalent of the poem's accompanying emblem of Mary. Norman K. Farmer, Jr., who argues that Crashaw likely made the emblem himself, describes the image and its function in relation to the poem in a way that clarifies how the text works to include the reader within its frame:

The Magdalen's head ... lies at an unusual angle in relation to the picture plane. The viewer is positioned slightly below, and to the left of the figure. She in turn faces slightly to her right. The position of her head means that if a line were drawn along *her* line of sight, it would bisect somewhere to the left of the viewer a level line passing (also leftward) across both the viewer's eyes. In defiance of this triangulation, however, the Magdalen's eyes seem to be cast upward, above the point toward which her face is directed ... The upward glance of the eyes in Crashaw's picture complements the position of the wings, a sign of ascent, upon the flaming heart beneath. Again, we find a sharp visual contradiction. For the upward thrust of the wings and the eyes is countered by the falling tears and the falling blood at the bottom of the heart ... we are given a complex visual experience before we read the comparably complex poem. This experience places a heavy emphasis on our imaginative role in the completion of the poem's meaning; we think visually as well as verbally.[36]

Crashaw's handling of prosopopeia structures and delimits the possibilities of this imaginative participation in the poem. The visual emblem and the final stanzas which are, in effect, word-emblems, include the reader within the interpretive frame, making the process of reading active to the point of being quasi-sacramental. The poem's pursuit of Christ's Real Presence brings into view the extent to which the poem's apostrophic structure works to interpellate the reader in relation to the invoked object. Culler describes how this process of interpellation is inherent to modes of address when he asserts that "the vocative of apostrophe is a device which the poetic voice uses to establish with an object a relationship which helps to constitute him. The object is treated as a subject, an I which implies a certain type of you in its turn. One who successfully invokes nature is one to whom nature might, in its turn, speak."[37] Crashaw's poem literalizes this dimension of apostrophe through prosopopeia as the invoked tears are made to speak. And yet these tears are made to deflect the desire that has accumulated around them to another, more real object – one that has been present and insistent throughout the poem but which has not been explicitly expressed until the final word of the final stanza. This final word substantiates the entire poem, reinforcing our sense that it is Christ's presence that has been communicated within and beneath Mary's voluptuous grief.

The poem's effort to create the effect that it is not just an object being perceived but a subject returning our gaze, is part and parcel of the way it communicates the saturation of experience that occurs in an encounter of the other's face that Southwell depicted in *St Peters Complaint*. In such an experience,

I cannot exactly locate myself outside in order to be in front of it, since it admits no "outside" and since I am irremediably in it and am it. I do not see it as a display, but I experience myself in and as it ... I cannot have vision of th[is] phenomenon, because I cannot constitute [it] starting from a univocal meaning, and even less produce [it] as [an] object. What I see of [it], if I see anything of [it] that *is*, does not result from the constitution I would assign to [it] in the visible, but from the effect [it] produces on me.[38]

Crashaw seeks to convey this saturation of meaning and its overwhelming of the perceiver's ability to synthesize the phenomena into a coherent set of objects in stanzas 2 and 3 of the poem:

> Heavens thy fair eyes be;
> Heavens of ever-falling starres.

'Tis seed-time still with thee
And starres thou sow'st, whose harvest dares
Promise the earth to counter shine
Whatever makes heavn's forhead fine.
But we'are deceived all.
Starres indeed they are too true;
For they but seem to fall,
As Heavn's other spangles doe.
It is not for our earth and us
To shine in Things so pretious.

Magdalene's tears are gazed at from every possible angle, from every position of anamorphic distortion, and through this accumulation of perspectives the whole picture comes closer into view – but at this point it still escapes unaided phenomenal perception: "It is not for our earth and us / To shine in Things so pretious." Peter Schwenger describes the multiplying and variously anamorphic perspectives on Magdalene's penitent tears in Crashaw's "The Weeper" as moving towards a Neoplatonic apotheosis, in which Magdalene's many tears reveal the transcendent unity of the One: "the accumulating marvel evoked by the sheer variety of metaphorical transitions as well as their witty illusionism [raises] Magdalene's tears from a literal level to the level of apotheosis."[39] Eugene R. Cunnar offers a related interpretation of Crashaw's anamorphic poetics in general when he observes that "Crashaw converges, transposes, and interpenetrates ... images in an affective and sacramental form of *ut pictura poesis*, designed to soften or wound the reader's heart in a reciprocal act of charity."[40] Appealing to both Neoplatonic *gnosis* and empathic apprehension, Crashaw envisions a poetic form that aspires to the kind of reading not unlike that expounded by Nicholas of Cusa, who insists that one reads like God when one does not move successively from word to word but grasps the entirety of a text at once.[41]

When Crashaw elsewhere tries to envision such a visionary mode of reading he turns to the image of the body as "all eye." In his epigrammatic response to Matthew 18:9: "*It is better to go into Heaven with one eye, &c*," he pictures the kind of full apprehension gestured at in the final stanza of "The Weeper":

One Eye? a thousand rather, and a Thousand more
To fix those full-fac't Glories, o he's poore
Of Eyes that has but *Argus* store,
Yet if thou'lt fill one poore Eye, with thy Heaven and Thee,
O grant (sweet Goodnesse) that one Eye may be
All, and every whit of me.

As in "The Weeper," the fullness of perception is expressed in this epigraph through the figure of the face – the "full-fac't" glories of heaven. The image of the face as an instance of full-Being, of the union of will and desire, is a common Crashavian trope, its clearest expression occurring in the Epiphany Hymn: "All-circling point. All centring sphear. / The world's one, round, Aeternall year. / Whose full and all-unwrinkled face / Nor sinks nor swells with time or place; / But every where and every while / Is One Consistent solid smile" (lines 26–31). No face is ever fully apprehended, ever fully perceived precisely because its own look cannot, itself, be regarded. As a result, the face is a phenomenologically appropriate image for conveying this sense of incomprehensible fullness. It is precisely this phenomenological principle that is conveyed in "The Weeper"'s emphasis on the dialectical nature of Magdalene's tears, their self-destroying/self-recreating power: "O cheeks! Bedds of chast loves / By your own showres seasonably dash't; / Eyes! nests of milky doves / In your own wells decently washt, / O wit of love! that thus could place / Fountain and Garden in one face"(15). This dialectical tension resolves in a way that sustains the phenomenological principle that Magdalene's face presents a saturation of meaning that is in excess of being absorbed by cognition; that is to say, it pushes toward paradox rather than synthesis as "Cheekes and Eyes / Close in kind contrarietyes" (16). The verb "close," which characterizes the union of "rain" and "sunshine" – of sorrow and joy – means "to include, [or] contain within itself," "to fill up (a gap or open place); to bound, shut in (often with the notion of filling up or completing)"; "to come close together in contact or union" (*OED*). Magdalene's face thus presents to us a logically impossible conjoining of oppositions – a mystery of incarnation that is designed to be experienced as an injunction rather than just a spectacle. In this respect, the depiction of Magdalene's face in "The Weeper" exemplifies the phenomenology of the other's face we saw at work in *St Peters Complaint* – a phenomenology in which "I do not approach it following my intention, but following its intentionality, because it is the face that asks me ... to renounce any mastery over it, and to distance myself from it – '*noli me tangere!*'"[42] Indeed, Crashaw's representation of seeing a saintly face draws on, even as it develops, Southwell's apostrophic poetics.

This phenomenology, however, is more fully realized in "The Weeper" than it is in *St Peters Complaint*. Crashaw deepens the rhetorical possibilities of prosopopeia by literalizing its figurative force. In the final stanzas of "The Weeper" the tears speak their desire, moving us towards the sacramental moment when the deepened sense of finitude they convey is figured as turning into full presence of the Word as figured by the "Eye." In these final stanzas, we see the apotheosis of the poem's theology of form and its metaphysics of grief: it presents to us the Eucharistic mystery of Real Presence as the fulfillment of the poem's kenotic motions. And throughout the poem, these motions poeticize the affective state of godly sorrow as a saturated phenomenon in which more meaning and more experience is felt than can be synthesized into a determinate object. In "The Weeper," godly sorrow has the ontological status of a poem.

NOTES

1 See Anthony Stafford, *Femall Glory* (London, 1635), C2.
2 To be clear, then, I am not suggesting that Crashaw belongs to an alien Catholic tradition that is divorced from English literary and religious culture. On the contrary, my view is largely consistent with John Wall's thesis that the intent in poems such as "The Weeper" and "An Apologie for the Precedent Himne" "is not to inhabit a Catholic spiritual life from afar but to bring the riches of this spiritual tradition into his own religious milieu." See John N. Wall, "Crashaw, Catholicism, and Englishness: Defining Religious Identity," *Renaissance Papers* (2004), 107–26, 119. Though, unlike Wall, I agree with Graham Parry that Laudianism should itself be viewed as a form of Counter-Reformation and not simply a product of puritan polemic. See Graham Parry, *The Arts of the Anglican Counter-Reformation: Glory, Laud and Honour* (Woodbridge: Boydell Press, 2006). For discussions of the different theological and devotional contexts informing Crashaw's verse, see Thomas F. Healy, *Richard Crashaw* (Leiden: E. J. Brill, 1986); Austin Warren, *Richard Crashaw: A Study in Baroque Sensibility* (Ann Arbor: University of Michigan Press, 1957) and R. V. Young, *Doctrine and Devotion in 17th-Century Poetry* (Cambridge: D. S. Brewer, 2000).
3 Jean-Luc Marion, *In Excess: Studies of Saturated Phenomena*, trans. Robyn Horner and Vincent Berraud (New York: Fordham University Press, 2002), p. xiv. For my reading of Southwell in relation to Marion, see Chapter 1.
4 In my view, "The Weeper" seeks to express the mystery of Real Presence in such a way as to position the reader in an active relation to the text but it is not, in any sense, a polemic for or against the specific modality of this presence, be it the Thomistic view of the Tridentine Catholic Church or the Laudian view of the Caroline Church. For related accounts of Crashaw's Eucharistic poems, see Thomas F. Healy, *Richard Crashaw*, pp. 139–40; Gary Kuchar, *Divine Subjection: The Rhetoric of Sacramental Devotion in Early Modern England* (Pittsburgh, PA: Duquesne University Press, 2005), chapter 2; Ryan Netzley, "Oral Devotion: Eucharistic Theology and Richard Crashaw's Religious Lyrics," *Texas Studies in Literature and Language* 44.3 (Fall 2002), 247–72. For a reading of Crashaw's Eucharistic poems as distinctly Thomistic in orientation, see R. V. Young, *Doctrine and Devotion*,

p. 156. Robert M. Cooper, *An Essay on the Art of Richard Crashaw* (Salzburg: Universität Salzburg, 1982), chapter 3, offers a related, if more generally focused, account of the poem's themes, as I do. Though I am in general agreement with Cooper's reading, I focus more attention on the way Crashaw expresses his theological views through tropes rather than through images.

5 Louis Martz, *From Renaissance to Baroque: Essays on Literature and Art* (Columbia: University of Missouri Press, 1991), p. 206.

6 This is not to imply that Herbert remains theologically uncommitted to a notion of Real Presence. Like Calvin and Hooker, Herbert subscribes to a view of the Eucharist as a sign of Christ's Real Presence, but this belief does not translate into the kind of isomorphic poetics Crashaw pursues in "The Weeper," especially not in "Grief." For a discussion of how Herbert's English-Protestant belief in Real Presence informs his poetry, see Robert Whalen, *The Poetry of Immanence: Sacrament in Donne and Herbert* (Toronto: University of Toronto Press, 2002).

7 For a discussion of the emblematic features of the epigram, see Leland Chambers, "In Defense of 'The Weeper'," *Papers on Language and Literature* 3 (1967), 111–12.

8 *New Oxford Annotated Bible* (New York: Oxford University Press, 2001). For an informed discussion of the poem in relation to the patristic tradition of describing penitent tears as "sweet," see Stephen Manning, "The Meaning of 'The Weeper,'" *ELH* 22 (1955), 34–47.

9 Many readers of "The Weeper" have commented on its apparently unruly structure. For critiques of these negative views which are different from but not incompatible with mine, see Marc F. Bertonasco, "A New Look at Crashaw and 'The Weeper'," *Texas Studies in Literature and Language* 10 (1968), 177–88, revised in *Crashaw and the Baroque* (Alabama: University of Alabama Press, 1971), chapter 3; and Chambers, "In Defense of 'The Weeper.'" For a discussion of the imagery of abundance in "The Weeper," see George W. Williams, *Image and Symbol in the Sacred Poetry of Richard Crashaw* (Columbia: University of South Carolina Press, 1963), pp. 94–104.

10 I follow J. Douglas Kneale's discussion of prosopopeia in *Romantic Aversions: Aftermaths of Classicism in Wordsworth and Coleridge* (Montreal: McGill-Queens University Press, 1999), chapter 1. Kneale corrects some definitional problems in Jonathon Culler's discussion of apostrophe in *The Pursuit of Signs: Semiotics, Literature, Deconstruction* (Ithaca, NY: Cornell University Press, 1981).

11 See Kneale, *Romantic Aversions*, chapter 1.

12 Culler, *Pursuit*, p. 152.

13 Bertonasco, *Crashaw and the Baroque*, p. 108.

14 Cited in Michael Riffaterre, "Prosopopeia," *Yale French Studies* 69 (1985), 107–23, 108.

15 Ibid., 108.

16 Herman Hugo, *Pia Desideria*, trans. Edmund Arwaker (London, 1686), p. 40.

17 Cristóbal de Fonseca, *Deuout Contemplations* (Oxford, 1629), p. 579.

18 Heinrich Wölfflin, *Renaissance and Baroque*, trans. Kathrin Simon (Ithaca, NY: Cornell University Press, 1964), p. 62 and p. 39. See also Warren, *Richard Crashaw*, p. 65.

19 Thomas Aquinas, *Summa Theologiae*, trans. Eric D'Arcy (New York: Blackfriars and McGraw-Hill, 1975), vol. 20, q. 4, a. 2.

20 See Roberto Bellarmino, "De Gemitu Combrae," in *Opera Omnia*, 12 vols. (Paris: Ludovicum Vivés, 1874), vol. 8, book 2, chapter 10, pp. 451–54.

21 See for example, Herbert's "Denial" and Henry Vaughan's "Distraction."

22 John Bucke, *Instructions for the Use of Beads* (Louvain, 1589), p. 14.

23 Williams, *The Complete Poetry of Crashaw*, p. 135 fn 5.

24 The same kind of pun occurs in the final stanza of "The Teare."

25 Culler, *Pursuit*, p. 152.

26 Robert Southwell, *Marie Magdalens Funeral Teares*, p. 69.

27 Swanston Hamish, "The Second Temple," *Durham University Journal* 25 (1963), 14–22, comes closest to making this observation when he observes that "It may ... be hazarded that, no less than Marino, Herbert, with his poems on *Marie Magdalene* and the wildness of his *Griefe*, influenced the conception of Crashaw's *The Weeper*," 21.

28 Elizabeth Clarke, *Theory and Theology in George Herbert's Poetry: "Divinitie, and Poesie, Met"* (Oxford: Clarendon Press, 1997), p. 122.

29 Culler, *Pursuit*, p. 153.

30 Cited in ibid., p. 153.

31 For a discussion of the way Crashaw breaks down the frame of his poems in ways analogous to baroque art, see Lorraine M. Roberts, "Crashaw's Sacred Voice," in John R. Roberts (ed.), *New Perspectives on the Life and Art of Richard Crashaw* (Columbia: University of Missouri Press, 1990), p. 72. Roberts does not discuss "The Weeper."

32 For a discussion of how different bindings of *The Temple* reflect different devotional dispositions, see Kathleen Lynch, "Devotion Bound: A Social History of *The Temple*," in Jennifer Anderson and Elizabeth Sauer (eds.), with afterword by Stephen Orgel, *Books and Readers in Early Modern England: Material Studies* (Philadelphia: University of Pennsylvania Press), pp. 177–97.

33 Wölfflin, *Renaissance and Baroque*, p. 31 and p. 33.

34 Valerie Lind Hedquist, "The Real Presence of Christ and the Penitent Mary Magdalen in the *Allegory of Faith* by Johannes Vermeer," *Art History* 23.3 (September 2000), 333–64, 343. I am grateful to Veronica Bishop for bringing Vermeer's painting to my attention.

35 Ibid., 343.

36 Norman K. Farmer, *Poets and the Visual Arts in Renaissance England* (Austin: University of Texas Press), p. 46.

37 Culler, *Pursuit*, p. 142.

38 Marion, *In Excess*, p. 113.

39 Peter Schwenger, "Crashaw's Perspectivist Metaphor," *Comparative Literature* 28 (1976), 65–74, 74. For a related reading of Crashaw's poetic, see Heather Asals, "Crashaw's Participles and the 'Chiaroscuro' of Ontological Language," in Robert M. Cooper (ed.), *Essays on Richard Crashaw* (Salzburg: Universität Salzburg, 1979), pp. 35–49.

40 Eugene R. Cunnar, "Opening the Religious Lyric: Crashaw's Ritual, Liminal, and Visual Wounds," in John R. Roberts (ed.), *New Perspectives on the Seventeenth-Century English Religious Lyric* (Columbia: University of Missouri Press, 1994), p. 262.

41 See Jasper Hopkins, *Nicolas of Cusa's Dialectical Mysticism: Text, Translation, and Interpretive Study of De Visione Dei* (Minneapolis: Arthur J. Banning Press, 1985) and Carl M. Selkin, "The Language of Vision: Traherne's Cataloguing Style," *ELR* 6 (1976), 92–104, 97.

42 Marion, *In Excess*, p. 117.

CHAPTER 3

The poetry of tears and the metaphysics of grief: Andrew Marvell's "Eyes and Tears"

If Crashaw reworks Herbert's "Grief" by substituting a poetics of difference for a Eucharistic poetics of similitude, then Andrew Marvell's "Eyes and Tears" responds to "The Weeper" by furthering the Calvinist ethos of *The Temple*. In the process, Marvell sums up the poetry of tears as a genre from a more discernibly Protestant viewpoint, giving the coincidence of "eyes and tears" a very different theological valence than their "kind contrarietyes" possess in Crashaw's "The Weeper."

Although Marvell's "Eyes and Tears" revises the poetry of tears as a genre, it is often seen as only marginally participating in the tradition of Southwell's *St Peters Complaint* and Crashaw's "The Weeper." For example, in his 2003 edition of Andrew Marvell's English poems, Nigel Smith glosses the subject matter of "Eyes and Tears" as secular with the proviso that stanza 8's description of Mary Magdalene is religious:

Marvell's poem begins and remains secular in subject-matter, like other similar examples in the period: see, e.g. Thomas Carew, "Lips and Eyes" (1640). Only stanza VIII, with the attached Latin version, is religious and certainly may be regarded as part of the English tradition inaugurated by the Elizabethan Jesuit Robert Southwell.[1]

Smith's account of "Eyes and Tears," one shared by other Marvell scholars, is inadequate not only because it begs the question of the poem's thematic integrity, but also because it elides how the poem revises the theological and devotional vision expressed in "The Weeper" and other more avowedly Catholic tear poems, especially William Alabaster's *Spiritual Sonnets*.[2] Marvell's entire poem, and not simply one of its stanzas, needs to be read as a critical reassessment of the English tradition inaugurated by Robert Southwell; for the poem revises the Catholic literature of tears tradition by putting verbal adaptations of anamorphic forms of representation in the service of a theological vision, whose irony, epistemological skepticism, and overall philosophy is distinct from previous Catholic and Laudian instances of the genre. In order to grasp how Marvell's meditation on tears translates anamorphosis into a poetic register we must return to Shakespeare's *Richard II*. By situating Marvell's poem in relation to both the poetry of tears tradition and Shakespeare's meditations on the anamorphic qualities of tears, we can better grasp Marvell's idiosyncratically Protestant and epistemologically skeptical answer to the Pauline question – inherent to the *ars lachrimandi* generally – what does it mean to weep in an authentically devout way, rather than in a narcissistically self-oriented way?

By considering how the poem's translation of anamorphic forms of representation into a verbal register differs from similar tropes in poems by Alabaster and Crashaw we can broaden, and yet at the same time refine, Barbara Lewalski's and Joan Hartwig's interpretations of "Eyes and Tears." Arguing for the poem's distinctly Protestant character, Lewalski asserts that Marvell's curiously reasoned speaker expresses how repentance provides "a means of clearer vision about natural order and its goods" – thereby deepening the reformation of tear poetry begun in Herbert's *The Temple*.[3] Examining the philosophical views expressed in the poem, Hartwig sees "Eyes and Tears" as expressing the view that "distortion through tears is a valid way of seeing, and that, if we could but put aside given ways of seeing, of perceiving reality, we might find that all is one – dualities are only apparent. There is no true 'this' and 'other.'"[4] Though Lewalski's and Hartwig's readings are notable insofar as they address the theological and philosophical issues at stake in Marvell's poem, neither examines how "Eyes and Tears" presents a thoroughgoing revaluation of the Neoplatonic vision and specific sacramental ethos visible in poems by Alabaster and Crashaw. For instance, Hartwig's thesis that "Eyes and Tears" arrives at the view that "all is one" collapses Marvell's ironic vision of the relations between divine and mundane orders with the effusively Eucharistic view forwarded in Crashaw's "The Weeper" and Alabaster's *Spiritual Sonnets* – thereby missing the distinct way in which the paradoxes of incarnationist theology are voiced in Marvell's poem.

Rather than articulating a theological view in which differences are only apparent, "Eyes and Tears" presses toward the position that the relation between earthly and heavenly orders is actually grounded in difference and should thus be predicated through what Luther calls the "category of relation" rather than that of substance.[5] For Marvell, as for Luther, the order of grace communicates with the order of nature through differential relations among signs and beings, rather than through analogical or isomorphic similitude. Unlike Augustine and Crashaw, who presuppose that the invisible truths of divine reality are conveyed analogically through their similitude with the visible realities of empirical existence, Marvell presupposes that difference clears the space for a relation with the order of grace that is radically incommensurable with the sensual appearances of earthly life. On the basis of this theology, Marvell accommodates the non-relation between divine and worldly orders with recourse to verbal adaptations of anamorphic forms of representation, which in Renaissance art generally present two profoundly dissimilar, often shockingly opposed, images. In other words, the difference between coexisting images within a single anamorphic perspective provides a vehicle for expressing the coexistence of human and divine orders within a single experience of grief. Developing the Reformation habit of radicalizing the kenotic tendencies within Christian traditions of godly sorrow, such as we saw in relation to Donne's "Jesus Wept," "Eyes and Tears" insists that the relation between the orders of grace and nature subsists not only between shadow and substance, subject and object, but *within* identity itself. Through a philosophical reflection on the anamorphically distorting/clarifying function of tears – a theme evident in the literature of tears tradition as early as Alabaster's Elizabethan poems – Marvell affirms the paradoxes of incarnationist theology by asserting that the breach separating material and spiritual orders constitutes the hinge by which the two are conjoined. In other words, it is not enough to say, as Hartwig does, that Marvell's poem articulates the view that "heaven and earth are the same thing once seen through the wisdom of tears,"[6] for this simply restates the question addressed in the poem's final stanza: what is the meaning of the word "same" when it is raised in the context of the relations between eternal and temporal orders, between God and humanity?

As I shall argue, Marvell explores the form of identity pertaining to the human–divine relation by inverting the Neoplatonic ontology and Eucharistic vision evident in Alabaster's and Crashaw's poems in the tear tradition. This inversion turns on Marvell's handling of the idea that tears distort (and yet clarify) perception in a way similar to the distortions inherent in anamorphosis.[7] Moreover, the epistemologically skeptical view expressed in "Eyes and Tears" echoes, even as its Protestant theology appears distinct from, Shakespeare's radically demystifying meditations on how the anamorphic properties of tears disclose the tragic conditions of the fallen world. In other words, I think Marvell learned how to address the relation between divine and mundane worlds from Shakespeare's meditations on anamorphosis. I thus begin my analysis of the complex literary history implicit in Marvell's poem by considering, in some detail, its Shakespearean background. By unpacking this literary-theological history, I hope to demonstrate how Marvell's "Eyes and Tears" incorporates into itself the competing answers writers working within the poetry of tears tradition give to such questions as: do we ever weep for anybody other than ourselves? And if we do, what is revealed by such an act? What makes such concern with otherness possible, especially the radical otherness of God?

VENUS' TEARS AND THE QUEEN'S SORROW

In a 1667 letter to Sir John Trott, Marvell distinguishes between weeping that springs "from tenderness only and humanity" and weeping that stems from "an implacable sorrow."[8] Among other things, "Eyes and Tears" is a meditation on how the first form of weeping affords perspective on the very meaning of the category "human." Because the question of weeping is so closely bound up with the question of the "human" for Marvell (as for western culture more broadly), he addresses it in relation to broader theological and metaphysical questions – questions of the relations between the order of grace and the order of nature.[9] As we have seen, Shakespeare also approaches weeping as a philosophical question. One such example is in *Venus and Adonis*, which, as several critics have observed, appears to inform the title as well as the first and last stanzas of "Eyes and Tears."[10]

   The passage from *Venus and Adonis* to which several scholars suggest the title of Marvell's poem alludes occurs near the end of the poem when Venus weeps over the slain body of Adonis: "O, how her eyes and tears did lend and borrow, / Her eye seen in the tears, tears in her eye, / Both crystals, where they viewed each other's sorrow" (962–63). As is often the case with Shakespearean characterization, the perversely self-propagating features of usury indicate that Venus remains caught within the horizon of her own narcissism. Presenting us with another demonic parody of Magdalene's compassionate weeping over the body of Christ – with whom these two pagan figures are generally identified via Christian typology – Shakespeare's Venus is repeatedly depicted as hopelessly solipsistic, such as when she looks into Adonis' dead eyes and sees: "Two glasses, where herself herself beheld / A thousand times, and now no more reflect" (1129–30).[11] These specular scenarios make it clear that Venus is guilty of the narcissism of which Southwell warns in a statement that, despite his Catholicism, encapsulates general attitudes toward grieving in Protestant England: "Much sorrowe for the dead is eyther the childe of selfe-loue, or of rash iudgement: if wee should shead our teares for others death, as a meane to our contentment, wee shewe but our owne wound perfit louers of our selues."[12] Although Venus' tears tend to serve as mirrors for self-reflection, they also perform another, potentially less self-absorbed, function. For while her tears continually blur her vision of Adonis' otherness, they occasion a more insightful, if ultimately incomplete, recognition of the tragic conditions in which she finds herself. Gazing upon Adonis' wound, Venus' tears magnify the gash in his body, thereby initiating the poem's articulation of a "breach" within the heart of creation itself:

> Upon his hurt she looks so steadfastly
> That her sight dazzling makes the wound seem three;
> And then she reprehends her mangling eye,
> That makes more gashes where no breach should be.
> His face seems twain, each several limb is doubled;
> For oft the eye mistakes, the brain being troubled. (1063–68)

Implying a half-acknowledged desire that Adonis' death bear with it a meaning that is not accessible empirically, Venus' tearful misperception anticipates the significance she later accords to his demise when she decrees that there will henceforth be a division in nature itself: "Since thou art dead, lo here I prophesy, / Sorrow on love hereafter shall attend ... / It shall ... set dissension 'twixt the son and sire, / Subject and servile to all discontents" (1136–37, 1160–62). Through the "breach" in Adonis' flesh, the immortal Venus proclaims the material origin of the humble conditions of mortal love. Adonis' death is thus presented as the reverse image of Christ's death, as it conditions loss and division rather than victory and communion. The tragic conditions arising from Adonis' death come into view through the quasi-anamorphic perspective afforded by Venus' tears as her exaggerated view of Adonis' wound leads her to proclaim that there will henceforth be a disjunction inherent to nature. Venus thus parodies two roles in Christian scripture: the role God plays in Genesis 3 when he proclaims that sorrow and death shall be Adam and Eve's inheritance, and the roles Mary Magdalene plays in John 20 and Luke 7, particularly as they are re-envisioned in the Renaissance, as we saw in relation to Southwell in Chapter 1. While the God of Genesis unites speech and being in each verbal act, Venus continually misfires at the level of the word as well as at the level of the body; and while Magdalene misreads Christ's death through agapic love, Venus' misprision is an expression of selfishness and frustrated lust.

The narrator of *Venus and Adonis* indicates that the goddess' pseudo-divine decree is more retrospective than proleptic when he relates Venus' plucking of the flower that, in Ovid's version of the story, serves as a lasting memorial of Adonis: "She crops the stalk, and in the breach appears / Green-dropping sap, which she compares to tears" (1175–76). The gulf inherent to human relations is now materialized not only by the wound in Adonis' flesh, but also in the "breach" within the very signifier of that wound itself. Just as Richard feels himself becoming a sign for another sign, so Adonis is now being used by Venus as a signifying thing, which perhaps is all she was capable of in the first place. Perhaps this is why Venus' comparison of the Green-dropping sap with "tears" calls attention to the retrospective character of her pseudo-prophetic utterance: just as the link between real event and its signification in nature appears as an arbitrary function of Venus' desire rather than an inherent part of nature's signifying power, so Venus' decree that all future love will be subject to death and discontent appears diagnostic rather than portentous. Rather than demonstrating any power over the world of love, Venus continues to appear subject to the dislocations within nature at several levels. She can maintain a relationship with Adonis neither at the real level of physical love nor at the symbolic level of the signifying "stalk."

The gulf between Venus and Adonis' memorial flower is evinced when she draws attention to the difference between symbol and symbolized, remarking that: "There shall not be one minute in an hour / Wherein I will not kiss my sweet love's flow'r" (1187–88). While emphasizing the metonymic rather than isomorphic relation between the stalk and Adonis, Venus also implicitly reminds us that the word "stalk" implies not only a "scape or flower-stem rising directly from the root" but also "a penis, especially one that is erect" (*OED*).[13] Eros thus turns into *thanatos* in the realm of bodies as well as that of signification: Venus becomes a living grave for Adonis, plucking the "purple flower" so that it might in the "hollow cradle" of her breast "take [its] rest" (1184).

That Shakespeare's poem is a pagan comi-tragedy, rather than a Christian tragi-comedy, is further evinced by the way Adonis' death serves only to reinforce, rather than alleviate, the conditions occasioning Eros' morphing into *thanatos*. Given the pagan landscape of the poem, Venus' distorting tears bring into view the tragic conditions of love in the fallen world without offering any alternative vision. Consequently, the prophetic authority her tears inspire is consistently undercut. Rather than appearing as an outward decree with proleptic force, her tearful pronouncements are inwardly oriented, retrospective assertions. In the final analysis, it looks as though Venus' "decree" that Adonis' death constitutes the origin of human discontent serves to obscure the arbitrary nature of Adonis' death – thereby evoking another palpable but, for this pagan goddess, illegible beginning before the beginning. By signifying the impossibility of interpreting and thereby gaining access to origins, Venus' cropped stalk denotes not the beginning of human discontentment but an always-already existent rupture. The originary wound that Venus' stalk brings into view not only occasions Eros' various misfirings in the poem, but it also denotes the irreconcilable gap severing past from future and mortal from immortal. What Venus' tears make visible is not the absolute beginning of human discontentment, but a tragic view of the originary difference severing past from future, life from death, mortal from immortal – a view that will come to haunt the lachrymose Queen in *Richard II*.

In other words, the disjunctions revealed by Venus' tears are those symbolized by the cropped flower, which comes to stand for the seemingly irreconcilable gulf that exists between "sweet beginning" and "unsavory end" (1138). By emphasizing the primordial "breach" between nature and Eros, the poem ends by emphasizing the differences rather than the similarities between Venus and Adonis and their Christian counterparts, Magdalene and Jesus. What is missing from Shakespeare's poem is the promise of renewal, that force of grace which conjoins rather than crops immortal and mortal realms. This absence of a redemptive force in the epyllion makes Venus and Adonis look remarkably similar to, if much more comic than, Richard and Isabel in the opening of Act 5 in *Richard II*.

The tragic scenario played out in *Venus and Adonis*, with its attendant distorting tears, morbid foreboding, and overall fascination with the "breach" or "nothing" at the heart of the fallen world, is replayed in *Richard II* in more explicitly anamorphic terms. Marvell will rework these terms by offering a skeptically Protestant (rather than outright tragic) view of the "breach" between temporal and divine orders. While Venus berates herself for multiplying Adonis' wound, so the courtier Bushy attempts to console Queen Isabel on the occasion of Richard's departure for Ireland by saying that her tears distort her perception in the manner of an anamorphic painting. Engaging in a form of anticipatory mourning, not only for Richard, but also, it would seem, for an heir who was never conceived, the Queen voices grief for something that was never present in the first place. Marvell, as we shall see, will redeploy this mourning of a "something-nothing" – this grieving for an origin that was never present as such – in an entirely different generic context:

QUEEN: Some unborn sorrow, ripe in Fortune's womb,
          Is coming towards me, and my inward soul
          With nothing trembles. At something it grieves
          More than with parting from my lord the King.
BUSHY: Each substance of a grief hath twenty shadows,
          Which shows like grief itself, but is not so;
          For sorrow's eyes, glazed with blinding tears,
          Divides one thing entire to many objects,
          Like perspectives, which, rightly gazed upon,
          Show nothing but confusion; eyed awry,
          Distinguish form. So your sweet majesty,
          Looking awry upon your lord's departure,
          Finds shapes of grief more than himself to wail,
          Which, looked on as it is, is naught but shadows
          Of what it is not. Then, thrice-gracious Queen,
          More than your lord's departure weep not. More is
          not seen,
          Or if it be, 'tis with false Sorrow's eye,
          Which for things true weeps things imaginary. (2.2.10–27)

Attempting to obscure the Venus-like insight of Isabel's tears, Bushy deploys an anamorphic analogy in order to sustain a Platonic distinction between shadow and substance that serves to authorize a distinction between true and false grief. The problem with Bushy's anamorphic conceit, however, is that the inconsistent value accorded to oblique perspective – to eyeing something awry – undercuts its own claim that direct or accurate perspective can be achieved. Consequently, Bushy further confuses, rather than resolves, the distinctions between true and false grief.

Appropriating Bushy's politically motivated anamorphic figure to her own purpose, Isabel responds to Bushy by demystifying his Platonic distinction between shadow and substance. She accomplishes this deconstruction by asserting that her grief is without precedent and hence originary: "nothing hath begot my something grief, / Or something hath the nothing that I grieve. / 'Tis in reversion that I do possess – / But what it is, that is not yet known what, / I cannot name. 'Tis nameless woe, I wot." (2.2.36–40). As Ned Lukacher observes, Isabel here presents a different view of "nothing" than Bushy.[14] Rather than seeing nothing as emptily void, as no-thing, she implies that "nothing" is the difference of something from itself. For Isabel, "nothing" names the condition of possibility for the meaning of her grief to be revealed "in reversion" or retrospectively. What Isabel finds disturbing, in other words, is not simply the transparently unfortunate nature of Richard's troubles, but the fact that the meaning of her grief cannot be determined until the events that have caused them are legible as *events* – as part of a completed chain of historical causation. Caught within the folds of unraveling time, Isabel is suspended in the difference of the singular moment from itself. Because the cause of her grief can only emerge once the effect is legible, Isabel voices the precise sense in which time is constitutively out of joint in Shakespearean tragedy. The meaning of the singular moment is illegible because it is non-coincident with itself. In other words, her anamorphic tears bring into focus the disjointedness of time that Crashaw's Magdalene perceived from the point of view of redemptive immanence, rather than ensuing tragedy. As we shall see, Marvell views this disjuncture within nature as conditioning the meaningfulness of weeping as the most distinctly human and the most properly faithful of acts.

By attending to the difference within the apparent identity of the self-same moment (what Aristotle designates in the *Physics* as the "now" or discrete unity discernible within the flow of diachronic time), Isabel's "nothing" appears like the "breach" in the cropped flower from *Venus and Adonis*. Rather than being totally vacant of, or replete with, significance, this "nothing" constitutes the apparent "origin" of a grief whose meaning is ultimately determined retrospectively. Not knowing whether her womb will constitute a beginning or an end, an origin or a tomb, she responds to Bushy by demystifying his distinction between substance and shadow. By doing so, she implies an ontology, to paraphrase Lukacher, in which singularities as apparently empty as "nothing" are pregnant with "something" – where one thing is never really simple, never fully substantial, but is always haunted by an other thing – where the act of naming is coincident with un-naming, just as the act of seeing is co-relative with not seeing.[15] In this respect, Isabel's speech employs anamorphosis as a way of visualizing and thereby conceptualizing an ontology in which appearance and reality, shadow and form, are involuted within one another in such a way that apparently discrete entities remain inconsistent with themselves. One thing may appear to be one thing, but when looked at more closely, it is actually two, maybe even many things. In the end, Isabel's lamentation of Richard's departure constitutes a profound meditation on the existential and epistemological conditions of finitude. For Isabel, as for

Venus, the "nothing" constituting these conditions becomes discernible only when the world is seen through tears.

Like Shakespeare's *Venus and Adonis* and *Richard II*, Marvell's "Eyes and Tears" is a meditation on the conditions of finitude that make grieving necessary and meaningful. By thinking about the conditions of finitude that occasion weeping and that make weeping an act that "speaks," Marvell follows Shakespeare in asking what it means to engage in an act of mourning without assuming one ever really knows what it is one mourns (even when one thinks one does). Like Isabel, the speaker of Marvell's poem reflects in a philosophical manner on the conditions that make mourning and weeping necessary, rather than assuming, from the beginning, one knows what it means to weep. Neither Isabel nor Marvell's speaker presumes to know what or whom is being grieved for exactly. The similarities between these texts become most visible, however, when we recognize that they all tend to approach the impossibly enigmatic question, "what does it mean to grieve?" by reflecting on the disjunctions between the world and our relation to it through anamorphic figures.

Eyes and tears

Working within the *contemptus mundi* tradition informing Shakespeare's *Richard II* – not to mention Holbein's anamorphic masterpiece "The Ambassadors," which may have inspired the Bushy/Isabel exchange[16] – the opening stanza of "Eyes and Tears" introduces the nameless loss, the general state of *vanitas*, motivating the poem. This stanza introduces this ontological breach by making the shortcomings of human knowledge the occasion not for poetic complaint as such, but for a meditation on why the question of human being is so deeply bound up with the question of weeping: "How wisely Nature did decree, / With the same Eyes to weep and see! / That, having view'd the object vain, / They might be ready to complain" (1–4). The poem begins with the speaker reflecting on "Nature's decree" that it is appropriate that tears – the primary symptoms of human finitude – should originate from eyes; for even as eyes are the central source of empirical knowledge, they nonetheless betray the limitations of human apprehension by viewing things "vainly." The subtle but crucial paradox here is that the disjunction between human perception and the world which occasions Nature's decree is a disjunction *internal* to Nature itself. In other words, Nature's decree that tears should flow from eyes presumes, or as it were evokes *post facto*, a *prior* decree regarding an original breach between human knowledge and the world as such. The self-reflexive logic of Nature's decree is thus reminiscent of Venus' decree: it speaks less of an objective, outward-oriented speech-act, than it does of the limited power of Nature to decree anything other than what is already the case.[17]

Nature's decrees, like Venus' promises, can only bring into being more of the same. Such impotence renders legible a breach inherent to Nature itself. This unnamed and strangely inaccessible breach, which is retro-actively evoked in the first stanza, is the basic focus of Marvell's medi-tation; for this loss at the heart of things occasions and renders potentially meaningful the act of weeping – a phenomenon that stanza 12 insists is the most distinctly human of all acts. To be precise, this prior breach in Nature brings into view the limits of human knowledge that the poem both diagnoses and seeks to mitigate by advocating rigorous attention to the paradoxes of incarnationist thought. This process involves a full recognition of the limitations of human knowledge as disclosed through the phenomenon of self-reflexivity, the tendency within human appre-hension to find its own image even when, indeed especially when, it pursues self-transcendence. Like Nature, Marvell's speaker cannot trick himself out of the limitations of finitude; he can only acknowledge such limitations in the act of weeping as a gesture of faith in the hope of grace. By doing so, he "knows with tears" rather than with the eye of reason.

The problem of reflexivity arises at the outset of the poem when the self-involving logic of Nature's decree is reinforced through the Latinate syntax of stanza 1, specifically the placement of the word "vain" in line 3: "How wisely Nature did decree, / With the same Eyes to weep and see! / That, having view'd the object vain, / They might be ready to complain" (1–4). Operating as both adverb and adjective, the word "vain" complicates what it is precisely that is without substance: the object being viewed or the subject doing the viewing. By modifying both the subject viewing and the object being viewed, the word "vain" calls attention to the self-reflexive dimensions of Ecclesiastes 1:14, to which the stanza alludes. "I haue seene all the workes that are done vnder the Sunne, and behold, all is vanitie, and vexation of spirit." By grammatically accommodating subject and object, the word "vain" calls attention to the self-reflexive dimension triggered by the word "all" in Ecclesiastes 1:14 – the fact that the speaker of Ecclesiastes is necessarily a part of the totality to which he refers. Thus, just as Nature's decree exposes the internal disjunctions that render its "decree" appropriate (not to mention determined), so the human I/eye that sees vainly betrays its own incapacity to say anything truly objective about "everything." Unlike Ecclesiastes, Marvell's poem is inviting us to consider the *position of enunciation* from which such statements regarding the vanity of *all* things can be made; for it is through the very act of recognizing the limits of human finitude, the poem continues to insist, that one comes to understand how God reveals himself to humanity.

The incarnational paradox underwriting Marvell's poem is that the continuity between the order of nature and the order of grace occurs only insofar as the order of grace opens itself to the lack in creation itself. In other words, the poem insists that it is by fully (rather than unwittingly) acknowledging the breach in Nature, and thus in one's self, that one comes to understand how the breach is mediated. At bottom, the self-reflexive logic of Nature's decree and of human perception implied in stanza 1 will be articulated in more fully thematic terms in subsequent stanzas. In later stanzas we learn that despite the perspectival limitations of human perception, one's tears can nonetheless purchase a form of insight in which the absent-presence of the "all-seeing" becomes discernible through the vanity that the "all-seeing" assumed in the Incarnation. Deepening the moral and ontological skepticism articulated in Ecclesiastes, stanza 1 voices – at the level of trope and diction – the incarnational paradoxes that make the act of weeping a potentially godly gesture of faith rather than an inevitably self-serving act of vanity. "Eyes and Tears" thus articulates the incarnational lesson that the failure of human knowledge and the ontological lack that failure implies is both the wound and the balm. To put this another way, consciousness of the vanity of things, the poem will continue to insist, is not simply an act of negating the world in favor of an all-embracing omnipotent God, but rather it is the way one comes to know how God communicates to man by opening himself to the vale of tears.

Victoria Silver addresses the issue of human finitude at stake here when she asserts that the beginning of religious wisdom within the Lutheran tradition, as within the history of tragedy, comes by knowing how "we are circumscribed and confounded by our mortality."[18] Paraphrasing Werner Jaeger, Silver asserts that "a delimited human being is a religious recognition even as human suffering is a religious problem, which is to say that the understanding commanded by the Delphic god and proffered us by tragedy delineates the extreme boundaries of rationality, where explanation and transcendence are brought not simply to an impasse but to an insuperable conflict."[19] In Marvell's poem, weeping is the emotional expression attendant upon the knowledge of such limitations and the existential conflicts conditioned by them. Tears demarcate, for Marvell, a form of understanding that is not propositional but expressive. This form of seeing is not unifying in the sense argued for by Hartwig, but rather it signals how the paradoxical nature of the Incarnation can be known at the level of lived experience in the act of weeping. Faithful tears, the poem tells us, are the emotional consequence of understanding a loss internal to the natural order – a loss that is both the breach and the bridge between temporal and eternal domains. This strange epistemology becomes clearer in stanza 2.

The incapacity of Marvell's speaker to take account of the "all" referred to in Ecclesiastes is developed in stanza 2 when a reference to the triangulating measurements of a sextant brings into further relief the impossibility, contra Florentine Neoplatonism, of encompassing the totality of creation through thought: "Thus since the self-deluding sight / In a false angle takes each height, / These tears, which better measure all, / Like wat'ry lines and plummets fall" (5–8). As stanza 1 made clear, there is nothing simple about the way the word "all" is operating here. While tears are presented as offering a clarity of which eyes are incapable, their accuracy – as the image of falling plummets implies – is not a function of perceiving "all" in the sense of everything at once, but rather they better measure "all" in the sense that they disclose how everything partakes of and is haunted by "nothing," just as weeping is opposite to and yet enigmatically continuous with laughter: "What in the World most fair appears, / Yea even Laughter, turns to Tears" (13–14). Just as George Herbert compares a plummet's descent with a Christian's measuring the depth of his sins through prayer ("The Christian plummet sounding heav'n and earth" ("Prayer (I)," 4)), so Marvell describes tears as "plummets" which allow a better view of the vanity within one's self and the world at large. The question for both poets is how one determines the relation between all and nothing, between grace and oblivion, through the "vain" resources of reason. For both Herbert and Marvell, one must suspend the logic of reason in order to make such a calculation. Consequently, one must turn inward in order to go outward just as one must weep falling tears in order to "measure" the upward movement of grace. This paradoxical economy, in which falling tears calculate the vanity of the temporal world and hence the divine alterity of God, occasions the poem's constant doubling of apparent singularities, as weeping and laughing, sorrow and joy, continually overlap: "Yet happy they whom Grief doth bless, / That weep the more, and see the less: / And, to preserve their Sight more true, / Bath still their Eyes in their own Dew (26–29). The paradoxes offered by the world's vanity demand not only lachrymal tendencies but an anamorphic turn of mind – a capacity to see the difference within identity.

The doubleness required of the eye of faith over and against the "self-deluding" singularity of the eye of reason is encapsulated in stanza 12, when Marvell's speaker gives himself the following imperative to weep: "Ope then mine Eyes your double Sluice, / And practice so your noblest Use" (45–46). The word "Sluice" indicates not only a dam or embankment for impounding the water of a river or canal (*OED*), but it also implies "a gap, breach, opening, or hole; a gash or wound" (*OED*). Hence to open the eye of faith through weeping is to acknowledge the vanity within, to open the very "breach" severing flesh from spirit. The kenotic paradox here is that by opening the "Sluice" – by acknowledging the indissoluble difference between human and God – one is doing what is most distinctly human and thus, paradoxically, most like Christ: "For others too can see, or sleep; / But only humane Eyes can weep" (46–47). For Marvell, the act of weeping discloses, even as it is occasioned by, the paradoxical immanence of the self and Christ, an immanence St. Paul articulates in Galatians 2:20, when he asserts that "I am crucified with Christ; nevertheless I live; yet not I, but Christ liveth in me: and the life which I now live in the flesh I live by the faith of the Son of God." This counter-intuitive relation of self as Christly other cannot be "understood" or "comprehended" in the form of a propositional statement; it must be lived through the experience of faith. Weeping, Marvell's poem tells us, is the expression of such an "understanding." The speaker's reasoned calculations are ironic precisely insofar as they dissolve under the weight of what faithful weeping reveals. Like the tears shed in Donne's "A Valediction: Of Weeping," Marvell's tears are not simply "Fruits of much grief" but "are emblems of more"; they constitute how the eye of faith becomes an instance of the mystery of the Incarnation rather than trying to comprehend such a mystery through the "captivating" eye of reason.[20]

The simultaneously distorting and clarifying effects Marvell attributes to tears recall, even as they reconstitute, the lachrymal visions of the Elizabethan Catholic poet, William Alabaster. The difference between Alabaster's and Marvell's tears is both soteriological and metaphysical (which should be understood here in the philosophical rather than literary-historical sense). In terms of soteriology, Alabaster forwards the view that tears of contrition can earn one grace, while the Protestant Marvell does not. What Marvell encourages is a meditation on weeping as a sign that reveals the lessons of *vanitas mundi* – rather than as a means of earning grace through *imitatio Christi*. In terms of metaphysics, Alabaster articulates a view of the perception afforded by penitent tears that is Plotinian in structure, while Marvell demystifies such a view. For Alabaster, the fully penitent subject catches a glimpse of quasi-divine perception through the perfecting of phenomenal modes of apprehension. In such a mode of Neoplatonic perception, there is no ontological distinction between seer and seen, between object and subject viewing. Marvell, as stanza 2 makes clear, demystifies the epistemological optimism of this form of Neoplatonism. What is perhaps most intriguing here is that these theological and epistemological differences get registered through a meditation on the enigmatic question of what it means to weep. In Sonnet 71, Alabaster suggests that the act of reflecting on the crucified Christ differs in terms of whether he perceives Christ with or without tears. In order to distinguish between empathic and unempathic modes of viewing Christ, Alabaster turns to anamorphic forms of representation or what he calls "optic works" – implying that seeing Christ fully means, paradoxically, seeing him anamorphically:

> When without tears I look on Christ, I see
> Only a story of some passion,
> Which any common eye may wonder on;
> But if I look through tears Christ smiles on me.
> Yea, there I see myself, and from that tree
> He bendeth down to my devotion,
> And from his side the blood doth spin, whereon
> My heart, my mouth, mine eyes still sucking be;
> Like as in optick works, one thing appears
> In open gaze, in closer otherwise.
> Then since tears see the best, I ask in tears,
> Lord, either thaw mine eyes to tears, or freeze
> My tears to eyes, or let my heart tears bleed,
> Or bring where eyes, nor tears, nor blood shall need.[21]

The mode of perception afforded by contrite tears in this sonnet is explicated in Thomas Lodge's 1596 work of Marian devotion, *Prosopopeia*, when the Virgin Mary asks "Shall I teach you how to bewaile Christ?" and responds by asserting that "when thou art converted into Christ, then mayest thou truely bewaile him. For the losse of things then neerest touch us, when they are best knowee [sic] unto us. Those that are one in affection, are one in passion, one in desires, one in teares."[22] Alabaster's anamorphic tears thus result in a form of vision that answers the question posed three sonnets earlier in "A Morning Meditation (I)": "how can clearness to my soul be brought, / To see and to be seen, that hath his sight / From Christ, and what it sees is his fair spright."²³ As Ceri Sullivan observes, Alabaster's tears constitute "a site for a union between divinity and humanity. They act as a species of ambiguous sacrament."²⁴ More precisely, Alabster's tears express the Plotinian desire for full identity – for a dissolution of the distinction between perceiving subject and object perceived. By seeking Christ's sight, he desires to see the position from which he sees – to see not perspectivally but to see wholly and completely. Alabaster desires to be brought to a state of apotheosis where neither eyes, tears, nor blood are needed. Plotinus describes a related form of hypostatic apprehension this way: "He who then sees himself, when he sees will see himself a simple being, will be united to himself as such, will feel himself become such. We ought not even to say that he will *see*, but he will *be* that which he sees, if indeed it is possible any longer to distinguish seer and seen, and not boldly to affirm that the two are one."²⁵ In this form of divine-like vision, the subject becomes totally homogenous with itself – so homogenous, in fact, that we cannot speak of a difference between the subject seeing and the object being seen. In Plotinian hypostasis, being becomes seeing, seeing being, and the subject becomes like an instance of pure light – a form of unmediated apprehension.

Alabaster's speaker expresses a direct desire to collapse the disjunctions that the first two stanzas of Marvell's "Eyes and Tears" delineate as the necessary conditions of weeping. Alabaster seeks God by seeking the truth that lies within and behind the world's vanity, whereas Marvell seeks God by deepening his awareness of the vanity inherent to human being. The primary difference between the modes of perception afforded by Alabaster's and Marvell's anamorphic tears is that with Alabaster two becomes One – as subject and object, devotee and Christ are united in a sacramental embrace, while in Marvell's poem, as in Shakespeare's work, One is always-already at least two – as the apparently discrete nature of specific entities infold upon themselves such that laughing turns into weeping and joy transmutes into grief. In "Eyes and Tears," the accent is continually placed on the way that Nature is non-coincident with itself in such a way that individual entities continually reveal that they are different from themselves; in Alabaster's sonnet, on the other hand, apparent differences are collapsible through the Eucharistic force of God's presence in the world. In short, Alabaster's tears reveal sameness, while Marvell's tears measure difference. Let me clarify what is at stake here through reference to stanza II.

In stanza II, Marvell uses a *trompe l'oeil* figure in order to invert the Plotinian form of apprehension operating in Alabaster's *Spiritual*

Sonnets: "The Incense was to Heaven dear, / Not as a Perfume, but a Tear. / And stars *shew* lovely in the Night, / But as they *seem* the Tears of Light" (42–45, my emphasis). In this stanza, tears become the means of communication between heavenly and earthly dialects. Thus just as light – the conventional figure of divine revelation – is revealed not in the self-beholding form of Plotinian emanation, but as a sign of the very breach that the Son/Sun heals by taking into his person, so incense is received not in the form of a fragrance but a tear. It is in difference rather than in likeness that a relation is established between human and divine orders. The parallelism in this stanza accentuates the extent to which tears – the very symptoms of finitude – are paradoxically the means of traffic between temporal and eternal orders. Rather than blinding us with the "all-seeing" force of the sun, as Southwell does in *St Peters Complaint*, this literary trick of the eye has us peer into the "Sluice" conditioning Nature's decree. In this way, Marvell's figure calls into question the Plotinian simplicity of Ficino's metaphysics, when the Florentine Neoplatonist says that "if the sun is the first among the light-bearing things it does not lack any degree of light."[26] Focusing on the absence within light, rather than the self-sameness of it, Marvell's speaker emphasizes how the order of grace inhabits, even as it is constitutively separated from, the order of nature. While Christine Rees is thus entirely correct in observing that this stanza "goes against the Baconian principle that 'the truth of being and the truth of knowing are one,'" she is wrong to deflate the importance of this image by asserting that the "poet's vision is admittedly subjective."[27] The entire poem is spoken from a self-consciously subjective point of view and this is the very point. The poet's misperception that light reveals itself in the form of tears is consistent with the poem's overall assertion regarding the incongruous relations between heavenly and earthly dialects. While the speaker of Herbert's "The Search" comes to realize that God is known qualitatively, not quantitatively, Marvell's speaker begins there.[28] Stanza 11, then, articulates the same sentiment expressed in stanza 6 in which the "all-seeing" sun mirrors the dew or tears reflected to it from the world – a sentiment that Rees interprets in terms of typological allusions to the Incarnation: "this divine alchemy signifies blessing – 'He shall come down like rain upon the mown grass: as showers that water the earth.'"[29] Whenever the presence of the divine is figured in the poem it is represented in thoroughly kenotic terms – in terms of the breach or "Sluice" opened within the divine for humanity – rather than through the realization or even direct promise of a hypostatic union of temporal and eternal orders.

By calling attention to the way that seeing is bound up with not seeing, Marvell's lachrymal vision is more rigorously anamorphic than Alabaster's. While Alabaster employs anamorphosis as a way of figuring the unity of ostensible oppositions, Marvell deploys it as a way of representing an ontological gap within an apparent identity. This re-visioning of the literature of tears tradition is preceded by and is generally consistent with Luther's understanding of the way human language accommodates divine revelation primarily through irony and difference rather than analogy and similitude. As Victoria Silver demonstrates in her discussion of Luther's reading of St. Paul's allegories, "Luther shows us that the same image or form of expression can be productive of profoundly different meanings, in a kind of figural adiaphorism. Thus, seen one way, Paul's New Jerusalem becomes the transcendent habitation of the saints; seen another, it expresses the actual ubiquity of the gospel in this world."[30] In the first perspective, Silver asserts, "God and value are translated out of the world, while in the second God and value are embedded in it."[31] In this respect, the first mode of reading "makes religion the perfection of the phenomenal or rational" while the second sets religion "against all such presumptive truths." The first "structures *invisibilia* after what can be seen," while the second "entirely distinguishes them from it."[32] While Alabaster pursues transcendence by perfecting phenomenal experience in the manner of Neoplatonism, Marvell does not. Marvell's poem suggests that it is in the very breach between experience and understanding that the tearful eye comes to a relation with, if not a rational apprehension of, divine revelation.

This awareness of the radical difference between the phenomenal world of appearance and the unknowable reality of deity is signaled in Magdalen's "wise" tears, which are shed in stanza 8 of "Eyes and Tears": "So *Magdalen*, in Tears more wise / Dissolv'd those captivating Eyes, / Whose liquid Chaines could flowing meet / To fetter her Redeemers feet" (29–32). The term "captivating" not only reminds us that Magdalene's repentance involves turning from physical to spiritual love, but it also implies that her tears are "wise" in the sense that they reflect her recognition of the radical insufficiency of reason to "comprehend" or take hold of Christ. Magdalene thus "fetters" Christ not through the captivating eye of reason nor through the beauty of the flesh, but through the tears of faith. In this respect, stanza 8 poeticizes the Pauline dictum expressed in 1 Corinthians 8:1–3: "knowledge puffeth vp, but loue edifieth ... [And] if any man thinke that hee knoweth any thing, hee knoweth nothing yet as hee ought to knowe. But if any man loue God, the same is knowen of him."[33]

The poem's voicing of differences within apparent identities continues in stanza 13. In this stanza, we are presented with a series of perspectives on the process of penitent weeping as it unfolds in time: "Now like the two Clouds dissolving, drop, / And at each Tear in Distance stop: / Now like two Fountains trickle down: / Now like two floods o'erturn and drown" (49–52). Unlike Alabaster's anamorphic tears, these "Eyes and Tears" are "frozen" in the "now" of consecutive moments, rather than the eternal "now" of hypostasis. In this way, Marvell's "now" is less like the "eternal now" of Plotinian vision, in which thought beholds itself beholding itself, than it is like the Aristotelian "now," which "measures time in so far as time involves a 'before and after.'"[34] Rather than expressing a desire to "freeze" time into perfect simultaneity, into the *Nunc-stans* of scholastic thought, Marvell's speaker sees the act of weeping as a means of exposing the disjointedness of time. Thus even this Aristotelian view of the "now" as the point that unites and distinguishes the seamless flow of diachronic time fails to fully accommodate the modality of the present evoked by Marvell's *tableaux vivants*. The "now" in which Marvell's tears are suspended is akin to the out-of-joint nature of time Isabel diagnoses in *Richard II*. Rather than seeking a point of view beyond time, these images fix the reader's gaze at a series of particular moments in the experience of godly sorrow. Unlike the dilation of time in stanza 24 of "The Weeper," where we are promised the *Nunc-stans* of eternal simultaneity, Marvell turns our gaze towards the "distance" or interval between moments and keeps it there. This "distance" – while itself "nothing" – is the breach separating the tear from itself as it changes in and through time. These figures of suspended animation call attention to the way that the singular moment is dislocated from itself, bringing into view the vanity that occasions faithful tears. Like Isabel's anamorphic tears, Marvell's tears are lachrymose signs of the I/Eye's self-difference as they seek to close the distance separating themselves from themselves even as they embrace it. Caught in the amphibian world between temporal and eternal orders, these figures of suspended animation are deeply liminal in nature. Each "now" through which the tear passes is different from itself as the movement from present to future alters the significance of the past perspective. Marvell's "now" is more anamorphic than it is Aristotelian; it appears different depending upon "when" one sees it.

This play of anamorphic perspective recalls, even as it reconstitutes, Crashaw's perspectivalism in "The Weeper," particularly the moment when "we are deceived all. / Starres indeed they are too true; / For they but seem to fall, / ... Upwards thou dost weep. / Heavn's bosome drinks the gentle stream. / Where th' milky rivers creep, / Thine floats above; and is the cream" (3–4). In Crashaw's quasi-anamorphic shift of perspective on Magdalene, the transcendent reality of penitent tears is disclosed through a continuing readjustment of one's apprehension of the physical world from a higher plane of perception. Temporal illusions, in Crashaw's poem, give way to the eternal realities behind them as the poem tries to shift from being a sign to being the thing itself. While Crashaw enacts a gradual perfecting of phenomenal experience on his way to an apotheosis of the many within the One, Marvell emphasizes an indissoluble gap between the captivating eye of reason and the pregnant eyes of faith. Where Crashaw pursues transcendence through an iso-morphic poetics of similitude, Marvell pursues it through an anamorphic poetics of difference. This difference in the position of the speakers vis-à-vis the question of transcendence results in different perspectives on what it means to weep faithful tears. According to Marvell's poem, faithful tears signal the promise of grace within a fallen world, while for Crashaw and Alabaster, faithful tears are said to disclose a transcendent actualization of such a promise. Marvell's tears are thus closer to the lachrymose sap of Venus' "stalk" than they are to Crashaw's Eucharistic "springs"; they bear within them the "breach" inherent to Nature, though unlike Venus' flower they disclose the Lutheran paradox that a "Lack of understanding is real understanding; not knowing where you are going is really knowing where you are going."[35]

Another way to approach the issue is to observe that Marvell's ana-morphic tears do with time what the anamorphic skull in Holbein's "The Ambassadors" does with space; they compound the ostensibly simple relations between "now" as a single self-same moment and "now" as the dreadful anticipation of future fulfillment. Marvell's images of suspended animation suggest that what a tear *is* depends on when and from what angle it is viewed. A tear, like the time in which it is wept, is never simple, never self-coincident. Marvell's tears reveal this very difference, rather than Plotinian self-sameness. While Marvell thematizes the epistemo-logically skeptical implications of anamorphosis, working such implica-tions into his poem and the vision of faith it implies, Crashaw and Alabaster elide such implications. Crashaw's and Alabaster's poems remain aloof from the fact that anamorphic perspectivalism participates in the emergence of a non-analogical view of the cosmos, an epistemolog-ically skeptical view, in which the relations between mind and world, let alone divine and mundane realities, become characterized by difference rather than similitude, by distance rather than legibility. As Claudio

Guillèn has observed, the very "idea of perspective can readily be associated with a growing epistemological dualism, with a rigorous split between subject and object as in the Cartesian distinction between mind and *res extensa*."[36] To the extent that Crashaw and Alabaster use perspectivalism as a way of predicating the transcendence of finitude, they draw on representational techniques which contribute to the production of a non-analogical view of the universe and of our understanding of it. In this respect, Crashaw and Alabaster have one foot in the medieval world of Aquinas and another in the early modern world of Holbein. Their poems are peculiarly symptomatic of the very modernity they seek to resist. Marvell, on the other hand, seems to have recognized, following Shakespeare, that anamorphosis appears to complicate presuppositions of continuity between mind and world – be it the world of physical or spiritual perception.

Marvell's emphasis on difference rather than likeness as the interpretive stance proper to faith is implied in the image of tears consuming themselves in a flood in stanza 13. The question that arises in this stanza, and in the poem as a whole, is: what is revealed through such inward-turning, self-annihilating, tears? What is to be learned from an image of tears overturning upon themselves like waves in a flood? The poem's final stanza suggests that what is revealed by a flood of faithful tears is a view of identity that can only be accommodated through a chiasmic-like exchange of differences within and between separate entities: "Thus let your Streams o'erflow your Springs, / Till Eyes and Tears be the same things: / And each the other's difference bears; / These weeping eyes, those seeing Tears" (53–56). Like the poem's opening stanza, these enigmatic lines recall the teary words of Shakespeare's Venus. Only now the exchange of eyes and tears occurs not in a specular register through which the weeper's narcissism is expressed, but through a physical analogy in which each entity is said to "bear" the "other's difference." Following the *OED*, each side of the opposition is said to "carry," "sustain," "bring forth," "take as a companion," or perhaps most appropriately, "keep in remembrance," the other's difference. The result of this shift from visual to physical metaphors is a conception of "the same" that does not derive its meaning through an exclusion of difference, but bears difference within itself. Articulating explicitly what has been implicit within the poem's central tropes, the speaker departs from the conception of identity outlined in Aristotle's *Metaphysics*, in which Aristotle sets out the principle of contradiction that states that "A is not not-A," a view that defines identity through the absence of difference.[37] Implying a more Heraclitean view of difference as the unity of opposites, Marvell's speaker configures the exchange between "Eyes" and "Tears," between the order of nature and the order of grace, here and throughout the poem as a whole, as a more paradoxical affair in which identity is always-already different from itself.

The revelation made possible by tears is that it is the difference within identity that allows the subject to postulate a relation with the eternal as different from and yet involved with the temporal. Marvell's poem is asking us to recognize something divine, even while acknowledging something mournful, in the mode of alterity that makes such "sameness" possible. The poem, in other words, suggests that by turning inward through authentic grief, one's eyes and tears make visible a view of identity that is based not on an act of exclusion, but on the principle that each side of an apparent opposition suffers the difference of the other. By acknowledging this internal difference through the act of weeping – this breach that lies at the origin of things and occasions all of the poem's major poetic figures – one becomes attuned to the manner in which God communicates himself to humanity. In the final stanza, the poem's ana-morphic texture – its constant doubling of singularities – reaches an "apotheosis" through a resolution that sustains difference in the very gesture of recognizing sameness.

Insofar as Marvell's anamorphic tears disclose the simultaneous con-tinuity and discontinuity between temporal and eternal orders, they stand between the hypostatic vision of Neoplatonic transcendence voiced in "The Weeper" and the skeptically tragic view of existence expressed by Shakespeare. Neither sacramental in the way that Alabaster's tears are, nor radically demystifying in the same way as Shakespeare's, Marvell's tears and the Protestant mentality they bear with them are positioned between these two extremes. Developing the poetics of difference discernible in Herbert's expression of godly sorrow in "The Search" and "Grief," "Eyes and Tears" does not forward a sacramental vision in which penitent tears render visible how all aspects of creation are analogically or contiguously identifiable with all other aspects, nor does it deploy anamorphosis as a way to radically demystify distinctions between shadow and substance. Instead, it enacts a way of relating to deity that is characterized by a rigorous reflexivity, a constant attention to the limitations of finitude encompassing, if not determining, the desire for such a relation. For Marvell, devout weeping signifies that one is beginning to move towards something inexpressible at the very heart of what the Protestant tradition means by the word "human."

NOTES

1 Andrew Marvell, *The Poems of Andrew Marvell* ed. Nigel Smith (London: Pearson Longman, 2003), p. 50.
2 Like Smith, J. B. Leishman, *The Art of Marvell's Poetry* (London: Hutchinson, 1966), p. 193, does not include "Eyes and Tears" among the six Marvell poems he defines as religious: "The Coronet," "On a Drop of Dew," "A Dialogue Between the Resolved Soul, and Created Pleasure," "A Dialogue between the Soul and Body," "Bermudas," and "Musicks Empire." Contrary to Leishman and Smith, I agree with Barbara Lewalski, "Marvell as Religious Poet," in C. A. Patrides (ed.), *Approaches to Marvell: The York Tercentenary Lectures* (London: Routledge, 1978), pp. 251–79, that "the canon of Marvell's religious lyrics [are] comprised of just those poems which the contemporary editor placed first (no doubt for this very reason) in the posthumous first edition of the *Miscellaneous Poems*: "A Dialogue Between the Resolved Soul, and Created Pleasure," "On a Drop of Dew," "The Coronet," "Eyes and Tears," "Bermudas," and "Clorinda and Damon,'" p. 251.
3 Lewalski, "Marvell as Religious," p. 253. For a brief but authoritative account of Herbert's Protestantizing of the literature of tears tradition, see Richard Strier, "Herbert and Tears," *English Literary History* 46 (1979), 221–47. By viewing the poem as part of the reformation of tear poetry, I am suggesting that terms such as "quasi-Catholic" do not provide a precise view of how this poem works in relation to the wider tradition of English tear poems. For the use of such a term see Christine Rees, *The Judgment of Marvell* (London: Pinter Publishers, 1989), p. 36.
4 Joan Hartwig, "Tears as a Way of Seeing," in Claude J. Summers and Ted-Larry Petworth (eds.), *On the Celebrated and Neglected Poems of Andrew Marvell* (Columbia: University of Missouri Press, 1992), pp. 70–85.
5 See the Introduction for a discussion of Luther's concept of the category of relation, pp. 22–3.
6 Hartwig, "Tears," p. 82.
7 Thomas Clayton, "'It is Marvell He Outdwells His Hour' Some Perspectives on Marvell's Medium," in Kenneth Fridenreich (ed.), *Tercentenary Essays in Honor of Andrew Marvell* (Hamden: Archon Books, 1977), pp. 46–75, briefly addresses anamorphosis in relation to "Eyes and Tears" arriving at the conclusion, articulated subsequently and in more detail by Hartwig, in "Tears," that "subject and object are syntactically as well as naturally one" p. 66. For other discussions of Marvell and visual perspective, see Donald M. Friedman, "Sight and Insight in Marvell's Poetry," in Patrides (ed.), *Approaches to Marvell*; Rosalie Colie, *"My Ecchoing Song": Andrew Marvell's Poetry of Criticism* (Princeton, NJ: Princeton University Press, 1970), pp. 306–30; Judith Dundas, *Pencils Rhetorique: Renaissance Poets and the Art of Painting* (Newark: University of Delaware Press, 1993), pp. 205–12; Lynn Enterline, *The Tears of Narcissus: Melancholia and Masculinity in Early Modern Writing* (Stanford, CA: Stanford University Press, 1995), pp. 146–88; Marshall

Grossman, *The Story of All Things: Writing the Self in English Renaissance Narrative Poetry* (Durham, NC: Duke University Press, 1998), pp. 93–103 and pp. 197–217; and Cynthia Chase, "A Stroke of the Scythe: Marvell's Mower Eclogues as Anamorphosis," *Enclitic*, 5.1 (Spring 1981), 55–65.

8 Cited in Clayton, "It Is Marvell," 65.

9 Tom Lutz, *Crying: The Natural and Cultural History of Tears* (New York: Norton, 1999), pp. 17–18, addresses the connections between weeping and the definition of the "human." For a discussion of moderation in English Protestant discourses on mourning, see G. W. Pigman III, *Grief and English Renaissance Elegy* (Cambridge: Cambridge University Press, 1985), pp. 27–39.

10 See for instance, Smith, *The Poems of Andrew Marvell*, 51 and Thomas Clayton, "It is Marvell," 65.

11 The tradition of associating Magdalene and Venus is evident in the title of Marjorie M. Malvern's, *Venus in Sackcloth: The Magdalene's Origins and Metamorphoses* (Carbondale: Southern Illinois University Press, 1975). For another study that confirms the associations between Venus and Magdalene, see Susan Haskins, *Mary Magdalen: Myth and Metaphor* (New York: Harcourt, 1993).

12 Robert Southwell, *The Triumphs ouer Death* (London, 1595), B2.

13 The *OED* cites line 147 of Shakespeare's *A Lover's Complaint* as a source for the word's slang meaning.

14 Ned Lukacher, "Anamorphic Stuff: Shakespeare, Catharsis, Lacan," *South Atlantic Quarterly* 88.4 (1989), 863–97, 871.

15 Ibid., 871.

16 For a discussion of the conceptual and historical relations between *Richard II* and Holbein's "Ambassadors," see Lukacher, "Anamorphic Stuff," 868–69 and Ernest Gilman, *The Curious Perspective: Literary and Pictorial Wit in the Seventeenth Century* (New Haven, CT: Yale University Press, 1978), p. 14, pp. 54–55, pp. 98–104.

17 For an analysis of Marvell's fascination with figures of self-reflexivity, see Christopher Ricks, "Its Own Resemblance," in Patrides (ed.), *Approaches To Marvell*, pp. 108–35.

18 Victoria Silver, *Imperfect Sense: The Predicament of Milton's Irony* (Princeton, NJ: Princeton University Press, 2001), p. 14.

19 Ibid.

20 Hartwig's reading of the "double-meanings" inherent in the images from stanza 5 is helpful here. She notices that "the syntax of these lines suggests a double meaning: that not only had the tears the power to 'draw off' the honey, but also that the only true honey is the tears themselves. Honey, in biblical contexts, suggests both the honeydew of paradise and the manna of sustenance and grace (Exodus 16, John 6), and the colors 'red' and 'white' reiterate the suggestion of sacramental food ... The kind of double meaning contained in the honey attaches itself to almost all of the images of tears in the poem" (Hartwig, "Tears," p. 76). Also consistent with my reading is her

observation that stanza 12 reverses Aristotle's view that reason is "man's noblest power" by making "weeping" the I/Eye's "noblest Use," p. 83.

21 William Alabaster, *The Sonnets of William Alabaster*, ed. G.M. Story and Helen Gardner (Oxford: Oxford University Press, 1959), p. 39.

22 Thomas Lodge, *Prosopopeia, Containing the Teares of the Holy, Blessed, and Sanctified Marie, the Mother of God* (London, 1596), E8v. Murray Roston cites two examples of anamorphic depictions of Christ in Renaissance art, Mantegna's *The Dead Christ* and a lost work by Gandenzio Ferrari, in which Christ achieves his proper proportions only when viewed through a viewing-hole in the frame. See Roston, *Renaissance Perspectives in Literature and the Visual Arts* (Princeton, NJ: Princeton University Press, 1987), p. 253, p. 361 fn. 19.

23 *Sonnets of William Alabaster*, ed. Story and Gardner, p. 38, lines 5–7.

24 Ceri Sullivan, "Penitence in 1590's Weeping Texts," *Cahiers Élisabéthains* 57 (April 2000), 36.

25 Cited in A. L. Clements, *The Mystical Poetry of Thomas Traherne* (Cambridge MA: Harvard University Press, 1969), p. 74.

26 Cited in Harold E. Toliver, *Marvell's Ironic Vision* (New Haven, CT: Yale University Press, 1965), p. 48.

27 Rees, *Judgment*, p. 40.

28 See the Introduction for my discussion of "The Search."

29 Psalm 72:6, in Rees, *Judgment*, p. 39.

30 Silver, *Imperfect Sense*, p. 224.

31 Ibid.

32 Ibid.

33 *Geneva Bible*.

34 Aristotle, "Physics," in *The Basic Works of Aristotle*, ed. Richard McKeon, introduction by C. D. C. Reeve (New York: Modern Library, 2001), p. 293 (4.11.219b). According to Aristotle, "every simultaneous time is self-identical; for the 'now' as a subject is an identity ... The now measures time, in so far as time involves the 'before and after,'" p. 293 (4.11.219b).

35 Martin Luther *Luther's Works*, ed. Jaroslav Pelikan, vol. 14, ed. Jaroslav Pelikan (Saint Louis, MO: Concordia, 1958), p. 152.

36 Claudio Guillèn, *Literature as System: Essays Toward The Theory of Literary History* (Princeton, NJ: Princeton University Press, 1971), pp. 292–93.

37 See Aristotle, "Metaphysics," in *The Basic Works of Aristotle*, pp. 737–38 (4.4.1006b).

CHAPTER 4

Sad delight: Theology and Marian iconography in Aemilia Lanyer's Salve Deus Rex Judaeorum

A majority of the texts we have examined thus far either focus on, allude to, or parody Mary Magdalene – the *Magna Pecatrix* and *Beata Dilectrix*. This focus on an important female saint makes clear that the early modern grammar of religious melancholy is often construed as "feminine." Throughout the literature of tears tradition, the ability to weep and the modes of pneumatic knowing revealed in and through weeping are thought to be "feminine" gifts. In this chapter, I would like to examine what is at stake in this gendering by making explicit the feminization of tears that has thus far remained relatively implicit. I will do this by examining what is arguably the most thoughtful, and certainly the most politically charged, early modern representation of godly sorrow as "feminine," namely Aemilia Lanyer's *Salve Deus Rex Judaeorum*. More precisely, I will consider how Lanyer grounds both her poetic and priestly authority, as well as the Virgin Mary's priestly authority, on the early modern practice of figuring divine sorrow as feminine.

In a recent summary of Aemilia Lanyer's well-documented efforts to represent women as possessing priestly authority, Micheline White observes that in *Salve Deus Rex Judaeorum* "the Countess of Cumberland exercises the healing power of St. Peter's keys ... the Countess of Cumberland and her daughter are 'shepherdesses' who heal and feed Christ's 'flock,' and [other] virtuous women are authorized to anoint themselves with 'Aaron's oil' and feed each other with the Word."[1] What White leaves out here, and what readers of the poem have not yet recognized, is the priestly role Lanyer attributes to Mary under the cross. By evoking a late medieval iconographical tradition, in which Mary's swoon under the cross signals her role as a priestly co-redemptrix, the opening stanza of the two-part section on Mary positions the Virgin at the center of Lanyer's overall project of imagining women in clerical roles. Seen from this perspective, the theological particularity of Lanyer's text comes into fuller view as she resorts to a pre-Tridentine depiction of Mary as co-redemptrix, in order to make the Lutheran promise of the priesthood of all believers genuinely meaningful for women, particularly for herself as poet-priestess and for at least two, perhaps three, of her dedicatees.

Mary's priestly role is alluded to in the first stanza of "The Salutation and Sorrow of the Virgin Mary," when Lanyer evokes the controversy over the Virgin's physical comportment and spiritual experience under the cross, specifically the question of whether or not she swoons in her grief. Once Lanyer's portrait of Mary is placed in the theological and iconographical context of the *lo spasimo* controversy – the controversy over whether she stands and thus transcends the effects of human grief or whether she swoons and physically suffers in tandem with Christ – it becomes clear that Susanne Woods' assertion that the poem "contains no hint of Mary as mediator or co-redeemer, but instead presents her as the chief exemplar of all the womanly virtues Lanyer praises throughout *Salve Deus*," needs to be rethought.[2] Indeed, when Lanyer's portrait of Mary is situated within the pre-Tridentine Mariological traditions and controversies being evoked in the opening stanza of "The Sorrow of the Virgin Mary," it becomes clear that the poem is not, as Elaine V. Beilin has argued, "ardently Protestant."[3] On the contrary, the poem's account of the Virgin Mary participates in a late medieval tradition of representing the Virgin as a physically anguished priestly co-redeemer – a role that is considerably at odds with the general Protestant view of her as having no active or direct role in the work of redemption.[4]

By grasping the theological significance of Lanyer's portrait of Mary's grief it becomes evident that the two-part section dedicated to Christ's mother constitutes one of the most crucial features of Lanyer's overall attempt, as White phrases it, "to uncover a tradition of female priestly gestures and symbols."[5] In particular, this representation of Mary in pre-Reformation terms is likely to have appealed to Queen Anne, who is believed to have converted to Catholicism in 1598–99,[6] and to Lady Arabella Stuart, who is believed to have shared some of Anne's Catholic sympathies.[7] At bottom, though, Lanyer's portrait of Mary is an effort to situate female authority in relation to a gendered form of *compassio* – what Lanyer identifies in the letter to Anne as a form of "sad delight," which is intuitively available to herself as a female poet and, by implication, to other women. Moreover, access to this empowering form of "sad delight" is figured, both in the letter to Anne and in the sequence on Mary, as a function of the affective and intellectual powers associated with motherhood. More precisely, Lanyer's claim to poetic and priestly power resides in her assertion that she has intuitive or unmediated access to the kind of sorrow exemplified by Mary under the cross – a grief, the poem tells us, that is deeply connected to the experience of maternal mourning.

MARY'S SWOON: THEOLOGY AND ICONOGRAPHY

The exclusion of women from ministerial responsibilities, which Lanyer implicitly challenges in *Salve Deus*, has long been defended on the grounds that Christ gave the male Apostles the "power of the keys."[8] Pope Innocent III, for instance, enshrined the exclusion of women from the priesthood on the grounds that "although the Blessed Virgin Mary surpassed in dignity and in excellence all the Apostles, nevertheless, it was not to her but to them that the Lord entrusted the keys to the kingdom of heaven."[9] While Pope Innocent III emphasized the non-priestly authority that Mary possessed in twelfth-century Catholic theology, a later and less official tradition would emerge in which Mary would come to play the role of priestly co-redeemer. Lanyer invokes this late medieval tradition when she describes how Christ's

> ... woefull Mother wayting on her Sonne,
> All comfortlesse in depth of sorrow drowned;
> Her griefes extreame, although but new begun,
> To see his bleeding body oft she swouned;
> How could shee choose but thinke her selfe undone,
> He dying, with whose glory shee was crowned? (94; 1009–14)

By portraying Mary as swooning, Lanyer situates *Salve Deus* within a highly charged debate that occurred within sixteenth-century Catholicism over the Virgin's experience during the Crucifixion. The question at the center of the *lo spasimo* controversy, which was known in seventeenth-century England as in most parts of Western Europe,[10] is whether Mary's cooperative role in the sacrifice is reflected by her firm, dignified pose before the crucified Christ or whether her participation in Christ's agony is best figured through her physical collapse. At stake in the debate is the precise nature of the Virgin's bodily purity and spiritual integrity; the question, more properly, is whether Mary's exemplarity is a function of her capacity to restrain her human passions, thereby transcending normal human grief, or whether her capacity to feel and express sorrow is superlatively intense and thus intimately related to Christ's agony. For Lanyer, it is the deeply human, physically anguished dimension of Mary's grief that best expresses the Virgin's exemplarity and best conveys her priestly role within the Crucifixion.

The *lo spasimo* controversy emerged as a result of fourteenth, fifteenth and sixteenth-century artistic representations in art and literature, in which Mary is figured as swooning. Due to the popularity of these images and the very human view of Mary they offered, Pope Julius II was petitioned to authorize the feast *De Spasimo Beatae Virgine Mariae* and to enrich it with indulgences.[11] In response to the petition, Pope Julius II charged Thomas de Vio, Cardinal Cajetan, to judge the canonical nature of Mary's swoon.[12] As Leo Steinberg observes, the official position regarding Mary's swoon "is set forth in an important epistle of July 17, 1506 (republished 1529) ... entitled *De spasmo gloriossime virginis mariae matris dei*."[13] Cajetan, as Harvey E. Hamburgh writes, concluded that not "only is the swoon contrary to the text of the gospel, for John (19:25–26) says that the Blessed Virgin 'stood near the cross' but 'in the strict sense used by physicians' the swoon is a morbid state resulting from the contractions of the sinews, and 'therefore it is not proper to attribute this to the Blessed Virgin.'"[14] Referencing the idea that the Virgin Mary is pure in body and thus not susceptible to a "contraction of the sinews," Cajetan rejected the argument that the enormity of the Virgin's sorrows caused her to swoon physically. Cajetan's resistance to the idea that Mary's sorrow is registered physically as well as spiritually brings into relief the precise theological significance attached to Lanyer's depiction of Mary; for anxiety over Mary's physicality stems from the strict limits placed on displays of female suffering in the post-Reformation era. And as Elizabeth M. A. Hodgson and Patricia Phillippy have shown in relation to Lanyer's work, these limits were repeatedly enforced in seventeenth-century England, even in Catholic texts such as those of Robert Southwell. By insisting on Mary's physical reaction to her emotional strife, Lanyer goes against the protocols of temperate mourning characteristic of post-Reformation homiletics.[15] More precisely, she resists the assumption that physical expressions of female grief are irrational – an assumption underlying Cajetan's assessment of the scriptural materials he marshals in defense of Mary's stoical comportment during the Crucifixion:

But in truth the Blessed Virgin did not swoon in this way ... for she was "full of Grace" (Luke 1). It is necessary to deny such a bodily defect in her because it would have impeded this plentitude and perfection of grace. It is plain that grief which would have made her "beside herself," would have impeded her use of reason at that moment when it was the time for her to meditate most intensely and intelligently on the passion ... It was more pleasing to God that Mary should have shared in the passion of her Son not only in her feelings but also in her mind since that is the nobler part of man in which merit and grace properly reside. Therefore, it was necessary that if the suffering of the Blessed Virgin should be most intense, then her whole lower affectivity should be governed and controlled by her fully conscious mind. This exercise and rule of reason over her lower sensitivities could not have occurred if her suffering had made her "beside herself." Therefore, a swoon, even in the popular sense of the term, seems very inappropriate to the Blessed Virgin.[16]

Cajetan's assessment of swoon iconography anticipates the general shift in attitudes regarding the embodied nature of devotion which Donna Spivey Ellington traces in her study of late medieval and early Renaissance Mariology. Ellington observes a trend within the Catholic Church and European Christianity generally, in which inner spirituality and virtue rather than external devotion are emphasized. As a result of this shift, proclamations of "the Virgin's shared flesh with her son and physical manifestations of her suffering were more at home in the world of late medieval piety. They did not typify the modest, restrained, and disciplined religious life sought by the Church after Trent." Ellington explains this shift by observing that the "downplaying of Mary's physical participation at the cross coincided with a growing suspicion of the body, and of women's bodies specifically, in European society as a whole."[17] Writing within a Protestant context far more hostile to physical displays of devotion and mourning than Counter-Reformation cultures, Lanyer resists her culture's homiletic protocols and the theological assumptions underlying them by situating Mary's authority in a physical response to grief that is an expression, not of irrationality, but of the Virgin's compassion and comprehension of the providential events in which she actively participates.

Though Cajetan expressed an unequivocal view on the issue of Mary's swoon, writers, preachers, and artists continued to represent Mary as swooning.[18] As art historians Otto G. Von Simson, Harvey E. Hamburgh, and others have concluded, the persistence of swoon imagery in sixteenth-century paintings was not simply a function of "popular sentimentality but the utmost theological importance" for Catholics.[19] According to Hamburgh, the theological significance of swoon imagery consists of three major points:

1) that Mary is understood as the figure of the church itself; 2) that through her participation on Calvary she has been seen as our *co-redemptrix* with Christ; and 3) that the image of *lo spasimo* is explained by the dual notions of *compassio* and the pain of childbirth under the cross which connect decisively with the first two concepts.[20]

Otto G. Von Simson cites Roger Van Der Weyden's fifteenth-century masterpiece, *Descent from the Cross*, as indicative of these Mariological themes.[21] In this painting, Simson writes, the "Virgin swoons, and in collapsing her body assumes an attitude almost identical with that of her dead Son." This view of Mary makes her an "almost independent center of attention, nearly as important to the composition as is the figure of Christ." The intensity of Mary's suffering, Simson remarks, "evokes, in striking and dramatic manner, the Virgin's supreme dignity as fifteenth century theology had come to formulate it: her share in the work of Redemption; more precisely, her dignity as *co-redemptrix* in virtue of her *compassion* on Calvary."[22] Such depictions of Mary as swooning express the Virgin's superlative capacity for compassion in a dramatically physical manner. As Cajetan's disavowal of such iconography makes clear, this physical component is absent from representations of her as a dignified, somatically controlled woman in the manner of *Stabat Mater*.[23] When Mary is represented as standing in a dignified manner she discloses an elegantly spiritual sorrow that is contained by her bodily purity and her knowledge of the atonement. In this respect, Lanyer's depiction of Mary is distinct from the Counter-Reformation view of her expressed by Francois de Sales, who insists that Mary "did not faint or make an excessive outward show of her grief, as some painters falsely portray."[24]

In the Protestant context of Jacobean England, Mary's experience under the cross is not generally the focus of devotional attention because, as Christine Peters observes, "the compassion of the Virgin Mary had to be distanced from ideas of maternal intercession with her Son."[25] Hence, the question of Mary's experience under the cross is generally of more homiletic than of theological interest. This is evinced by the fact that when Mary's experience under the cross does appear in official English Jacobean Protestant contexts, it is often to foreground Christ's suffering as the greatest of agonies and her sorrow as the greatest of empathic responses to his suffering. For example, in one of the rare instances that Lancelot Andrews addresses Mary's experience under the cross, the discussion of the Virgin serves, not as a distinct site of devotional or homiletic focus, but as a way to cast Christ's suffering into greater relief:

Truly Simeon saith to the blessed Virgin by way of prophecy, that "the sword should go through her soul," at the time of His Passion. And as the sword through hers, so I make no question but the spear through His. And if through hers which was but *anima compatientis*, through His much more, which was *anima patientis*; since compassion is but passion at rebound. Howbeit, it is not a sword of steel, or a spear-head of iron, that entereth the soul, but a metal of another temper.[26]

Andrews – who is generally recognized as a precursor of the High Church sensibilities which characterize the Caroline Church – not only distinguishes Christ's agony as more immediate, and thus more intense than Mary's, he also emphasizes the spiritual nature of Mary's sorrow – focusing little to no attention on her physical suffering. Unlike De Sales and Andrews, Lanyer returns to a more late medieval form of Marian devotion – focusing on Mary's active, embodied, and cooperative role in the Passion.

By returning to a pre-Tridentine vision of Mary as a swooning co-redemptrix, Lanyer presents a vision of the Virgin that is consistent with, and was likely informed by, Thomas Lodge's implicitly Catholic and anonymously published prose work, *Prosopopeia Containing the Teares of the Holy, Blessed, and Sanctified Marie, the Mother of God* (1596). Dedicated to the Countess of Cumberland as well as "The Mother Countesse, Countesse of Darby" (the openly Catholic and politically disgraced Margaret Stanley), Lodge depicts Mary as speaking in the voice of her son, as "immaculate," and as "the mediation and head of grace." Lodge concludes his depiction of Mary with the dramatic image of the swoon:

Thus plagued in bodie and distressed in soule, sate poore *Marie* (a holy and happie virgin) enacting hir griefe with her armes ... The image of her griefe before her, and the domage of her losse within her, shee sownded on the sen-selesse earth, and being conueied to her oratorie by the holy assistance, the sacred bodie of Christ was bound up and borne to the sepulchre.[27]

In Lodge's work, the swoon encapsulates the priestly, co-redeeming role attributed to Mary throughout the text as a whole, a role vividly expressed, among other ways, through the analysis of the Crucifixion as "one massacre."[28] Given the pre-Tridentine character of Lodge's depiction of Mary's physically registered participation in the Crucifixion, it is not surprising that he follows his anticipation of Protestant hostility to his work by anticipating critique from certain Catholic readers, those inter-preters who "will accuse me for writing these teares, desiring rather with [the Lutheran theologian] *Brentius* to impaire the honor of the mother of God, than with *Bernard* to inhance it." Such readers, Lodge fears, "will accuse the stile, as to stirring," and "the passion, as too vehement."[29] Lodge's prefatory material along with the text itself make clear that the theological controversy surrounding the nature of Mary's grief remained a vital issue for Elizabethan Catholics, an issue that Lanyer would put to work to very different ends than Lodge.

While there are many similarities between Lodge's and Lanyer's por-traits of Mary as actively participating in the work of sacrifice and atonement, Lanyer situates her account of the Virgin Mary's priestly functions at the center of a larger effort to imagine women in ministerial roles. Moreover, this effort to position women in roles of authority is grounded in the Lutheran promise of the priesthood of all believers rather than in any fidelity to the Catholic faith itself.[30] Thus, while Lodge's portrait of Mary is primarily an effort to recuperate Catholic devotional traditions, Lanyer's vision of the Virgin is primarily an effort to empower women as priests.

MARY AS PRIESTLY MOTHER

Like the Catholic Lodge, Lanyer depicts Mary's sorrow not as a second-hand reflection of Christ's agony in the Protestant manner of Andrews, but as an intensely participatory form of suffering – one that is physical and spiritual in nature. The first stanza in the sequence begins with Mary, "wayting on her Sonne" (94; 1009), and ends by claiming that "None ever lost so great a losse as shee, / Beeing Sonne, and Father of Eternitie" (95; 1014–15). The phrase "wayting on her Sonne," along with the act of swooning, initiates Mary's active role in the Crucifixion as she "stands at the watch," observing attentively (*OED*).[31] This scene precipitates the sequence's later focus on the active nature of the Virgin's gaze itself, "When thy faire eies beholds his bodie torne" (100; 1131), which develops and grounds the emphasis on the female gaze expressed in the "tears of the daughters of Jerusalem" whose "Eagles eyes did gaze against this Sunne" (94; 991).[32] Such focus on Mary's attentiveness is characteristic of late medieval Marian devotions. As Christine Peters observes,

The increasingly Christocentric focus of late medieval piety, with its emphasis on the suffering Christ of the Crucifixion, promoted a re-evaluation of the role of Mary: she became primarily a witness who was intimately involved with the sufferings of Christ, and well placed to communicate her anguish to the human race.[33]

In Lanyer's poem, Mary's witnessing of the Crucifixion becomes an active participation in it.

This participation in her Son's pain begins with Mary's "griefes extreame" that are "but new begun" – a phrase that recalls how Mary's swoon is traditionally interpreted as a sign that under the cross she experiences the childbirthing pains that were absent during the original birth of Jesus, as alluded to in Revelation 12:2 and as fulfilled in Simeon's prophecy in Luke 2:35,[34] and which Lanyer refers to in line 1083 of *Salve Deus*. In her recent study of the connections between Mary's swoon and the Virgin's physical experience as a mother, Amy Neff cites many medieval and early Renaissance examples of Mary's maternity on Calvary, beginning with Rupert (d. *c*.1135), Benedictine abbot of the Rhineland monastery of Deutz, who offers an interpretation of John 16:21 that focuses on Mary's *compassio* in terms of her physical pain as a mother. In John 16:21–22 Jesus explains to the Apostles:

A woman when she travaileth, hath sorrow, because her hour is come: but when she hath brought forth the child, now she remembreth not the anguish for joy, that a man is born into the world. And you therefore, now indeed you have sorrow, but I will see you again, and your heart shall rejoice.

As Neff observes, Rupert sees these words as fitting not only the Apostles, but even more so Mary:

[At the foot of the cross, Mary] is truly a woman and truly a mother and at this hour, she truly suffers the pains of childbirth. When [Jesus] was born, she did not suffer like other mothers: now, however, she suffers, she is tormented and full of sorrow, because her hour has come ... [I]n the Passion of her only Son, the Blessed Virgin gave birth to the salvation of all mankind: in effect, she is the mother of all mankind.[35]

Consistent with this tradition of identifying Mary's swoon with the delayed effects of her physical suffering during childbirth, the Virgin's "new begun" agony in Lanyer's depiction of the Passion suggests that her sorrow is the fulfillment of the Annunciation. And whether or not this symbolic association accounts for Lanyer's reversing of the chronological order of events – a narrative decision which certainly emphasizes the symbolic relations between Mary's role under the cross and her role as Mother of God – her physically registered sorrow recontextualizes the Passion from Mary's perspective. Read in this manner, Mary's woeful tending to Christ's crucified body functions as a way of helping birth the redemption just as she birthed the "blessed infant" (97; 1071).

Mary's active participation in the work of the Crucifixion is further expressed in the following stanza, when she protects Christ's blood and body so that its redeeming power might be gathered like a ripened flower. This representation of Mary as spiritual gardener, and the swoon iconography which it thematically supports, is consistent with conventional Catholic associations of her as a figure of the (Mother) Church. This portrait of Mary is also continuous with the poem's overall conflation, as Elizabeth Hodgson puts it, "of virtuous women with the Church ... and the priestly and prophetic powers of its ministers."[36] Moreover, Mary's role as spiritual gardener further suggests that she actively assumes her role within providence. This active assumption is centered on Mary's maternity of Christ – a participatory role alluded to in the figure of Christ as a flower that needs to be gathered at the proper hour, just as she protects his body through the nurturing power of her tears:

> Her teares did wash away his pretious blood,
> That sinners might not tread it under feet
> To worship him, and that did her good
> Upon her knees, although in open street,
> Knowing he was the Jessie floure and bud,
> That must be gath'red when it smell'd most sweet:
>   Her Sonne, her Husband, Father, Saviour, King
>   Whose death killd Death, and tooke away his sting. (95; 1017–24)

The representation of Christ as "floure and bud" is based on Catholic translations of Isaiah 11:1, which form part of the basis of flower symbolism in Christological and Mariological devotions: "there shall come forth a rod out of the root of Jesse, and a *flower* shall rise up out of his root" (Douay-Rheims). In Catholic traditions, this passage is generally interpreted as a prophecy of the Incarnation, in which Christ's lowly beginnings as the son of a Virgin Mother parallel David's humble beginnings from the Patriarch Jessie. As St. Ambrose puts it in *On the Holy Spirit*, "The root of Jesse the patriarch is the family of the Jews, Mary is the rod, Christ the flower of Mary, Who, about to spread the good odour of faith throughout the whole world, budded forth from a virgin womb, as He Himself said: 'I am the flower of the plain, a lily of the valley.'"[37] This rendering of Isaiah appears in Lodge's *Prosopopeia*, when the narrator proclaims to Mary, "thorough the vapour of the holy Ghost the flower sprong: A branch shall springe out of the roote of Jesse, and a flower shall ascende from the roote, as faith [*sic*] Esaie. And what other is this braunch … but thy selfe the virgine of God: what this flower but thy sonne?"[38] It also appears in the conclusion to Southwell's poem on the Virgin's birth called "Her Nativity": "For heavenly flowre shee is the *Jesse* rod, / The child of man, the parent of a god" (17–18). These renderings of Isaiah 11:1 are distinct from the translation and glosses in the 1560 Geneva Bible. The Geneva translation has "grase" rather than flower (the King James uses the term "branch," as does Lodge) and more importantly the gloss elides altogether the Virgin Mother's role in the Incarnation:

Because the captivitie of Babylon was a figure of the spiritual captivitie Under sinne, he sheweth that our true deliverance must come from Christe for as David came out of Isaiah a man without dignitie: so Christ should come of poore carpenters house as out of a dead stocke.

Lanyer's focus on Mary's role as the first person to prepare for the gathering of Christ's blood serves as a visible form of the iconographical significance implied by the Virgin's swoon.

The Virgin's priestly authority is further signaled when Mary kneels before Christ "in open street," an image that recalls how Lodge's Mary cries, "Let the voice of my mourning bee heard in your streets, for the noise of tribulation is harbored in my heart."[39] This active, visible, and corporeally expressive Mary is distinct from the "silent, self-controlled, and obedient" Mary that predominates in post-Reformation culture.[40] Indeed, Lanyer's Mary, who kneels and protects Christ "in the open street," is closer in nature to late medieval views of Mary, in which the Virgin, as Ellington observes, "gave public, ritual expression to the people's grief for the innocent suffering of her son on their behalf."[41] More strikingly, Lanyer's focus on how Mary's knowledge of providence affects her inward experience, and consequently her outward displays of motherly compassion and protection, suggests, contra Cajetan and other Counter-Reformation authorities, that there is no opposition between Mary's intense emotion and her profound spiritual understanding. In this way, Lanyer's depiction of Mary is consistent with the epistemological view that the emotive faculties are not extensions of the sensitive appetite, as in Aristotle and Aquinas, but are a function of the will, as in Augustine and the Franciscan tradition.[42] Lodge outlines this view when he depicts Mary as claiming that "Philosophie concents to my sorow, for mine eies increase in griefe, my passions are intollerable, beeing afflicted in al my senses, my loue quickens my passions, my deuotion nourisheth my loue, my teares beautifie my affection."[43] Such an epistemology is in keeping with Lanyer's representation of Mary as suffering, like Christ, in her body as well as in her spirit. For Lanyer, as for the Catholic Lodge, intense and gendered grief constitutes its own form of non-propositional, and hence properly spiritual, apprehension. What differentiates Lanyer's text from Lodge's, though, is that this combination of emotion and reason, affect and comprehension, supports her effort of imagining women as bearing clerical authority rather than as a way of recovering Catholic devotional practices.

MARY AND FEMALE POETIC AUTHORITY

A key part of Lanyer's effort involves exhorting her patrons to play clerical roles, as evinced in the letter to the Countess of Dorcet. The gardener imagery used to express Mary's priestly authority closely echoes the imagery Lanyer uses in her exhortation to Dorcet to adopt the role of a priestly healer. Lanyer calls on Ladie Anne to "Bind up the broken, stop the wounds that bleeds, / Succour the poore, comfort the comfortlesse, / Cherish faire plants, suppresse unwholsom weeds" (44; 276–78). As Micheline White observes, this gardening imagery "echoes Matthew 13:24–32, 36–43, a parable frequently used to discuss an English priest's responsibility to 'exhort by wholesome doctrine . . . [and] put to silence such as speak against it. The devil . . . ceaseth not at all time to sow his weeds, tares, and cockle in the Lord's field.'"[44] Lanyer's exhortation to Dorcet to play the role of spiritual gardener finds its theological ground in the Virgin Mary's priestly role as the protector and first gatherer of Christ's blood. Perhaps most importantly, Lanyer situates her own authority as poet-priestess in relation to Isaiah 11:1. In the prefatory letter to the Countess of Cumberland, Lanyer implies a parallel between the humble roots of Christ and her own socially marginal position:

The sweet incense, balsums, odours, and gummes that flowes from that beautifull tree of Life, sprung from the roote of *Jessie*, which is so super-excellent, that it giveth grace to the meanest & most unworthy hand that will undertake to write thereof. (pp. 34–35)

Lanyer locates her poetic and quasi-priestly powers in the grace bestowed from one ostensibly abject figure to another. The paradoxes of authority in weakness, strength in compassion, are most clearly embodied in the Virgin Mary who, like Lanyer, participates in offering Christ up for others to witness. For, just as Christ is figured as a flower who springs from meek beginnings, so Lanyer secures the authority of her poem by remarking that "there is hony in the meanest floweres" (30; 196). While ostensibly downplaying the power of her verse, this figure implies that her poem's origins are comparable to Christ's humble beginnings, thereby furthering her claim to a quasi-priestly function.

Lanyer's reference to Mary's kneeling posture before Christ is also a significant indication of Mary's priestly role at the Crucifixion (30; 1020). Having fallen to her knees in order to protect Christ's blood in a priestly gesture of devotion, the narrative again emphasizes her physical reaction to Christ's suffering. This physical gesture recalls the Catholic practice of genuflection which early modern Calvinists repudiated. As with the controversy over Mary's swoon, what is at stake in the controversy over genuflection is the value of physical, outward acts of devotion – acts which Calvinist Reformers often characterized as effeminate and excessively ostentatious.[45] Embodying such outward displays of piousness, Mary exemplifies a form of piety more in keeping with late medieval than with Protestant devotions as she weeps, kneels, gathers, and protects Christ's body. By doing so, Mary authorizes an emotionally expressive piety that, in post-Reformation contexts (especially in the context of English Calvinism) was derogatorily associated with the feminine and with women more generally. By re-authorizing this emotionally and physically expressive form of devotion, Lanyer's text works to empower women as agents of an empathic and feminized Christ – a Christ whom Mary parallels through her physical and spiritual suffering.[46]

While Lanyer turns to Catholic translations of Isaiah 11:1 in order to express both her confidence as a poet and the Virgin Mary's authority as a priestess, she also identifies her poetic powers in terms of a "sad delight" – a form of affect that is a function of both feeling and knowledge, emotion and cognition. Such is the state, I have been arguing, exemplified by Lanyer's swooning Mary. Indeed, the poem's representation of Mary's authority provides theological support for Lanyer's own claims to poetic and priestly powers, particularly in the letter to Queen Anne. In her letter to Anne, Lanyer establishes her own poetic and spiritual authority on the grounds that Nature, as opposed to Art, has yielded her a "sad delight":

> And pardon me (faire Queene) though I presume,
> To doe that which so many better can;
> Not that I Learning to my selfe assume,
> Or that I would compare with any man:
> But as they are Scholers, and by Art do write,
> So Nature yields my Soule a sad delight. (9; 145–50)

The phrase "sad delight" upon which Lanyer hinges her authority is a pregnant one. It signifies a culturally unmediated relation to the paradoxes of joy in sorrow, victory in defeat, power in submissiveness that is the essence of incarnational theology. Moreover, the phrase implies that her "sad" soul is "steadfast, firm, constant, valiant, grave, serious," and perhaps most importantly, "of trustworthy character and judgment" (*OED*). By implying that her authority rests on an unmediated access to Christly virtues, Lanyer distinguishes the precise nature of her authority as a female poet from the authority male poets achieve through learning and rhetoric (through scholarship and art). This passage is thus consistent with Marshall Grossman's reading of "The Description of Cookeham," in which he demonstrates that Lanyer uses the "opposition between culturally mediated and naturally immediate discourse as a way of figuring difference; that is, of figuring the feminine as difference."[47] Locating her authority in a proximate, even immediate, relation with nature – which she refers to in the next stanza as the "Mother of Perfection" (10; 152) – Lanyer identifies with a creative force that is presented as the progenitor of Art, in order to present herself as a distinctly female writer. This intimacy with nature, this unmediated state of joy-in-sorrow, she tells us, makes her different from, but no less authoritative than, male poets, who stand at one remove from nature.

By locating her authority in an intuitive understanding of the paradoxes of incarnational theology that are yielded to her by Nature, Lanyer presents an alternative to Sir Philip Sidney's view that a poet's authority ultimately transcends Nature. For Sidney,

Only the Poet disdaining to be tied to any such subjection [to Nature], lifted up with the vigor of his own invention, doth grow in effect into another nature, in making things either better then nature bringeth forth, or, quite anew, forms such as never were in nature, as the Heroes, Demigods, Cyclops, Chimeras, Furies, and such like: so as he goeth hand in hand with nature, not enclosed within the narrow warrant of her gifts, but freely raunging within the Zodiack of his owne wit.[48]

Unlike Sidney, Lanyer's authority derives from an immediate proximity to rather than a transcendence of nature. The "sad delight" that Nature affords Lanyer signifies a paradoxical state of affectively based knowledge that closely aligns her and those of her gender with Christ and the unmediated authority associated with him. In this way, her ostensibly humble admission of having less learning and art than men occasions a confident identification with the creative force of Nature and with the ability to understand the paradoxes of scripture arising from this identification. This identification of herself with a personified Nature and men with Art in the letter to Anne may explain Lanyer's later claim, in her letter to Pembroke, that the ladies in her dream vision insist that Nature and Art be equal, no one being subject to the other: "And therefore will'd they should for ever dwell, / In perfit unity by this matchless Spring: / Since 'twas impossible either should excel, / Or her faire fellow in subjection bring" (25; 89–92). The sacred spring in which Nature and Art are united not only offers a vision of equality among opposites, but it also shows women determining the relation between these forces and the power possessed by them: "But here in equall sov'raigntie to live, / Equall in state, equall in dignitie, / That unto others they might comfort give, / Rejoycing all with their sweet unitie" (25; 93–96). While Sidney emphasizes the true poet's capacity to transcend, rather than be subject to,

Nature, Lanyer identifies poetic authority in terms of her intuitive relation to Nature, a relation that is not figured in terms of subjection and transcendence, but in terms of Nature's logical, if not metaphysical, priority, over Art.[49]

Given Lanyer's difference from Philip Sidney on the question of the poet's relationship to Nature, it is perhaps not surprising that Lanyer uses the trope of poetry as birth in a different way than Sidney does in the opening stanza of *Astrophel and Stella*. In the letter to Anne, Lanyer asserts:

> And since all Arts at first from Nature came,
> That goodly Creature, Mother of Perfection,
> Whom *Joves* almighty hand at first did frame,
> Taking both her and hers in his protection:
> Why should not She now grace my barren Muse,
> And in a Woman all defects excuse. (10; 151–56)

Here again, Lanyer's authority as a poet is a function of her intimacy with Nature, the "Mother of Perfection." The implication here is that as a woman and mother[50] Lanyer has more immediate access to the creative force behind Art than do male poets, particularly the male poet who labors so intensely in Sidney's sonnet sequence. In the opening sonnet of *Astrophel and Stella*, Astrophel's initial inability to birth a persuasive form of praise is not due to a lack of learning, but quite the opposite; he must abandon the weight of the past, look into his heart, and thereby give birth to a new expression of love. Astrophel's lack of invention is a function of his alienation from Nature through too much study: "Invention, Nature's child, fled stepdame Study's blows; / And others' feet still seemed but strangers in my way. / Thus, great with child to speak, and helpless in my throes, / Biting my truant pen, beating myself for spite: / 'Fool,' said my Muse to me, 'looke in thy heart, and write!'"[51] Astrophel's capacity to write truthfully occurs once he outstrips past authorities by turning into himself, locating truth as a function of his own experience. Astrophel has an entirely different relationship to history and, by extension, Nature than does Lanyer. What is remarkable about Lanyer's account of her authority is that it is grounded on the claim that she does not suffer the kind of alienation from Nature that Astrophel expresses. As a result she, as a woman and mother, is able to identify with Nature as the "Mother of perfection" in a way that is different than male poets. This difference is implied in the pointed question: "Why should not She [Nature] now grace my barren Muse?" Ostensible humbleness masks a confident re-appropriation of male discourse's tendency to appropriate female experience and characteristics.

The "sad delight" that Lanyer locates as Nature's gift to her, and the quasi-priestly authority that extends from it, is embodied in and exemplified by Lanyer's portrait of the Virgin Mary.

Indeed, the priestly role that Mary plays when she protects Christ's blood from the feet of sinners mirrors, in reverse, the protective role that the hand of Jove plays in relation to Nature and all of Nature's offspring: while the father protects the mother in the dedicatory letter to Anne, it is the mother who protects Christ, "Beeing Sonne, and Father of Eternitie," in the section on the sorrow of the Virgin Mary (95; 1016). The poem thus presents a reciprocal relation between God's protective role of Mother Nature and Mary's protective role of Christ. It is precisely this reciprocity that is embodied in the iconography of the swoon. More to the point, Lanyer's casting of Mary in a priestly role calls attention to the fact that male clerical responsibilities often entail an appropriation of conventionally female characteristics – an appropriation not unlike Sidney's use of pregnancy as a figure for the desire to write. As Ellington observes of late medieval Catholicism, to

cast Mary as a priest was to place her in a male role with female characteristics. In the place of women, men who are priests must now lay the table and prepare the food for the people to eat. Medieval mystical literature at times used such gender reversal to speak of the clergy as pregnant with Jesus, or as cooks who prepared Christ as food.[52]

By figuring herself as the priestess who invites women readers to the feast of her text[53] and by figuring Mary as the priestess who shelters Christ's body, Lanyer reclaims for women those ministerial roles that have long been associated with femaleness. Thus, just as Lanyer makes the case for her poetic power by reclaiming the male appropriation of metaphors of maternity, so she also makes the case for women as priests on the ground that such roles have always demanded characteristics more traditionally associated with women, particularly mothers.[54]

THE SALUTATION OF THE VIRGIN MARIE

The reciprocity between Christ and Mary figured in the swoon assumes that Mary actively agrees to the message of the Annunciation and hence to her role as *Mater Dolorosa*. Catholic readings of Mary as playing a cooperative role in the Passion generally presume that Mary's submission to the message of the Annunciation involves a positive assertion of agency rather than a passive acceptance of God's will. In his 1606 work, "Miracles Lately Wrought by the Intercession of the Glorious Virgin Marie, at

Mont-aigu," for instance, Philips Numan describes Mary's role in the Annunciation as a function of her active agreement to participate in providence. As Frances E. Dolan remarks, Numan's text offers an interpretation of "Mary's response to the Annunciation, 'fiat' or 'let it be,' not as submissiveness but as an assertion of agency equal to God's creation of the world: 'By his Fiat, he made the world and man, by her Fiat, God entered into the world, and became man.'"[55] Protestants, on the other hand, tend to view Mary as a passive vehicle of the divine plan, downplaying any active role on Mary's part. Luther, for example, remarks in a sermon that "Mary does not desire to be an idol; she does nothing; God does all. We ought to call upon her that for her sake God may grant and do what we request. Thus also, all other saints are to be invoked, so that their work may every way God's alone."[56] Lanyer addresses this issue in one of the stanzas leading up to "The Salutation of the Virgin Marie":

> Most Blessed Virgin, in whose faultless fruit,
> All Nations of the earth must needes rejoice,
> No Creature having sense though ne'r so brute,
> But joyes and trembles when they heare his voice;
> His wisedome strikes the wisest persons mute,
> Faire chosen vesell, *happy in his choice*:
>   Deere Mother of our Lord, whose reverend name,
>   All people Blessed call, and spread thy fame.
>   (95; 1025–32, my emphasis)

That Mary is figured here as actively assuming her role is evident in the phrase "happy in his choice," which indicates not only "having good 'hap' or fortune, blessed, or beatified," but it also indicates "having a feeling of great pleasure or content of mind, arising from satisfaction with one's circumstances or condition" (*OED*). This focus on Mary's active assumption of her role in providence becomes more explicit six stanzas later when the Virgin inquires how it could be that she should bear God in her womb and she concludes that it is the most extraordinary of blessings: "Thy virgin did thinke, none could impart / This great good hap, and blessing unto thee" (97; 1075–76). The Virgin's "chaste desire" (97; 1079) is fulfilled through her role as God's mother, as suggested when Mary is told that "He is with thee, behold thy happy case" (96; 1043). Throughout this sequence, Lanyer focuses on Mary's experience during the Annunciation and Crucifixion, an experience that is repeatedly figured as active rather than passive.

By reading Mary's acceptance of the message of Annunciation as a positive act of will we can see how the stanza quoted above establishes the context for the following stanza's focus on her active role in inspiring

God's choice of making her the "Blessed vessel": "Thy lowly mind, and unstain'd Chastitie / Did pleade for Love at great *Jehovaes* gate" (95; 1034–35). While the emphasis in this stanza is clearly on God's magnification of Mary, which is broadly consistent with both Protestant and Catholic traditions, it shows clear similarities with late medieval and Counter-Reformation traditions of presenting Mary as appealing to God through her virtue as a virgin – a tradition which grants Mary a more active and thus central role in providence than Protestant tradition tends to. Robert Southwell expresses this tradition of granting Mary an important place in the divine hierarchy in his poem, "The Virgins Salutation":

> O virgin breast the heavens to thee incline,
> In thee their joy and soveraigne they agnize
> Too meane their glory is to match with thine,
> Whose chaste receit God more then heaven did prize,
> Haile fairest heaven, that heaven and earth dost blisse,
> Where virtues starres God sunne of justice is. (7–12)

Though Lanyer's poem does not go so far as to place Mary above the heavenly host, it does imply that Mary's virtue "pleads" with God – thereby configuring Mary as possessing the desire to participate in the fulfillment of providence. The "of" in Lanyer's "The Salutation of the Virgin Marie" can thus be read as either subjective or objective genitive. It is not only the angel of Annunciation's greeting that is expressed, but also, as Southwell's title suggests, the Virgin Mary's own salutation. When read together these elements make clear that Mary is presented as cooperating in Christ's suffering, and thus the work of atonement.

At the conclusion of this stanza, Mary's authority is summed up in terms of her role as the "most beauteous Queene of Woman-kind," to which "The Angell did unfold his Makers mind" (95; 1039–40). In this respect, Mary is identified as embodying the best of womanly virtues and power and as possessing knowledge of providential design. Moreover, her proximity to Christ is expressed in terms of the physical suffering she underwent with Christ at the Crucifixion – traditionally a sign of her priestly role within the atonement.

This account of Mary's authority through suffering and acceptance of God's plan initiates Lanyer's depiction of the salutation of the Virgin Mary. The line that begins this stanza opens with the language of the rosary taken from the Douay-Rheims translation of the Bible: "Hail *Mary* full of grace." What is most notable about this stanza is not its evocation of the rosary – a predominantly, if not distinctly, Catholic form of prayer – but its substitution of the word "worlds" for the terms "generations" and "ages" in the allusion to Luke 1:48 that concludes the stanza. While the 1587 Geneva Bible depicts Mary as claiming that "henceforth shall all *ages* call me blessed," the King James and Douay-Rheims translations say that "all *generations* shall call me blessed." Lanyer, however, glosses Luke 1:48 differently:

> What endlesse comfort did these words afford
> To thee that saw'st an Angell in the place
> Proclaime thy Virtues worth, and to record
>   Thee blessed among women: that thy praise
>   Should last so many worlds beyond thy daies. (96; 1044–48)

The word "worlds" not only implies a "period or age of human history characterized by certain conditions" (*OED*), but it also signifies "eternity" as in English translations of the Latin *in secula seculorum, in seculum seculi* (*OED*). Lanyer's rendering of Luke 1:48 thus sustains a reading of Mary's authority extending beyond a solely temporal perspective into a more eternal point of view – an idea embodied in the Catholic theme of the Assumption. Perhaps most importantly, the word "worlds" is often used, as the *OED* has it, "with reference to birth or death especially *to bring into the world*, to give birth to." Like the adjective "happy," the substitution of "worlds" for "generations" or "ages" indicates that Mary is to be read as playing a physical and spiritual role in the redemption. This stanza thus continues the sequence's focus on the comfort that Mary takes in the Word. By doing so, it furthers the poem's focus on Mary's experience as a distinct site of devotional meditation.

This focus on Mary's subjectivity continues in the following stanza as the Annunciation is presented from the Virgin's point of view:

> Loe, this high message to thy troubled spirit,
> He doth deliver in the plainest sense;
> Sayes, Thou shouldst beare a Sonne that shal inherit
> His Father *Davids* throne, free from offence,
> Call's him that Holy thing, by whose pure merit
> We must be sav'd. (96; 1049–54)

The stanza following also focuses on the effect that receiving the Word has on Mary: "He cheeres thy troubled soule, bids thee not feare" (96; 1057). The poem's focus on Mary's subjectivity becomes most ideologically charged three stanzas later, when she is presented in a state of spiritual genuflection, this time voicing her "chaste desire": "When on the knees of thy submissive heart / Thou humbly didst demand, How that should be?" (97; 1073–74). If Mary's authority is earlier presented in terms of her physical suffering alongside Christ, it is now voiced in terms of her physical and spiritual distance from the corrupting force of men: "Farre from desire of any man thou art, / Knowing not one, thou art from all men free: / When he, to answere this thy chaste desire, / Gives thee more cause to wonder and admire" (97; 1077–80). The focus here is on Mary's affective experience, just as the initial focus was on her physical and emotional suffering at the Crucifixion. Mary's experience at this point culminates in an act of joyful weeping, an expression of the kind of sad delight Lanyer uses to distinguish her poetic authority from that of male poets: "Could thy faire eyes from teares of joy refraine, / When God look'd upon thy poore degree?" (97–98; 1085–86). Through the salutation, the first of Mary's joyful mysteries, Mary is afforded a relation to God that is based on an affective experience similar to the "sad delight" that Nature is said to afford Lanyer in the letter to Anne. In this respect, the depiction of Mary as an expressive and active player in providence, a priestess who protects Christ's body and helps ensure that his gifts are bestowed to others, provides historical and theological precedent for Lanyer's claim to priestly power, as she says in her letter "To the Ladie Margaret Countesse Dowager of Cumberland," the power to "present unto you even our Lord Jesus himselfe" (34; 7). In both cases, female authority is figured in terms of *compassio* – an ability to feel and express joy-in-sorrow.

As the flashback to the Annunciation ends, the poem returns again to the scene of Christ's death and the iconography of the swoon. This transition unfolds from Mary's perspective as she witnesses Christ's walk to Golgotha:

> How canst thou choose (faire Virgin) then but mourne,
> When this sweet of-spring of thy body dies,
> When thy faire eies beholds his bodie torne,
> The peoples fury, heares the womens cries;
> His holy name prophan'd, He made a scorne,
> Abusde with all their hatefull slanderous lies;
>   Bleeding and fainting in such wondrous sort,
>   As scarce his feeble limbes can him support. (99–100; 1129–36)

Mary's physical and priestly participation in Christ's agony is consummated now as Christ is depicted as bleeding and fainting in "wondrous sort" thereby paralleling Mary's physical posture earlier in the poem. The structure of Lanyer's sequence on the Virgin Mary thus bears a close relation to the many late medieval and early Renaissance visual depictions of Christ and Mary as sharing in physical agony and thus spiritual responsibility.

By figuring Mary as swooning due to her participation in Christ's suffering, Lanyer accomplishes a number of things. First, Mary's swoon implies the Virgin's priestly participation in the Passion – an active role that provides theological and iconographical authority for Lanyer's own reclamation of a quasi-priestly power. When read this way, the opening line of the stanza just quoted implies that Mary has made an active choice and thus the narrator stands in awe of her, evoking empathic identification with the *Mater Dolorosa*. Moreover, the iconography of the swoon condenses the poem's whole thematics of female suffering and the religious authority such suffering wields in the text. In sum, the swoon situates the poem's veneration of motherhood in a popular and powerful iconographic tradition that grounds Mary's spiritual authority in her physical experience as a loving and suffering mother.

CONCLUSION: THE QUESTION OF PATRONAGE

At the start of this chapter, I indicated that the Catholic dimensions of Lanyer's representation of the Virgin Mary are presumably intended to appeal to at least two of Lanyer's readers – Queen Anne and Lady Arabella Stuart. Bearing in mind Lanyer's explicit concern with female patronage, her poem supports Peter Davidson and Thomas M. McCoog's thesis that "Anne's Catholicism must be one of the factors which informs the debate about her cultural patronage."[57] Indeed, it is worth pointing out in this context, Davidson and McCoog's discussion of the gift Anne received on April 11, 1609 during a Jonsonian entertainment at Britain's Burse, put on by Robert Cecil, Earl of Salisbury. The gift was a silver bas-relief plaque of the Annunciation. This gift, Davidson and McCoog contend, "is a representation of Scriptural narrative, and, as such, theoretically tolerable in a Protestant context. It is also clearly open to interpretation as essentially Catholic; the first Joyful Mystery of the Rosary, the moment of the utterance of the 'Ave Maria.'"[58] Lanyer's depiction of a swooning, priestly Mary clearly presents a more complicated theological text than the gift Davidson and McCoog speak of – reclaiming as it does a pre-Reformation view of the Virgin. Yet given the relative subtlety of swoon iconography, especially in post-Reformation cultures, along with the careful diction and allusiveness Lanyer uses in her representation of Mary as priestly co-redeemer, combined with the theological freedom made possible by poetry (a fact evinced by the publication of Southwell's "The

Virgins Salutation" and other clearly Catholic Marian poems in England),[59] it is not altogether surprising such a portrait could circulate in print without fear of censorship or reprisal. In any case, Lanyer's portrait of Mary does not seem intended to line up with specific confessional or doctrinal positions so much as it works to foreground female spiritual power. Such power, her poem insists, is no longer readily available in either official Protestant or Catholic doctrines, but it could be reconfigured by synthesizing varying discourses of godly sorrow, from the "sad delight" of Nature's authority to the Virgin's priestly swoon under the cross.

While the two sequences on the Virgin Mary in *Salve Deus* were likely fashioned in order to appeal to Anne's religiosity, Lanyer also seems to have connected the symbology of the Virgin Mary to her representation of the virtues of Lady Arabella Stuart, who is believed to have shared at least some of Anne's Catholic sympathies.[60] The letter to Arabella depicts the King's cousin as a Phoenix and as a Morning Sun, traditional symbols of the Virgin Mary and of female learning more generally.[61] And like Lodge, Lanyer may have presented a powerful image of the Virgin Mary in the hopes that it would be received as appropriate praise of Margaret Clifford's power as a matriarch, particularly Clifford's fashioning of "a matrilineal heritage and kinship network." As Barbara Lewalski has demonstrated, "Anne Clifford was profoundly grateful to her mother [Margaret] for beginning and carrying forward ... lawsuits in her behalf, and admired her enormously for her patience in adversity and for her exemplary courage and firmness in opposing the patriarchal power structure."[62] Taken together, the patronage context informing Lanyer's depiction of Mary appears highly overdetermined.

Yet perhaps the most important observation to be made in relation to Lanyer's depiction of Mary's physical suffering under the cross is that it circumvents, somewhat, the reasons many historians of religion have argued that the cult of Mary has had detrimental effects on the lived experience of women.[63] Insofar as Mary constitutes an impossible ideal of chastity, bodily perfection, and self-sacrifice, she stands at the center of a religious regime that is destructively asymptotic in nature – leading faithful women to strive for a form of being that is, by its very nature, impossible to attain. By drawing on an iconographical tradition that emphasizes Mary's physical suffering – a tradition Counter-Reformation authorities disavowed precisely because it calls Mary's bodily perfection into question – Lanyer presents a version of Mary that is more deeply human and thus more relevant to the lived experience of women than the other-worldly Mary venerated in the official post-Tridentine tradition.

In this light, perhaps the best way to read Lanyer's depiction of Mary is as an attempt to imagine a vision of female authority that is configured not as a disembodied ideal, but as a physically real, emotionally expressive, and intellectually engaged exemplum of female spiritual power – one who can be seen as playing an active rather than passive role in the work of redemption. Such a figure, Lanyer's poem tells us, was not available in either of the official doctrines on Mary in post-Reformation Europe; though something like it could be envisioned through an imaginative synthesis of pre-Reformation traditions and the newly emergent idea of the priesthood of all believers; both of which are depicted in the poem as being mediated by the gendered language of godly sorrow.

NOTES

1 Micheline White, "A Woman with Saint Peter's Keys? Aemilia Lanyer's Salve Deus Rex Judaeorum (1611) and the Priestly Gifts of Women," *Criticism: A Quarterly for Literature and the Arts* 45.3 (2003), 323. For other readings of Lanyer's representation of herself and her patrons as priests, see Kari Boyd McBride, "Sacred Celebration: The Patronage Poems," in Marshall Grossman (ed.), *Aemilia Lanyer: Gender, Genre, and the Canon* (Lexington: University of Kentucky Press, 1998), pp. 60–82; Lynette McGrath, "'Let Us Have Our Libertie Againe': Aemilia Lanier's 17th-Century Feminist Voice," *Women's Studies* 20 (1992), 342; and "Metaphoric Subversions: Feasts and Mirrors in Aemilia Lanier's *Salve Deus Rex Judaeorum*," *LIT* 3 (1991), 101–13; Wendy Wall, *The Imprint of Gender: Authorship and Publication in the English Renaissance* (Ithaca, NY: Cornell University Press, 1993), pp. 319–30; Catherine Keohane, "'The Blindest Weakness Be Not Over-bold': Aemilia Lanyer's Radical Unfolding of the Passion," *ELH* 64 (1997), 359–89.
2 Susanne Woods, *Aemilia Lanyer: A Renaissance Woman Poet* (New York and Oxford: Oxford University Press, 1999), p. 138.
3 Elaine V. Beilin, *Redeeming Eve: Women Writers of the English Renaissance* (Princeton, NJ: Princeton University Press, 1987), p. 182.
4 My reading of the poem provides concrete evidence for Achsah Guibbory's claim that "Lanyer's extended attention to this 'Blessed' 'Mother of our Lord' (ll. 1032, 1031) recalls and perhaps revives the devotion to the Virgin Mary that blossomed in medieval Catholicism but withered with Protestantism." Achsah Guibbory, "The Gospel According to Aemilia: Women and the Sacred," in Grossman (ed.), *Aemilia Lanyer: Gender, Genre, and the Canon*, p. 198.
5 White, "A Woman," 336.
6 See Peter Davidson and Thomas M. McCoog, SJ, "Father Robert's Convert," *Times Literary Supplement* (Nov. 24, 2000), 16–18.

7 For a recent account of the religious politics surrounding Arabella, see Sarah Gristwood, *Arbella: England's Lost Queen* (London: Bantam Press, 2003), pp. 89–98. Michael Morgan Holmes, "The Love of Other Women: Rich Chains and Sweet Kisses," in Grossman (ed.), *Aemilia Lanyer: Gender, Genre, and the Canon*, p. 188, hints at the importance of Lanyer's Catholic readers to our understanding of the poem when he remarks that "the fact that Lanyer's father, Baptist Bassano, was a Venetian and her husband, Alfonso Lanyer, a Roman Catholic, might suggest the poet's awareness of, and interest in, Catholic devotion."

8 See White, "A Woman," 339.

9 Cited in White, "A Woman," 339 fn. 9.

10 For a discussion of the swoon controversy in relation to some of its English contexts, specifically the work of Richard Crashaw, see Eugene R. Cunnar, "Crashaw's 'Sancta Maria Dolorum': Controversy and Coherence," in John R. Roberts (ed.), *New Perspectives on the Life and Art of Richard Crashaw* (Columbia: University of Missouri Press, 1990), pp. 99–126.

11 Harvey E. Hamburgh, "The Problem of *Lo Spasimo* of the Virgin in *Cinquecento* Paintings of the *Descent from the Cross*," *Sixteenth-Century Journal* 12.4 (1981), 45. See also, Charles Journet, "Notre Dame des Sept Douleurs," *Les Cahiers de la Vierge* II (1934), 56.

12 Hamburgh, "The Problem," 45.

13 Leo Steinberg, "Pontormo's Capponi Chapel," *Art Bulletin* 56 (1974), 386–87.

14 Hamburgh, "The Problem," 46.

15 See Elizabeth Hodgson, "Prophecy and Gendered Mourning in Lanyer's *Salve Deus Rex Judaeorum*," *SEL* 43.1 (2003), 101–16; Patricia Phillippy, *Women, Death and Literature in Post-Reformation England* (Cambridge: Cambridge University Press, 2002), pp. 39–48.

16 Cited in Hamburgh, "The Problem," 46. A full translation of Cajetan's treatise appears in Harvey Hamburgh, "Aspects of the *Descent from the Cross* from Lippi to Cigoli" (Ph.D. dissertation, University of Iowa, 1978), pp. 750–54.

17 Donna S. Ellington, "Impassioned Mother or Passive Icon: The Virgin's Role in Late Medieval and Early Modern Passion Sermons," *Renaissance Quarterly* 6.22 (1995), 254.

18 The popularity of such imagery led the Jesuit Peter Canisius to reiterate Cajetan's point more forcefully in 1577 (Hamburgh, "The Problem," 47).

19 Hamburgh, "The Problem," 51. See also, Otto G. Von Simson, "*Compassio* and *Co-Redemptio* in Rogier Van Der Weyden's *Descent from the Cross*," *Art Bulletin* 35 (1953), 9–16.

20 Hamburgh, "The Problem," 51.

21 For discussions of other examples of this iconography and its theological implications, see Cunnar, "Crashaw's 'Sancta Maria Dolorum'"; David Baier, "Mary at the Foot of the Cross," *Franciscan Studies* 23.2. (March 1942), 3–11; J. B. Carol, "Our Lady's Part in the Redemption According to Seventeenth-Century Writers," *Franciscan Studies* 24 (1943), 3–20; Paul Y. Cardile, "Mary

as Priest: Mary's Sacerdotal Position in the Visual Arts," *Arte Cristiana* 72 (1984), 199–208.

22 Von Simson, "*Compassio*," 11. Along with Lodge's 1596 *Prosopopeia*, this late medieval way of depicting Mary's experience is expressed in England in the 1519 prose meditation, "The lamentacyon of Our Lady," which depicts the Passion from Mary's point of view. In this early Renaissance text, Mary's participation in the Crucifixion is figured by having her faint five times – each symbolically corresponding with Christ's five wounds.

23 "Juxta crucem tecum stare, / Et me tibi sociare / In planctu desidero [I long to stand with you by the Cross, and to be your companion in your lamentation]." Cited in Eamon Duffy, *The Stripping of the Altars: Traditional Religion in England c.1400–c.1580* (New Haven, CT: Yale University Press, 1992), p. 259.

24 Cited in Ellington, "Impassioned," 245.

25 Christine Peters, *Patterns of Piety: Women, Gender and Religion in Late Medieval and Reformation England* (Cambridge: Cambridge University Press, 2003), p. 237.

26 Lancelot Andrews, *Ninety-Six Sermons* (Oxford: John Henry Parker, 1841), vol. 2, p. 123.

27 Thomas Lodge, *Prosopopeia, Containing the Teares of the Holy, Blessed, and Sanctified Marie, the Mother of God* (London, 1596), C8r, D1v, D4v, D1r, H8r.

28 Ibid., D6v.

29 Ibid., A5v.

30 Recall for instance the anti-Catholic rhetoric used in the letter "To the Ladie Susan, Countesse Dowager of Kent": "From *Romes* ridiculous prier and tyranny, / That might Monarchs kept in awfull feare" (p. 25).

31 Micheline White, "A Woman," observes, in relation to these lines, that women in the poem are praised "for displaying watchfulness, the very virtue that the disciples lack," 333.

32 For a discussion of the politics of Mary's gaze in medieval literature, see Sarah Stanbury, "The Virgin's Gaze: Spectacle and Transgression in Middle English Lyrics of the Passion," *PMLA* 106 (1991), 1083–93.

33 Peters, *Patterns of Piety*, p. 74.

34 See Cunnar, "Crashaw's 'Sancta Maria Dolorum,'" 106.

35 Amy Neff, "The Pain of *Compassio*: Mary's Labor at the Foot of the Cross," *Art Bulletin* 80.2 (June 1998), 256.

36 Hodgson, "Prophecy," 105.

37 St. Ambrose, *On the Holy Spirit*, in *New Advent Catholic Encyclopedia*, 2v-r, http://www.newadvent.org/fathers/34022.htm (accessed April 11, 2004).

38 This distinctly Catholic rendering of Isaiah 11:1 also appears in a 1598 English version of the Rosary: "The Virgin has given birth to the Savior: a flower has sprung from Jesse's stock and a star has risen from Jacob. O God, we praise you." *A Methode, to Meditate on the Psalter, or Great Rosarie of our Blessed Ladie* (Antwerp, 1598), A4.

39 Lodge, *Prosopopeia*, B5r. Micheline White makes a related point when she observes that "Lanyer's depiction of Mary's grief is striking in that she

positions her 'in open street' (1020), and in contrast to the disciples who 'waited on' Christ yet failed to understand his mission (577)" ("A Woman," p. 334).

40 Donna Spirey Ellington, *From Sacred Body to Angelic Soul: Understanding Mary in Late Medieval and Early Modern Europe* (Washington, DC: Catholic University of America Press, 2001), p. 148.

41 Ibid., p. 79.

42 For a discussion of Augustine's faculty psychology in relation to the expression of religious experience in the Renaissance, see Debora Shuger, *Sacred Rhetoric: The Christian Grand Style in the English Renaissance* (Princeton, NJ: Princeton University Press, 1988), p. 133.

43 Lodge, *Prosopopeia*, D6v.

44 White, "A Woman," 328. White is quoting here from Thomas Beacon, *The Catechism of Thomas Becon ... With Other Pieces Written by Him*, ed. John Ayre (Cambridge: Cambridge University Press, 1844), p. 322.

45 For discussions of the misogynistic nature of Calvinist polemic against Catholic and High Church devotions, see Francis E. Dolan, *The Whores of Babylon: Catholicism, Gender, and Seventeenth-Century Print Culture* (Ithaca, NY: Cornell University Press, 1999).

46 For a discussion of Lanyer's feminization of Christ and the practice of blazoning attendant upon it, see Wendy Wall, "The Body of Christ: Aemilia Lanyer's Passion," in *The Imprint of Gender*, pp. 319–30.

47 Marshall Grossman, "The Gendering of Genre: Literary History and the Canon," in *Aemilia Lanyer: Gender, Genre, and the Canon*, p. 133.

48 Philip Sidney, "An Apology for Poetry," in *The Golden Hind: An Anthology of Elizabethan Prose and Poetry*, ed. Roy Lamson and Hallett Smith (New York: W. W. Norton, 1956), p. 275.

49 For a discussion of the broader theoretical issues at stake in Lanyer and other women writers claiming a less mediated relation to nature, see Grossman's discussion of Luce Irigaray in "The Gendering of Genre," pp. 132–33.

50 For a discussion of motherhood in *Salve Deus*, see Naomi J. Miller, "Mother Tongues: Maternity and Subjectivity," in Grossman (ed.), *Aemilia Lanyer: Gender, Genre, and the Canon*, pp. 143–66.

51 Philip Sidney, "Astrophel and Stella, Sonnet I," in *The Golden Hind*, p. 236, lines 10–14.

52 Ellington, *From Sacred Body*, p. 90.

53 For discussions of Lanyer's feast imagery, see Kari Boyd McBride, "Sacred Celebration," and Lynette McGrath, "Metaphoric Subversions."

54 For a discussion of how male religious roles and experience were represented in female terms in late medieval culture, see Caroline Walker Bynum, *Jesus as Mother: Studies in the Spirituality of the High Middle Ages* (Berkeley: University of California Press, 1982).

55 Dolan, *Whores of Babylon*, p. 104.

56 Thomas O'Meara, *Mary in Protestant and Catholic Theology* (New York: Sheed and Ward, 1966), p. 117.

57 Davidson and McCoog, "Father Robert's Convert," 17. For a recent study of Anne's patronage of the arts, see Leeds Barroll, *Anna of Denmark, Queen of England: A Cultural Biography* (Philadelphia: University of Pennsylvania Press, 2001).
58 Davidson and McCoog, "Father Robert's Convert," 17.
59 As William L. Stull observes, the 1635 edition of Donne's collected poems includes a hyperbolically Catholic sonnet called "On the Blessed Virgin Mary," which Stull identifies as the work of Henry Constable (William L. Stull, "'Why Are Not Sonnets Made of Thee?' A New Context for the 'Holy Sonnets' of Donne, Herbert, and Milton," *Modern Philology* 80.2 (Nov. 1982), 129–35).
60 For a recent account of the religious politics surrounding Arabella, see Gristwood, *Arbella*, pp. 89–98.
61 For a discussion of such symbols in England, see Helen Hackett's *Virgin Mother, Maiden Queen: Elizabeth I and the Cult of the Virgin Mary* (New York: St. Martin's Press, 1995).
62 Barbara Lewalski, "Re-writing Patriarchy and Patronage: Margaret Clifford, Anne Clifford, and Aemilia Lanyer," *Yearbook of English Studies* 21 (1991), 92.
63 See for instance, Marina Warner, *Alone of All her Sex: The Myth and the Cult of the Virgin Mary* (New York: Vintage Books, 1976); Merry Wiesner, "Luther and Women: The Death of Two Marys," in Jim Obelkevich, Lyndal Roper, and Raphael Samuel (eds.), *Disciplines of Faith: Studies in Religion, Politics, and Patriarchy* (London: Routledge, 1987). This same attitude underlies Ellington's study of Mary, *From Sacred Body*. For a psychoanalytic account of what is both satisfying and oppressive about varying versions of the Virgin Mary for women and men, see Julia Kristeva, "Stabat Mater," in *Tales of Love* (New York: Columbia University Press, 1983), pp. 234–63.

CHAPTER 5

Petrarchism and repentance in John Donne's Holy Sonnets

By making unusually explicit the shared cultural assumption that the capacity for godly sorrow is tensed as feminine in early modern England, Lanyer figures women as possessing a greater ability to experience the reciprocity of empathic, selfless, love for Christ than men. If Lanyer had seen any of John Donne's *Holy Sonnets* in manuscript, she would have had good reason for making such a gendered claim. For Donne, the *compassio* that Lanyer depicts as "feminine" in nature is psychically violent, even traumatizing. In this respect, the same cultural discourse that provided Lanyer with a way of representing women as having unmediated access to the sad delight of incarnationist theology, inspired in Donne a psycho-spiritual crisis. Like Lanyer's depiction of men in *Salve Deus*, the speakers of Donne's *Holy Sonnets* are not naturally inclined to the life of faith, especially when it comes to opening themselves to the terrifying intimacy of God within the soul. On the contrary, most of the poems depict the devotional life as a counter-intuitive struggle. And whereas Lanyer takes the theological and devotional amorphousness of Jacobean England as an occasion for synthesizing pre-Tridentine iconography with Lutheran ecclesiology, Donne experiences the multiplicity of coexisting devotional practices and theological systems in early seventeenth-century England as a significant religious problem.

In this chapter, I explain how Donne depicts godly sorrow as a deeply ambivalent phenomenon – one that is terrifyingly bound up in a dialect of repentance which is, itself, complicated by coexisting, and in certain cases, mutually exclusive, devotional, and soteriological regimes. Throughout the *Holy Sonnets* Donne increases the sense of psycho-spiritual complexity in the poetry of tears tradition by applying the demystification of Petrarchism advanced in the *Songs and Sonets* to the terrifying experience of being God's lover. In particular, this application of post-Petrarchan poetics to the *Holy Sonnets* deepens, to an extraordinary degree, the gap between intention and meaning characteristic of the poetry of tears. In short, Donne's *Holy Sonnets* derive much of their power of fascination by the way they enact and diagnose penitential sorrow as a deeply ambivalent and anxiety-producing affair.

OPUS ALIENUM DEI

Luther believed that the process of justification is experienced as a dialectic in which, as Alister McGrath explains, "an action which is alien to God's nature (*opus alienum Dei*) results in an action which belongs to his very nature (*opus proprium Dei*): God makes a person a sinner in order that he may make him righteous."[1] Few English writers are more sensitive to the dialectical process by which deity is said to inhabit the repenting soul than John Donne, who often expresses reticence, even as he voices awe, over the simultaneously consoling and terrifying nature of God's presence in the subject. In *Devotions Upon Emergent Occasions*, for instance, Donne expresses the dialectic of regeneration by expostulating to God:

Thou wouldst have thy corrections taste of *humiliation*, but thou wouldest have them taste of *consolation*, too; taste of *danger*, but taste of *assurance* too... [while] these corrections ... have shewed us, that we are nothing in our selves, they may also shew us, that thou art all things unto us.[2]

The twofold structure of the Word of which Luther and Donne speak when describing repentance not only rests on the Pauline depiction of the Word as a double-edged sword,[3] but also on the idea that God is immanent within the soul at the same time as he is radically transcendent to the self. Augustine characterizes this potentially disturbing dimension of divinity when he says that God is "more inward than my most inward part, higher than the highest element within me" (*interior intimo meo et superior summo meo*).[4] Subscribing to Augustine's notion of God's immanence, Luther and Donne both portray the presence of deity within the soul as simultaneously terrifying and reassuring. The metaphysically comforting promise that God is "all things unto us" is first revealed through the narcissistically traumatic and thus anxiety-producing insight that "we are nothing in our selves."

This dialectic is a general feature of all the specific (and in certain instances mutually exclusive) soteriological regimes that have been used to explain the depiction of repentance in the *Holy Sonnets*. Whether we view the *Holy Sonnets* within the context of Richard Hooker's view of contrition,[5] a modified or orthodox version of Calvin's *ordo salutis*,[6] or a more broadly conceived "Augustinian spirituality"[7] (all of which inform but none of which seem to determine the *Holy Sonnets*) we still come up against a basic ambivalence at the heart of the poems: the speaker wants to express full contrition for his sins (either as a way to participate in or to be assured of salvation) at the same time as he experiences terror over the narcissistically traumatic insight that such contrition entails. In this respect, the fundamental drama of the *Holy Sonnets* is characterized by the speaker's terrifying recognition that repentance requires him to experience his lack of autonomy – to undergo a psychically violent process, in which he comes to realize, existentially as well as cognitively, that in himself he is nothing.

A key feature of this spiritual drama that has not been adequately explained involves the speaker's appropriations of Petrarchism. In "O Might Those Sighes and Teares," Donne's speaker represents the desire for conversion in self-consciously Petrarchan terms, calling for a shift from the idolatrous tears of the secular lover to the penitent tears of the devotional supplicant; while in "What If This Present," "If Faithfull Soules," and "Since She Whome I Lovd," a distinctly Petrarchan image of the courtly lover is evoked as a means of distinguishing between human and divine love. In each case, Donne's speaker employs the language of Petrarchism – its vocabulary as well as its thematic topoi – not only as a way of trying to cope with fear of God's judgment but also as a way of defending against anxiety over his own ontological and soteriological lack of self-sufficiency. Mary Ann Koory anticipates this point when she observes that "Donne uses Petrarchan poetics ... to shelter himself from the force of God's love," adopting "Petrarch's strategies from the *Rime Sparse* for imitating and resisting Augustine's self-representation from the *Confessions.*"[8] While Koory notices the Petrarchan thematics at work in the *Holy Sonnets*, she largely ignores the theological differences between Petrarch's and Donne's contexts. As a result, Koory does not situate Donne's resistance to conversion within the dialectical pattern of Prot- estant regeneration that forms an integral part of how the *Holy Sonnets* depict the experience of repentance. Moreover, Koory does not situate Donne's use of Petrarchism in the *Holy Sonnets* in relation to its uses in the *Songs and Sonets*. In my view, Donne's expression of ambivalence over regeneration in Petrarchan terms in the *Holy Sonnets* needs to be grasped in the context of Donne's parodies of Petrarchan solipsism in the *Songs and Sonets* which provide an important subtext to the anxiety and fear of God in the divine verse. What follows is an attempt to demonstrate that the theologically mediated anxiety expressed over the loss of perceived autonomy in the *Holy Sonnets* gets expressed in the Petrarchan terms that Donne parodies in the *Songs and Sonets*.

MY TEARS HAVE BEEN MY MEAT

The language of Petrarchism that Donne employs in the *Holy Sonnets* is inherently bound up with the theme of *metanoia*, the penitential turning from worldly things to God. The overall structure of the *Rime Sparse* evinces this crucial theme as the collection concludes with a prayer to the Virgin, in which Petrarch asks Mary to "fill my weary heart with holy repentant tears, let at least my last weeping be devout and without earthly mud, as was my first vow, before my insanity ... Lead me to the better crossing and accept my changed desires."[9] While this conversion scene is generally interpreted as a failed or incomplete one, as are virtually all such scenes in the *Canzionere*, it registers what Robert Durling views as the "central theme" of the *Rime Sparse*, namely "the unresolved conflict between Petrarch's love and his religion." Petrarch's verse is saturated by and gains much of its rhetorical force from its "Christian anguish,"[10] particularly its parodic inversions of the godly sorrow expressed in the psalms.

In Sonnet 342, for example, Petrarch begins by translating the image of "tears" as spiritual sustenance expressed in Psalm 42 to a secular and ultimately more narcissistic register – a register which the speaker of "O Might Those Sighes and Teares" will adopt. As we have already seen, Augustine interprets verse 3 of Psalm 42 as signifying the psalmist's state of *caritas*, as expressing how the psalmist's sustaining of his thirst for God signifies the divine, rather than worldly, modality of his desire: "[David] said not, 'My tears became my drink,' lest he should seem to have longed for them, as for the 'water-brooks,' but still retaining that thirst wherewith I burn, and by which I am hurried away towards the water-brooks ... And assuredly he does but the more thirst for the water-brooks from making his tears his meat."[11] For Augustine, then, the psalmist's tears are an expression of the way his desire is for the radical otherness of God, rather than for the self or for any worldly object by which one can love oneself. By contrast, Petrarch experiences his tears as a deepening of his self-indulgent grief. Rather than revealing *caritas*, they imply that a mode of self-love is at work here: "With the food of which my lord is always generous – tears and / grief – I feed my weary heart, and I often tremble and often / grow pale thinking of its cruel deep wound."[12] Despite this difference, Petrarch experiences the act of weeping in similarly kerygmatic terms as the psalmist (be he interpreted as a subjective individual or the corporate voice of Israel). Like the psalmist, Petrarch depicts weeping not as one emotion among others, but as a state that sets forth something essential about the relationship between desire and being, between the soul and God. In both psalmic and Petrarchan traditions, tears are revelatory, disclosing the alterity that grounds the suppliant's being. But whereas the psalmist's tears reveal the other-oriented nature of his divine desire or *caritas*, Petrarch's tears disclose a tendency towards solipsism.

In this respect, Petrarch self-consciously turns the "godly sorrow [that] worketh repentance" into the "worldly sorrow [that] worketh death."[13] In doing so, Petrarch cultivates what Siegfried Wenzel describes as a psychologically enriched version of the medieval sin *accidia* – a *voluptas dolendi* in which the sufferer "feeds with a dark craving upon his tears and pains" to such a degree "that he is loath to leave [his misery]."[14] If Petrarch does move – at least in part – from worldly to godly grief, it is by ascending out of the mode of *cupiditas* expressed in Sonnet 342 to *caritas*. Whether this final movement is fully achieved in Petrarch or not, it is clear that the speaker's claim to autonomy, and with it his well-known literary subjectivity, emerges from the way Petrarch manipulates and oscillates between profane and sacred modalities of grief. More importantly for a reading of Donne's post-Petrarchan poetics is that much of the rhetorical and psychological power of Petrarch's verse lies in his articulation of a modality of sorrow in which he claims to "feed upon my tears and sufferings with a morbid attraction [*atra quadam cum voluptate*] that I can only be rescued from ... despite of myself."[15]

While Donne's Petrarchan-inflected *Holy Sonnets* also gain much of their literary power from the way they articulate varying modalities of godly and worldly sorrow, they do so with an even greater degree of self-awareness about the psychological and theological dynamics of Petrarchism than we find in the *Rime Sparse* itself. Donne deepens the already self-conscious forms of subjectivity in the *Rime Sparse*, as well as many subsequent responses to it. By employing Petrarchism as a way of conveying the experience of repentance, Donne poeticizes his own version of what Luther refers to as the "delicious despair" of *Anfechtung* – the ambivalent sorrow of spiritual crisis. In the process, Donne demonstrates how the self-annihilating terrors of godly sorrow can be defended against by means of a "vehement grief" that appears in the guise of "holy discontent." Much of the dramatic power of Donne's *Holy Sonnets* emerges as a result of the psychological ambivalence articulated through the intersecting discourses of Protestant regeneration and Petrarchan modalities of sorrow.

Before we consider how Donne appropriates Petrarchan modalities of sorrow and their accompanying forms of psychic defensiveness in the *Holy Sonnets*, it is helpful to see how Donne diagnoses such defensiveness in the *Songs and Sonets*. The speaker of several *Holy Sonnets* tries to sustain the kind of narcissism that Donne explodes in the *Songs and Sonets*. More precisely, the speaker seeks to avoid the self-negating half of the dialectic of regeneration by cultivating the kind of Petrarchan solipsism that Donne parodies in the *Songs and Sonets*. Thus just as certain Petrarchan speakers in the *Songs and Sonets* use the discourse of Petrarchism to establish a sense of autonomy and differentiation from the women they ostensibly love, so the speaker of certain *Holy Sonnets* uses the discourse of Petrarchism as a way of avoiding the negative, self-dissolving half of the dialectic of regeneration. In short, the speaker of several *Holy Sonnets* marshals the psychically defensive resources of Petrarchism in an attempt to resist the force of God's will in the process of regeneration.

PERVERSE IT SHALL BE WHERE IT SHOWS MOST TOWARD

As we know, Donne's engagement with Petrarchism is ironic and self-conscious for at least two reasons. First, because it comes at a late point in the tradition[16] and second, because he was writing for a coterie audience "that was fond of antisentimental Ovidianism."[17] As a result of his literary-historical belatedness and cultural context, as well as his innate psychological perspicuity, Donne often does much more than repeat Petrarchan conventions; he diagnoses them, offering us a symptomatic reading of the morbidity at work within the tradition itself. As William Kerrigan has argued, Donne's critique of Petrarchism is part and parcel of the way he championed mutual love, refusing "for fame or for contemplative beatitude, [to] abandon his partner."[18] Part of this revision of the language and philosophy of love consists of parodying Petrarchan conventions, revealing the forms of defensive narcissism inherent within the traditional stance of the Petrarchist. One of Donne's favorite ways of doing this involves literalizing Petrarchan conceits. As Patricia P. Pinka has observed, Donne's more parodic Petrarchan verses "mock the hyperbolic language of the conceits by pretending to accept them literally."[19] This stance subverts the idealizing pretensions of Petrarchism, not through direct Ovidian irony, but through an exaggeration of and over identification with Petrarchism's own terms. In this way, poems such as

"The Computation" and "The Expiration" enact a specific variation of the transgressive principle that Robert Southwell summarizes when he warns that "too much of the best is evill, and excesse in virtue, vice."[20] Given the poems that Pinka focuses on ("The Computation," "The Expiration," "Witchcraft by a Picture," and "The Paradox"), she concludes that, for Donne, Petrarchism is a cynical "stratagem for luring women to bed."[21] Yet Donne's anti-Petrarchan parodies reveal greater psychological insight than simply observing a latent, unavowed, Ovidianism functioning within Petrarchan idealizations.

As Kerrigan and Braden have demonstrated, Donne, like other post-Petrarchists, understood that one of the great temptations of Petrarchism is to become wholly enamored with the image, or phantasm, of the beloved – thereby relinquishing any relationship with the lady herself. According to Kerrigan and Braden, "the psychological transaction by which the image becomes preferable to the woman herself is only latent in Petrarch, but emerges openly in the tradition he inspired."[22] Kerrigan and Braden cite John Hoskyn's "Absence, Hear Thou My Protestation" (a poem sometimes attributed to Donne) as an important example of the Petrarchan tendency to idolize the image of the beloved as a way of cultivating a self-protecting narcissism in the name of love for the other:

> By absence this good means I gain,
>   That I can catch her
>   Where none can watch her,
>
> In some close corner of my brain;
>   There I embrace and kiss her,
>   And so I both enjoy and miss her.[23]

By this point in the tradition, Petrarchism has been revealed as a solitary enterprise where the emotional and sexual satisfactions (not to mention tensions) of reciprocated love give way to the solipsistic pleasures of fantasy. From this perspective, Petrarchism is not disguised Ovidianism, but something much more perversely, if intransigently, narcissistic.

What Kerrigan and Braden do not mention, however, is that Donne's critique of Petrarchism goes one step further than pointing out the dangers of losing the beloved in her poetic image. In "Negative Love," Donne's speaker is devoted not to a simulacrum of his lady, but to something more ineffable yet. By applying the apophatic principles of negative theology to a woman rather than to God, "Negative Love" reveals the narcissistic inner workings of Petrarchan sublimation more profoundly than most, if not all, others. Aptly titled in some manuscripts as "The Nothing,"[24] "Negative Love" outgoes conventional Petrarchan poems by pursuing increasingly sublimated forms of love – concluding that the only way to properly represent the beloved is in terms of negation. In this respect, Donne's poem is a *reductio ad absurdum* of the sentiment expressed in Sonnet 15 of the *Rime Sparse*, that lovers have the privilege of being "released from all human qualities."[25] Applying the principles of the *via negativa* to a secular context, Donne's speaker renders the beloved "nothing" in the sense that she remains ineffable and thus immune to verbalization in the way that God is thought to be in apophatic theology. While the poem's heightening of Petrarchan sublimation has been read as a sincere exploration of the metaphysics of love,[26] it seems more likely to be a critique of the narcissistic nature of Petrarchism. Perhaps it's best to say that the poem is designed to function like an anamorphic painting, offering two, perhaps even three, radically incongruous images, depending on how it is viewed. From one perspective, the poem appears as a sincere application of Neoplatonic apophaticism to the context of secular love; from a second perspective, the poem appears as an obscenely solipsistic retreat into oneself. And when viewed from a third perspective, the Neoplatonic vision is exploded altogether as the "nothing" is a coarse pun on vagina. In short, the poem's wit lies in the way that it is designed to be read as simultaneously earnest, symptomatic, and vulgar, where one interpretation negates the other depending on one's perspective. A striking example of early modern "negative capability," Donne's poem asks us to sustain radically opposing readings simultaneously. My focus here is on the symptomatic dimensions of the poem:

> I never stoop'd so low, as they
> Which on an eye, cheeke, lip, can prey,
>   Seldom to them, which soare no higher
>   Then vertue or the minde to'admire,
> For sense, and understanding may
>   Know, what gives fuell to their fire:
> My love, though silly, is more brave,
> For may I misse, whene ere I crave,
> If I know yet, what I would have.
>
>   If that be simply perfectest
>   Which can by no way be exprest
>   But *Negatives*, my love is so.
>   To All, which all love, I say no.
> If any who deciphers best,
>   What we know not, our selves, can know,

> Let him teach mee that nothing; This
> As yet my ease and comfort is,
> Though I speed not, I cannot misse.

If the speaker of "Air and Angels" weighs "love's pinnace" down by focusing too much on the body, then the speaker of "Negative Love" lets his object float entirely away through the insubstantial nothingness generated by the periphrastic motions of negative theology. His love is indeed "silly," not only in the intended sense of "plain" or "unsophisticated" (definitions which do not accurately describe the poem's complex apophaticism) but in the unintended though more literal senses of "foolish" and even more appropriately "deserving of compassion, pity," "poor," "weak" (*OED*).[27] Similarly, his play on the outbidding topos in which he describes his love as more "brave" than traditional Petrarchists should be taken as signifying not only an ironic claim to "courageousness" but also "showy, grand, fine" (*OED*). Thus just as "The Apparition" literalizes the Petrarchan figure that rejection by the beloved equals death, so the speaker of "Negative Love" concretizes the already hyperbolic, Neoplatonizing idealizations of the Petrarchan lady. By sublimating her out of existence altogether, the speaker reduces the beloved to, as the secondary title puts it, "Nothing." Thus when viewed "awry," the word "Negative" in the title should be read in moral as well as apophatic senses.

By the second stanza of this poem the speaker has managed to talk himself out of loving all existents, saying no "To All, which all love" (13). Thus if the speaker of "Air and Angels" ends by ballasting love between spiritual and physical domains and between male and female lovers, this speaker loses love in the firmament of his own cleverness. What he gains though, is a parodic version of the poetic autonomy often associated with Petrarch's *Rime Sparse*. By taking the Petrarchan scenario to its logical limit, Donne's speaker is left in a position where success and failure, absence and presence, all and nothing, bravery and cowardice, lose their distinctiveness and hence their meaning. The effect is a parody of the self-generating, monumental subjectivity that John Freccero sees at work in the *Rime Sparse* when he asserts that once the moral and spiritual torment of the *Canzoniere* are demystified their "poetic mechanism is revealed: the petrified idolatrous lover is an immutable monument to Petrarch, his creator and namesake."[28] Behind this "poetic mechanism," Donne's "Negative Love" insists, is not only a form of idolatry that demands deconstruction, but a deluded claim to psychological autonomy that requires demystification.[29] This demystification is called for when the speaker of "Negative Love" "bravely" offers up the apophatic challenge: "If any who deciphers best / What we know not, our selves, can know, / Let him teach mee that nothing" (14–16). The earnest reading of this impossible to fulfill challenge might be paraphrased: If any other lover can better decipher that ethereal thing which we do not yet know cannot be known then let him teach us that unknown and unknowable thing. The more critical reading, however, would render these lines reflexively, so that the awkward syntactical placement of "our selves" signals that it is "we" "ourselves" that remain truly "unknown." The lines might thus also be paraphrased as inadvertently signifying: if any one can better decipher how we Petrarchists do not know ourselves then teach me that which we do not know about ourselves. Read this way, the speaker's challenge to find even more remote "nothings" to love is just one more absurd looping back upon his own solipsism – one more betrayal of his own lack of self-knowledge. The speaker of the *Holy Sonnets* will cultivate exactly this kind of solipsism as a way of expressing ambivalence over the dialectic of regeneration.

By the end of the poem, we are left with "nothing" but the gap between lover and beloved, the negative space in which Petrarchan desire has been revealed to work. By taking Petrarchan sublimations to their logical end, the poem paradoxically announces, in effect, the desublimation of Petrarchan poetics. As a result, the poem offers not a rarified image of love, but a bare rhetorical structure. What we are left with is the naked verbal mechanism of how Petrarchan idealizations work to keep the beloved at a distance from the poet. Such distance not only keeps desire in play in the Freudian sense that obstacles are a necessary feature of sexual enjoyment, but it also allows the speaker to sustain his sense of individuation.[30] What is achieved by the deferral of reciprocity is not just a potential heightening of desire, but rather the speaker is able to maintain a sense of differentiation, a sense of autonomy distinct from the object of his desire. The absence of reciprocity has the paradoxical effect of increasing the speaker's claim to autonomy. Gordon Braden makes a related point about Petrarch when he observes that "what is at work [in Petrarchism] is a narcissistic regression of an especially powerful sort, the active withdrawal of libido from an object-choice that was itself probably narcissistically based." While Braden emphasizes the way that Petrarchan solipsism is linked to a drive "for self-bestowed immortality,"[31] I wish to emphasize the more strictly psychological observation that the "failure" to seduce the beloved means that the Petrarchist will not suffer the symbolic or psychical death implied by the sexual meanings of "die" in the seventeenth century. The result of such deferral in the case of "Negative Love" is that we see quite clearly how the work of Petrarchan sublimation is bound up with the work of differentiation. The speaker of "Negative Love" sustains the illusion of autonomy by generating an absolute metaphysical difference, rather than mitigating a more fluid gender difference, between the self and the female other. Donne's poem implicitly warns against the excesses of such differentiation, implying that a certain permeability within the self–other relation is necessary to love as lived experience rather than as poetic conceit.[32] It is precisely this resistance to love as a recognition of one's constitutive dependence upon the other that godly sorrow is thought to overcome – a process which the speaker of the *Holy Sonnets* experiences with pronounced ambivalence.

By exposing the pretensions behind Petrarchan idealizations, Donne's poem discloses how the Petrarchist, like the religious melancholic described in *Devotions*, "counterfeyt[s] the *Plague* in a *vowe*, and mistake[s] a *Disease* for *Religion*."[33] In this respect, "Negative Love" demystifies Petrarchism in a manner that closely parallels Slavoj Žižek's diagnosis of courtly love:[34]

What the paradox of the Lady in courtly love ultimately amounts to is ... the paradox of *detour*: our "official" desire is that we want to sleep with the Lady; whereas in truth, there is nothing we fear more than a Lady who might generously yield to this wish of ours – what we truly expect and want from the Lady is simply yet another new ordeal, yet one more postponement ... The Lady therefore functions as a unique short circuit in which *the Object of desire coincides with the force that prevents its attainment* – in a way, the object, "is" its own withdrawal, its own retraction.[35]

For Žižek, the courtly lover is attached not to the lost or absent woman (and certainly not to the woman herself) but to the original gesture of her loss, to an experience of absence that is determined by its never having been present as such. This is precisely what occurs when apophatic theology is applied to a secular love object in "Negative Love." As I have suggested, what is being desired is not the woman herself, but the negative space between the speaker and the beloved – the space in which both desire and the appearance of autonomy are maintained.

Donne's speaker thus positions his beloved in the same structural role that Jacques Lacan accords to the lady of courtly love. Developing Lacan's reading of courtly love, Žižek argues that the traumatic nature of sexual difference gets inscribed in courtly love through the lady who is "not our 'fellow-creature'" but who is an other "with whom no relationship of empathy is possible."[36] In other words, the idealizations of courtly love register, even as they defend against, the traumatic origins of Eros – the fundamental antagonism between the sexes that Shakespeare's Venus proclaims when she prophesies over Adonis' slain body that "Sorrow on love hereafter shall attend ... Perverse it shall be where it shows most toward" (1136–37, 1157). Shakespeare's formulation of the tragic origins of love follow the same basic structure of Petrarchan desire that Žižek articulates when he describes the courtly lady as "a unique short circuit in which *the Object of desire coincides with the force that prevents its attainment*."[37] As the perfect embodiment of an object which appears compliant when it is really most froward, the Petrarchan lady not only serves as the site of narcissistic projections and defenses, but she is also a sublimation of the radical negativity around which masculine desire is constituted. As Žižek's formulation implies (and as Donne's "Negative Love" corroborates), the Petrarchan lady stands in for the unsymbolizable gap around and against which masculine desire forms itself; she is a name for the irreducible antagonism within desire itself. In Lacan's terms, "she is that which cannot be crossed," a "limit" or deadlock within the structure of masculine desire and within the accommodating power of language.[38] Hence the strange appropriateness of apophatic theology to Petrarchan poetics.

For Lacan, as for the speaker of "Negative Love," an encounter with the unmediated reality of the lady of courtly love would constitute a limit point of symbolization and desire. More importantly, such an encounter would be anxiety-producing in the precise sense that anxiety is an affect signal or warning that the borders between self and other are dissolving. As Roberto Harari explains with regard to Lacan's *Seminar X*, anxiety "is the signal of something that believes itself to be sufficiently divided, differentiated in psychic life, but that at a certain point tends to erase its boundaries; that is why it is a 'border or edge phenomenon.'"[39] Like an encounter with the overpowering force of God's will, a direct encounter with the lady of courtly love unsettles the very distinction between self and other. Viewed this way, it becomes clear that the courtly lady is positioned within the field of Petrarchan signification in the same place as God is positioned within the field of penitential prayer – as both cause and effect of the discourse itself, an extreme limit beyond which there is no passage.

This means that like God, the lady is anxiety-producing insofar as she represents not merely an object of desire, but the origin or traumatic cause of desire itself. Her ideality conceals a radical otherness that is utterly asymmetrical with respect to the speaker's subjectivity. Petrarchism thus shares a basic structural affinity with the Pauline penitential theology underwriting Donne's *Holy Sonnets*:[40] it positions the lady in a transcendent place that can be appealed to but never actually inhabited, addressed but never fully embodied in material terms. We have now arrived at a more exact sense in which Petrarchism is a desacralization of *metanoia*. Where the psalmic–Pauline–Augustinian tradition of repentance presumes that the Christian soul emerges "by an external traumatic encounter, by the encounter of the Other's desire in its impenetrability,"[41] Petrarchism works primarily by deferring such an encounter; and by deferring it the Petrarchist is able to hold onto a certain form of autonomy. Petrarchism might thus be understood as a misprision – a secular and psychically defensive misreading – of Pauline *metanoia*. Donne's *Holy Sonnets* testify to the way that he grasped the psychically defensive possibilities of Petrarchism more completely than virtually any other English writer in the period.

Žižek's recent discussion of Pauline conversion brings the structural parallels and ideological differences between courtly love and penitential theology which are implicit in "O Might Those Sighes and Teares" into better view. Describing Pauline *metanoia* (or what he translates as "new creation"), Žižek discusses how the process of conversion involves an encounter with the radical negativity that he argues elsewhere is sublimated in courtly love through the elevation of the lady to the dignity of a sublime object:

The term "new creation" is revealing ... signaling the gesture of *sublimation*, of erasing the traces of one's past ("everything old has passed away") and beginning afresh from a zero-point: consequently, there is also a terrifying *violence* at work in this "uncoupling," that of the *death drive*, of the radical "wiping the slate clean" as the condition of the New Beginning.[42]

While courtly love and its Petrarchan variations situate the lady in the place of the Real (the domain of the death drive) as a way of avoiding its terrifying violence, Pauline Christianity situates deity as a dialectical being who recreates through the force of the death drive. Where the Petrarchist fetishizes the gap between desire and the Real – thereby defending against the anxiety-inducing overpresence of the other within the economy of one's own narcissism – the Pauline penitent seeks an encounter with God's overpresence within the self, calling for rather than retreating from the anxiety-producing overpresence of a God who is "*interior intimo meo et superior summo meo*." Thus while Petrarchism is characterized by a stance in which acts of idealization insulate the speaker from the desire of the lady, Pauline *metanoia* calls for a direct encounter with the desire of God as other – a traumatizing encounter with negativity that "wipes the slate clean," leaving one forever changed. Where Petrarchan love exists as a way of sustaining the male fantasy of self-sufficiency, Pauline conversion calls for the obliteration of such self-sufficiency.

Donne's *Holy Sonnets* testify to the drama of such a process, especially as experienced by a speaker who is self-assertive, intelligent, and prone to narcissistic defensiveness. "O Might Those Sighes and Teares" is a particularly effective example of this drama because it unfolds by playing the structural affinities of Petrarchism and Pauline *metanoia* against their soteriological and psychical differences, making the incongruity between these two discourses the operative scheme within the poem.

LACHRIMAE ANTIQUAE NOVAE

In the course of "O Might Those Sighes and Teares," Donne's speaker evokes the discourse of Petrarchan anguish in order to try to evade the double-edged sword of the Word in the very gesture of asking to be healed by it. Petrarchan conventions are thus employed as a way of trying to avoid full contrition in the very gesture of petitioning God for the prevenient grace necessary for the "godly sorrow that worketh repentance":

> O MIGHT those sighes and teares returne againe
> Into my breast and eyes, which I have spent,
> That I might in this holy discontent
> Mourne with some fruit, as I have mourn'd in vaine;
> In my Idolatry what showres of raine
> Mine eyes did waste? what griefs my heart did rent?
> That sufferance was my sinne I now repent,
> Because I did suffer'I must suffer paine.
> Th'hydroptique drunkard, & night-scouting thiefe,
> The itchy Lecher, and selfe tickling proud
> Have the remembrance of past joyes, for reliefe
> Of coming ills. To (poore) me is allow'd
> No ease; for, long, yet vehement griefe hath beene
> Th'effect and cause, the punishment and sinne. (1635, 1–14)

The internal drama of this penitential prayer is determined by the way the speaker conflates even as he tries to contrast the idolatrous sufferance of the complaining lover with the "holy discontent" of the Christian supplicant. In the process of confessing his sins amidst a prayer for grace, the speaker concludes by curiously blurring the "vehement grief" of unrequited love with the "holy discontent" of the devotional supplicant – leading us to ask if the differences between idolatrous and penitential grief are "Apparent in [*him*] not immediately" ("If Faithfull Soules," 1635, 7). By dwelling on the continuity of his own emotional state in the very process of asking to suffer a fundamental change from one modality of sorrow to another, the speaker betrays the "pensive" rather than sincere nature of his repentance. Moreover, by repeating the same Petrarchan state he has long been guilty of in the very gesture of calling for a radical change, Donne's poem reproduces the kind of stasis characteristic of the *Rime Sparse*, such as in Sonnet 118 which concludes:

> Now here I am, alas, and wish I were elsewhere, and wish I
> wished more, but wish no more, and, by being unable to do
> more, do all I can;
> and new tears for old desires show me to be still what I used to
> be, nor for a thousand turnings about have I yet moved.[43]

What emerges from this poem is that Petrarch really does not *want* to change, at least not enough to actually change. He enjoys his symptoms, admitting that what "is bitter is sweet to me, and my losses useful."[44] Donne's poem risks the same sentiment. His speaker more than intimates that he enjoyed not the full reciprocity of love but the "vehement grief" of unreturned passion: "long yet vehement grief hath been / The effect and cause, the punishment and sin" (13–14). Evoking the "vehement grief" of Petrarchan *accidia*, the speaker reveals that his melancholy is not simply a consequence of unreciprocated passion but it is a motivating factor for further melancholy. His sadness is a "cause" as well as an "effect" of his self-absorbing *tristia*. As both punishment and transgression, both pain and pleasure, "vehement grief" appears as the speaker's real, if slightly obscured, purpose. Rather than being an inadvertent effect of his idolatrous desire for women (as we would expect) the sufferance of unrequited love is positioned as the source as well as the effect of his sin. The psychological complexity conveyed in the poem's final lines lies in the way they manifest the speaker's desire for autonomy. They expose his "vehement grief" as the true, yet weirdly reflexive, aim of his desire, at the same time as they betray the speaker's inability to will himself to change. Like Petrarch, Donne's speaker "feed[s] upon [his] tears and sufferings with a morbid attraction [*atra quadam cum voluptate*] that [he] can only be rescued from ... despite of [himself]."[45]

Donne's speaker is thus melancholic in the precise sense that his grief serves as a substitute object of desire. As Robert Burton says of himself in the preface to *The Anatomy of Melancholy*, the speaker's grief has become "his mistress."[46] By taking grief as an object of desire, Donne's speaker tries to defend against being absorbed in and by *amor dei*, thereby exemplifying the symptomology that Julia Kristeva identifies as characteristic of narcissistic modalities of melancholy. In such melancholy, sadness can become a "substitute object ... the sole object" that protects against a wound at the origin of one's identity.[47]

While Donne repeats the Petrarchan structure of stasis in the very gesture of asking for conversion, he does so within the context of a series of poems that self-consciously engage questions of Reformation soteriology. Thus the meaning of "sufferance" and the structure of stasis signify differently in the *Holy Sonnets* than they do in the *Rime Sparse*. To begin with, Donne's poem evokes, even as it complicates, the soteriologically comforting position Richard Hooker forwards when he says that "a grieved spirit is ... no argument for a faithless mind." For Hooker, who follows the basic Reformation view that the regenerate Christian is *simul justus et peccator* (both justified and a sinner), grief over one's lack of devotion betrays an underlying, undetected fidelity. Putting his own stamp on the Pauline/Reformation view that the Holy Spirit intercedes "for us with sighs too deep for words," Hooker insists that God's presence within the self exceeds our consciousness and as a result there is greater significance to our grief than we often recognize:

there is no doubt, but that our faith may haue and hath her privie operations secret to vs, in whom, yet knowne to him by whom they are. Tell this to a man that hath a mind deceaved by too hard an opinion of himselfe, and it doth but augment his griefe: he hath his answer ready; will you make mee thinke otherwise then I find, then I feel in my self? I haue thoroughly considered and exquisitely sifted all the corners of my heart, and I see what there is: never seek to perswade me against my knowledge; *I doe not, I knowe I doe not beleeve*. Well, to favour them a little in their weaknesse: let that be granted which they doe imagine; bee it that they are faithlesse and without beleife. But are they not grieved for their vnbeleife? They are. Do they not wish it might, and also striue that it may, be otherwise? We know they doe. Whence commeth this but from a secret loue and liking which they haue of those things that are believed? No man can loue things which in his owne opinion are not. And if they thinke those things to be, which they shew that they loue, when they desire to beeleve them; then must it needs be that by desiring to beleeve, they prove themselves true beleevers.[48]

While Hooker emphasizes how the godly motions of the Word within the soul can go undetected by the believer himself, Donne's poem implies that the worldly motions of the defensive psyche can also be in excess of one's immediate awareness – that the very gesture of seeking a "holy discontent" can betray a half or unacknowledged anxiety about the costs of such a grief. The question raised by "O Might Those Sighes and Teares" is precisely which of these preconscious forces are at work in the speaker – the privy operations of faith or the oblique operations of self-deceit? What is not in question, though, is that unlike Hooker, Donne's speaker is rather queasy about the Reformation proposition that the regenerate soul is *simul justus et peccator*.[49] This speaker seems to find it difficult to believe, or at least finds it distasteful that he should be weak and full of sin and yet possibly regenerate at the same time.

Because the sonnet raises but does not answer the question of the speaker's regenerate state, we cannot know whether the poem is the beginning of godly sorrow or whether it is an example of the self-deceit that Daniel Dyke speaks of in his posthumously published 1614 treatise, *The Mystery of Self-Deceiving*. Following generally Calvinist principles, Dyke explains that self-deceit takes one of two forms in the context of repentance, either false sorrow or feigned desire. "O Might Those Sighes and Teares" raises the possibility that the speaker is deceiving himself in his petition for godly sorrow just as the speaker of "Oh, To Vex Me" explicitly thematizes the inconstancy of his desire for God. According to Dyke, godly sorrow marks the beginning of "the terrors and horrors that are in the consciences of the Elect,"[50] while "Temporarie" or "aguish" sorrow leads one to flee "when God shootes his arrow into the syde of [the] conscience ... as a Dog from him that striketh him with a cudgell, and seekes anywhere for relief than at his hands."[51] That Donne's speaker may be retreating from the terror of his conscience in the very gesture of seeking its "arrows" is indicated by the moral decline traced in the poem. As Mary Ann Radzinowicz observes, the "sonnet opens with its strongest point; it does not close with it."[52] Despite making this key observation, Radzinowicz sees the poem as a relatively unambiguous expression of "sorrow over wasted sorrow." The poem's dramatic power clearly lies, however, in the possibility that the speaker's moral decline in the course of the sonnet may signify that he is symptomatically repeating the "wasted sorrow" he ostensibly claims to be repenting. The poem thus raises the possibility that he is not even in a precipitous possession of godly sorrow which, as Dyke says, "respects the sin more than the punishment, caring not for the outward suffering that is experienced."[53] In this respect, Donne's speaker is distinct from the speaker of Herbert's "Affliction (I)," who is more clearly regenerate precisely because he is not permitted the psychically defensive pleasures of eroticized grief: "Yet lest perchance I should too happy be / In my unhappiness, / Turning my purge to good, thou throwest me / Into more sicknesses" (49–52).

Although the speaker of "O Might Those Sighes and Teares" repents his "suffrance," he concludes that this gesture of repentance will not result in any discernible change of his emotional state. In the past, his heart did "rent" griefs not so much in the sense that he was torn up by love, but rather that his griefs were fleeting, taking up momentary residence within his heart. Rather than expressing an authentic desire to convert from loving an idolatrous to a divine *object*, the speaker betrays the possibility that he really just wants to substitute one form of insincere desire, one form of unrequited *love*, for another. Thus in the process of stating that he wants to change his object from an idolatrous to a divine one, he inadvertently betrays a desire to change one form of solipsistic love for another. In this respect, the speaker's prayer avoids articulating any feeling of contrition, even as it says that he wants to feel such contrition.

Like the Petrarchist of "Negative Love," this speaker avoids the traumatic object of his desire in the very gesture of asking for its presence. In the act of confessing his sins, the speaker raises the possibility that he is a Petrarchan variation of the religiously morbid man who finds "Vertue in *Melancholy*, and only there," as Donne says in "A Letter To the Lady Carey and Mrs. Essex Riche."[54] As a result of his desire, he offers up a "confession" that dissolves into a self-indulgent form of self-description – what C. S. Lewis calls in reference to Milton's Satan, "incessant autobiography."[55]

By the end of his petition, the speaker ends up in the perversely comfortable position of the Petrarchan wooer who complains about the absence of his beloved even as he secretly prefers such absence over what the Ovidian-turned-quasi-Petrarchist of "Love's Deitie" calls the "deeper plague" of her presence. The difficulties of tone and meaning that arise from the complex ambivalence that I have just delineated would seem to verify George Williamson's preference for the 1635 edition of "O Might Those Sighes and Teares" as opposed to Grierson's and Gardner's more popular editions. The lack of punctuation and the overall syntax of the 1635 edition conveys the speaker's ambivalence about conversion and points to the sense of stasis for which I have been arguing. Line 7 of 1635 reads: "That sufferance was my sinne I now repent." Gardner's edition places a comma after "sinne" and puts the deictic "now" before the first person pronoun, thus creating a stronger sense of opposition between past and present, and lessening the ambiguity enacted in the poem. In her edition, line 7 reads: "That sufferance was my sinne, now I repent."[56]

If the Petrarchan speaker of "O Might Those Sighes and Teares" is anxious about his regenerate state and if he is uneasy with the Reformation notion that he is justified and a sinner, then the speaker of "If Faithfull Soules" appears to move toward a possible, though still slightly ambiguous, resolution. This poem alludes to the Petrarchan scenario of "O Might Those Sighes and Teares" by asking how one's state of salvation can be interpreted if the outward signs of "idolatrous lovers" appear the same as those who do not feign devotion. He answers this question by appearing to recognize that God is immanent even as he is transcendent and that by turning inward to God he is simultaneously turning outward toward deity in the manner of Psalm 42. An important, but by no means unambiguous, structural difference is thus initiated between the Petrarchan stasis of "O Might Those Sighes and Teares" and the announced desire to turn towards deity in "If Faithfull Soules." In the previous poem, no discernible movement is made or even announced, as indicated by the fact that what appears to be an initiating of the *anima mea* tradition of soul dialogue is really an address to the self: "To (poore) me is allow'd / No ease" (12–13). In "If Faithfull Soules," however, the speaker clearly apostrophizes his soul as the repository of God's regenerative force, opening up an internal dialogue that appears to unsettle, if not break, the Petrarchan solipsism governing "O Might Those Sighes and Teares." By clearly initiating the *anima mea* tradition of interior dialogue between the self and the soul, "If Faithfull Soules" begins to reveal the psalmic and Augustinian subtexts within and behind the Petrarchan language he has been speaking. Even more importantly, the speaker initiates his interior dialogue by confessing his dependence on God for knowledge of his own sincerity, thereby implying at least a cognitive recognition of the renunciation of autonomy necessary to Protestant regeneration, if not a devotional or existential realization of such:

> ... Idolatrous lovers weepe and mourne
>   And vile blasphemous coniurers to call
>   On Iesus name; and Pharisaicall
> Dissemblers faine devotion: then turne
> (O pensive soule) to God, for he knowes best
> Thy greife, for he put it into my brest. (1635, 9–14)

Although this poem clearly expresses a greater degree of self-awareness than "O Might Those Sighes and Teares," and although the speaker announces his desire to submit to God's authority by its end with no clear sense of anxiety, the poem does not perform the "turn" of conversion; on the contrary, it simply expresses a desire to do so, while also admitting that if such a turn happens it will be, in large part, God's will realizing itself through him. In this respect, the Petrarchan structure of stasis is weakened but not undone. In subsequent poems, however, the same sense of stasis visible in "O Might Those Sighes and Teares" recurs in similarly Petrarchan terms.[57]

For example, "What If This Present were the Worlds Last Night?" alludes to Petrarchan conventions in order to evade the negating force of God's will:

> What if this present were the worlds last night
>   Mark in my hart, O Soule where thou dost dwell
> The picture of Christ crucified, and tell
>   Whether that countenance can thee affright.
> Teares in his eyes quench the amazeing light,
> Bloud fills his frownes which from his pierc'd head fell
> And can that tongue adiudge thee vnto hell
> Which prayed forgiuenes for his foes fierce spight?
> Noe, noe, but as in my Idolatrie
>   I said to all my Profane Mistresses,
> Beauty, of pitty; foulness only is
>   A signe of rigor; soe I say to thee
> To wicked spiritts are horrid shapes assign'd,
>   This beauteous forme assures a pitious minde. (Revised, 1–14)

Interrogating the status of his soul, the speaker initiates an Ignatian meditation upon the Passion that is framed within the hypothetical setting of judgment day. But rather than visualizing Christ's suffering as a way of generating the *compassio* that would verify his repentant, and thus redeemed, status, he veers away from the image of Christ's suffering in order to persuade himself of the heterodox idea that Christ is incapable of damning souls as such. He thus answers the opening interrogatives by speaking on behalf of Christ's prerogative to save or damn souls as the divine will sees fit: "No, no." He justifies this defensive reaction to his interrogation by drawing an analogy between Christ and his "Profane Mistresses." But as Koory observes, "In the context of Petrarchan idolatry ... contemplation of the beloved's image cannot assure the poet of his beloved's pity, in fact, quite the contrary."[58] The tortured syntax of lines 11 and 12 betrays the incongruity of this Petrarchan analogy, reminding us, as Stachniewski remarks, that "the love poems by no means unequivocally suggest that the beauteous form of his mistress did in fact bespeak a piteous mind."[59] This failed analogy thus reveals that the speaker's efforts at meditation appear evasive rather than revelatory, wishfully persuasive rather than genuinely consolatory.

More complexly, the speaker's recourse to an analogy between Christ's appearance and his merciful judgment exposes the contradictions between

Ignatian and Protestant meditative traditions. Just as "Batter My Heart" expresses confusion over Catholic and Calvinist views on reason – on whether reason is "weak" or "untrue" as Strier emphasizes[60] – so "What If This Present" exposes the tensions between the Ignatian dependence on sense experience and Protestant disavowal of such experience. In other words, Donne's meditation fails because it oscillates between a Catholic meditative tradition that is predicated on an Aristotelian epistemology and a Protestant tradition based on an Augustinian epistemology. This confusion becomes legible when the speaker attempts to read God through analogy between his appearance and his essence. This Ignatian mode of reading leads the speaker to the doctrinally heterodox view about universal mercy and by doing so calls attention to the Protestant critique of such analogical thinking. As Victoria Silver explains,

Luther and Calvin ... reject the ethical model of monasticism, in which celibacy and the mortifying of the flesh are cultivated as a veritable *imago Dei*. Indeed, they regard it as a species of idolatry, since monastic practice not only asserts an equivalence between divine and human righteousness – a doctrine of works – but also assigns Christ a single, definable, and purely palpable identity as a celibate or ascetic; monasticism chooses to confine the deity of the incarnate God by analogy to what we can see of him, so that the Christ is worshipped as an image of human suffering which we at once emulate and transcend by renouncing a peccant world. But adoring Jesus' appearances is no less idolatrous than worshipping the place where God reveals himself.[61]

From this Reformation view, the speaker's meditation was bound to fail from the start not only because its particular analogy is inappropriate but because any analogy between Christ's appearance and his essence is bad Protestant thinking. Indeed, rather than being a straightforward failure as an Ignatian meditation, the poem enacts the difficult fit between the sense-based Aristotelian epistemology of the Ignatian method and the Protestant hermeneutic which disavows analogy as a means of bridging human and divine relations. Unlike Ignatian meditation, Protestant traditions of meditative prayer avoid the composition of place and the use of sense experience as a means of accessing divinity. They do so because Protestants generally presume an Augustinian–Platonic epistemology that downplays the role of the senses rather than an Aristotelian epistemology that relies on sense experience. Like many of the *Holy Sonnets*, the poem fails devotionally because its speaker is caught within competing traditions.[62]

While it is certain that the speaker's turn away from Christ's suffering is a poeticization of the general soteriological axiom that fear of divine punishment denotes either failed or improper repentance,[63] it is less apparent that the poem expresses anxiety over the overpresence of God within the soul. In other words, "What If This Present" not only conveys terror over the possibility of reprobation, but the darkening of the soul and the overall unwillingness to carry through with the meditation – expressed through the devotionally deflationary sestet – also expresses anxiety over the dissolution of the I as an individuated being. This anxiety arises through the speaker's identification with Christ in his suffering as suggested in the image of Christ's very human "Tears" quenching "the amazing light" of his divinity at the moment of his death. Alluding to Gospel accounts of the sky's darkening during the Crucifixion,[64] the speaker expresses terror at the drowning out of divine light within the soul. This darkening of the soul initiates the first half of the dialectic of regeneration as it functions through an identification with the dying Christ. But rather than seeking to further implicate himself in Christ's suffering and death, Donne's speaker resists such identification – positioning Christ as a Petrarchan lady, whose beauty is believed to emanate from a transcendent mercy. Viewed this way, the Petrarchan analogy betrays a meaning altogether opposed to the speaker's intentions as the promise of mercy is conventionally deferred or thwarted in Petrarchism. Just as the repetition of "No, no" may imply an affirmation in the form of a double negative, so the Petrarchan analogy may signal the absence rather than the presence of divine mercy.

By objectifying Christ in Petrarchan terms rather than subjectifying his suffering, Donne's speaker fails to experience the kind of identification with the dying God that is required by Ignatian meditations on the Passion. This resistance to identification and the deflating response to his own question signal the speaker's anxiety, both of reprobation and of the de-individuation necessary to fully experience God's immanence in the process of regeneration. As Donne's poem implies, the immanence of a divine being within one's soul can generate a disturbing sense that the soul is not in possession of itself but is subject to a radical interiority that is "more oneself than oneself."[65] The anxiety arising from God's immanence is implied by the very structure of apostrophes to the soul, which generate a separation between self and other *within the soul*: "Mark in my hart, O Soule, where thou dost dwell" (2). As the differentiating movement of apostrophe implies, the soul constitutes an inwardness so intimate that its presence does not directly coincide with the speaker as subject. The image of the Passion within the heart should appear from elsewhere, even as the entire *mise-en-scene* must occur inwardly. Apostrophes to the soul thus disclose how the Augustinian subject is constantly "beside itself" in the sense that the soul is more the self than the self and that God is more the soul than the soul.

Michel de Certeau expresses the ethical challenges posed by the exstatic structure of the soul when he asserts that the soul is "the place in which that *separation of self from itself* prompts a *hospitality*, now 'ascetic,' now 'mystic,' [a place] that *makes room* for the other. And because that 'other' is infinite, the soul is an infinite space in which to enter and receive visitors."[66] As I have argued elsewhere, Donne's "Batter My Heart" makes clear that this opening of the soul to God's infiniteness is both terrifying and redeeming, destructively violent and recreative. It is precisely the terrifying dissolution of self that is necessary in order to make room for the other that is depicted in "What If This Present were the Worlds Last Night?" – a terror that is defended against through recourse to the psychically defensive conventions of Petrarchism.[67] Like Milton's Satan, Donne experiences anxiety in the Kierkegaardian sense of the term in which "Anxiety is a desire for what one fears, a sympathetic antipathy; anxiety is an alien power which grips the individual, and yet one cannot tear himself free from it and does not want to, for one fears, but what he fears he desires."[68]

In each of the three *Holy Sonnets* that I have discussed, Petrarchism is evoked as a way of expressing the speaker's ambivalence about conversion. This distinctly Petrarchan way of expressing ambivalence about the process of regeneration is given its most moving expression in "Since She Whome I Lovd." As Heather Dubrow has observed, this sonnet "recalls Petrarch's own lyrics on the death of Laura and specifically her position as intercessor, a role often associated with the *donna angelicata*."[69] What Dubrow and other critics have not fully acknowledged, though, is that this sonnet not only mourns the loss of a beloved woman, but it also laments the impossibility of the Petrarchan conversion elegy as a literary form. Indeed, Donne's sonnet bitterly expresses the loss of the onto-theological conditions of possibility for the work of mourning made possible by the Petrarchan conversion elegy. To be more precise, Donne's poem records the impossibility of mourning the beloved according to the Augustinian–Neoplatonic principle that love for a human in the mode of *cupiditas* can lead one to the love of God in the mode of *caritas*. In other words, critics have not fully demonstrated how the poem stages the impossibility of writing, in a Reformation context, the kind of elegiac conversion sonnet that Petrarch wrote of Laura.[70]

John Stachniewski comes closest to my view when he asserts that the poem begins in a Neoplatonic mode, where God can be reached through a process of mediation by worldly things, but that this conception of God "is replaced by a stiffly Protestant conception of God as jealously intrusive. Instead of a source of benignity, to which he applies, God has become a character whose love has plans of its own."[71] While I agree that the poem's purposeful failure consists of a bitter shift from a Neoplatonic metaphysic to a Lutheran/Calvinist one, I do not think this shift can be accounted for without reference to the poem's Petrarchan intertexts.

As I have already indicated, Donne's speaker finds it difficult to fully absorb the Reformation thesis that the regenerate Christian is *simul justus et peccator*. In "O Might Those Sighes and Teares," this reticence is expressed in terms of the speaker's confused stance vis-à-vis his own grief. In "Since She Whome I Lovd" a similar reticence is expressed, but there it does not have to do with the modalities of love that the human subject is believed to be capable of. One of the consequences of Luther's Pauline thesis regarding regeneration is that it renders the Augustinian-Neoplatonic interpretation of *caritas* moot. For Augustine, and much of the medieval tradition after him, including Petrarch, *caritas* denotes "the motion of the soul toward the enjoyment of God for His own sake, and the enjoyment of one's self and of one's neighbor for the sake of God."[72] In the Lutheran/Calvinist tradition, however, the emphasis is laid on the descending love of God to man, the self-emptying or kenotic love of *agape*, with little or no focus on a reciprocal ascending love from the regenerate soul. This Reformation view of man's inability to ascend to love of God in the Augustinian modality of *caritas* follows from what is perhaps the most central thesis Luther ever forwarded, namely that "Flesh and Spirit must not be understood as if flesh had only to do with moral impurity, and spirit only with the state of our hearts. Rather, flesh, according to St. Paul ... means everything that is born from the flesh, ie. the entire self, body, and soul, including our reason and all our senses."[73] The consequences that Donne's speaker thinks this thesis has on his experience of love and conversion unsettle the work of mourning and regeneration in "Since She Whome I Lovd." For him, this Lutheran deflation of the human will inspires resentment of and ambivalence about God. As a result, the process of mourning engaged in the poem remains as ambiguous as the desire for conversion in "O Might Those Sighes and Teares."

Although the poem opens as if it were a Petrarchan sonnet in praise of the deceased beloved, there is a bitterness latent within the opening quatrain that would be somewhat out of place in the *Rime Sparse*: "Since She whome I lovd, hath payd her last debt / To Nature, and to hers, and my good is dead / And her Soule early into heauen rauished, / Wholy in heauenly things my Mind is sett" (Westmoreland, 1–4). While many critics, including Stachniewski, describe the tone of these lines as "serene," such an interpretation overlooks several crucial, if subtle, features. First, the beloved's death is figured as untimely, implying that her "ravishment" is in danger of being perceived less as ecstatic than as violent and immoral. Second, the speaker admits that his "good is dead," a sentiment that conflicts with and thus stops in its tracks the movement from *cupiditas* to *caritas* implied in the opening. Such a Neoplatonic movement requires that the poet-convert realize that God is his *summum bonum*, not his female beloved. Yet, what the lines say is that his "good" (in which there may be an aural and idolatrous pun on "God") is dead and that he has "set" in the sense of "resigned" himself on "heauenly things." Indeed, the word "set" not only implies "focused" or "properly oriented," but also "descended to" or "sunk." The verb thus contradicts the upwardly moving nature of the *caritas* love apparently being expressed. The failed conversion that becomes explicit in the sestet is already latent in the opening quatrain.

While it is a convention of Petrarchan poetry to express the loss of the beloved as the loss of one's "good," the tone of Donne's poem is more despairing and bitter than one normally sees in the *Rime Sparse*. The latent bitterness in these opening lines contrasts sharply with the genuine serenity Petrarch expresses in Sonnet 346, in which Laura's role as mediatrix provides Petrarch with confidence and a sense of sacramental participation between earthly and heavenly love: "The elect angels and blessed souls who are citizens of Heaven, / the first day that my lady passed over, came around her full of wonder and reverence ... She, glad to have changed her dwelling, is equal to the most / perfect souls, and still from time to time she turns back, / looking to see if I am following her."[74] The advantage that Petrarch has over Donne's speaker is that his female-beloved plays the role of sacramental mediator, a role eschewed in the Calvinist emphasis on St. Paul's declaration in Romans 8 that nothing worldly should "be able to separate us from the love of God."[75]

As a result, Donne's speaker experiences the properly insatiable nature of divine love as a punishment rather a gift of grace. As we saw Augustine claim in relation to Psalm 42, true divine love is insatiable in nature. The proper love of God registers as something painfully pleasurable because it is beyond fulfillment or satiation in this world. This is what Augustine takes Ecclesiasticus 24:29 to mean when he adduces it to define faith as constant searching: "They that shall eat me, shall yet hunger, and they that drink me, shall yet thirst."[76] In the absence of a female mediator, though, Donne's speaker finds this state of insatiable divine love not intoxicating but unambiguously anguishing, producing a "holy thirsty dropsy": "Here the admyring her my Mind did whett / To seeke thee God; so streames do shew the head, / But though I haue found thee,'and thou my thirst hast fed, / A holy thirsty dropsy melts me yett" (5–8). It is as though the speaker is saying that the insatiable love of God is only tolerable if such love is mediated through something earthly, something accessible to the senses. Here again, Donne's speaker resents the dissolution, or in this case liquefaction, of self inherent in divine love. This resentment is expressed in the verb "melts," which in this context denotes "to be overwhelmed or dismayed by grief" as in the Geneva translation of Psalm 129, "My soule melteth" (*OED*). The opening octave thus enacts the impossibility of mourning according to Petrarchan-Neoplatonic principles when one is committed to a distinctly Reformation view of the world. Just as meditations on the Passion are complicated in the *Holy Sonnets* by the coexistence of competing epistemologies within Ignatian and Protestant traditions, so the work of mourning is complicated by contradictions between Petrarchan and Reformation metaphysics.

The bitterness that has been relatively contained in the opening octave, explodes in the concluding sestet. By the end of the poem, Donne's speaker appears to experience the Reformation critique of Neoplatonic *caritas* as existentially unbearable. He thus berates this Calvinist God for pettiness, even implying that such a "jealous" God must be weak if he is so concerned about being "put out" by "the World, the fleshe, yea Deuill" (14). These final lines literalize the consequences of Luther's critique of medieval interpretations of "flesh." Indeed, they border on blasphemy, implying that such a God would have to be weak to be threatened by "My love to Saints and Angels." The speaker's theological sophistication is evident here as he claims that his love is "to" not "of" "saints and angels," thus implying a traditional Catholic distinction between direct worship of God or *latria* and the veneration proper to saints or *dulia*. This distinction implies that there should be nothing wrong with such mediated forms of worship (a view expressed in less defensive terms in "The Cross"), and that a God who prohibits such devotion must be tyrannical and hence weak himself.

Donne's poem thus ends by enacting the failure, or at the very least the incomplete nature, of his regeneration according to generally Protestant terms. Such an ending contrasts with the more confident ascending of Petrarch's desire at the conclusion of Sonnet 346, where he says "I raise all of my desires and thoughts toward Heaven, / for I hear her even pray that I may hasten."[77] Rather than undergoing a Petrarchan–Dantean conversion from love of Laura–Beatrice to love of God, Donne's speaker ends by sustaining a sense of his autonomy even at the price of despair. He paradoxically maintains this claim to self-authority by expressing resentment at the thought of a God who renounces human will and with it the possibility of *caritas*. The result is a poem that laments not only the death of a woman, but the death of the world view that made the Petrarchan elegy possible.

The phenomenology of repentance expressed in *Holy Sonnets*, as well as other religious works by Donne, particularly *Devotions Upon Emergent Occasions*, is characterized by a profound sensitivity to the anxiety-producing dimensions of penitential experience and the theology of immanence informing it – to the fear that arises when the borders separating self from other are compromised. This anxiety is expressed by, even as it is defended against, the affect of delicious despair – the *accidia* that is the emotional mark of one's vain attempt to sustain the illusion of autonomy in the process of regeneration. The dialectic of regeneration I have been tracing might be redefined now as involving the two faces of vanity, the nothingness of non-existence and the life-giving overpresence of *amor dei*. As Jean-Luc Marion puts it, "the experience of vanity indicates that even that which is finds itself disqualified as if it were not, so long as it does not have added to its status as a being the dignity of that which finds itself loved."[78] Some of the most dramatic moments in the *Holy Sonnets* arise when Donne's speaker recoils in the face of God's love, asking him to make "of ... my tears ... a heavenly Lethean flood, / And drowne in it my sinnes black memorie."[79] And as "Since She Whome I Lovd" discloses, Donne sometimes appeared to feel that the Lutheran/Calvinist disavowal of Neoplatonic ontotheology made this violent love spiritually unbearable. Indeed, Donne's "Since She Whome I Lovd" registers how Luther's critique of *caritas* amounted to a desublimation of the Petrarchan conversion elegy. After the Reformation, the poem insists, it became impossible to elevate one's beloved to the point of beatification, to the dignity of a sublime object; and in the absence of such sublimation Donne's speaker falls into a state of despair and self-conscious poetic impotence. Viewed this way, Frank Kermode's sense that the poem is "extremely flat and laboriously worked out" and Barbara Lewalski's feeling that the sonnet "seems less unified and effective than usual" reflect not an inadvertent failure on Donne's part, but the poem's purposeful diagnosis of the need for a new kind of elegiac conversion poem, one capable of mitigating the desublimating and potentially desacralizing consequences of Reformation thought.[80] It is paradoxically from such apparent failure that the poem derives its effect of sincerity and hence its emotional power. Thus if "Negative Love" confidently, even parodically, announces the desublimation of Petrarchan poetics, then "Since She Whome I Lovd" painfully records the stakes of what exactly has been lost. This desublimation is, perhaps paradoxically, the most devastating example of how Donne expresses the psychically violent nature of repentance and the complex play of self-denial inherent to *metanoia* in Petrarchan terms.

NOTES

1 Alister E. McGrath, *Luther's Theology of the Cross: Martin Luther's Theological Breakthrough* (Oxford: Basil Blackwell, 1985), p. 151.
2 John Donne, *Devotions Upon Emergent Occasions*, ed. Anthony Raspa (Montreal: McGill-Queen's University Press, 1975), pp. 39–40.
3 See Hebrews 4:12.
4 St. Augustine, *Confessions*, trans. Henry Chadwick (Oxford: Oxford University Press, 1991), book 3, chapter 6, paragraph 11.
5 See Douglas L. Peterson, "John Donne's Holy Sonnets and the Anglican Doctrine of Contrition," *Studies in Philology* 65 (1959), 504–18. For an authoritative critique of Peterson's depiction of Hooker's thought and a discussion of Donne's awkward acceptance of Hooker-style English Protestantism, see Richard Strier, "John Donne Awry and Squint: The 'Holy Sonnets,'" *Modern Philology* 86 (1989), 357–84. My reading of Donne's use of Petrarchism in the *Holy Sonnets* builds on Strier's thesis that Donne's devotional poems express anxiety about the Reformation view of imperfect sanctification, that the saved are both justified and sinful.
6 John Stachniewski, "John Donne: The Despair of the 'Holy Sonnets,'" *ELH* 48.4 (Winter 1981), 677–705 and John Stachniewski, *The Persecutory Imagination: English Puritanism and the Literature of Religious Despair* (Oxford: Clarendon Press, 1991); Paul Cefalu, "Godly Fear, Sanctification, and Calvinist Theology in the Sermons and 'Holy Sonnets' of John Donne," *Studies in Philology* 100.1 (Winter 2003), 71–86; revised in *Moral Identity in Early Modern English Literature* (Cambridge: Cambridge University Press, 2004), chapter 4. Barbara Lewalski, *Protestant Poetics and the Seventeenth-Century Religious Lyric* (Princeton, NJ: Princeton University Press, 1979), p. 256.
7 See Patrick Grant, "Augustinian Spirituality and the Holy Sonnets of John Donne," *ELH* 38.4 (December 1971), 542–61; Terry Sherwood, *Fulfilling the Circle: A Study of John Donne's Thought* (Toronto: University of Toronto Press, 1984), chapter 6; and Angus Fletcher, "Living Magnets, Paracelsian Corpses, and the Psychology of Grace in Donne's Religious Verse," *ELH* 72.1

(Spring 2005), 1–22. For a reading of the sequence in relation to post-Tridentine soteriology, see R. V. Young, "Donne's Holy Sonnets and the Theology of Grace," in Claude Summers and Ted-Larry Pebworth (eds.), *Bright Shootes of Everlastingness: The Seventeenth-Century Religious Lyric* (Columbia: University of Missouri Press, 1987), pp. 20–39.

8 Mary Ann Koory, "'England's Second Austine': John Donne's Resistance to Conversion," *John Donne Journal* 17 (1998), 144, 149. For brief discussions of Petrarchism and poetic subjectivity in the *Holy Sonnets*, see Anne Ferry, *The 'Inward' Language: Sonnets of Wyatt, Sidney, Shakespeare, Donne* (Chicago: University of Chicago Press, 1983), chapter 5 and Heather Dubrow, *Echoes of Desire: English Petrarchism and its Counterdiscourses* (Ithaca, NY: Cornell University Press, 1995), pp. 226–28. For a reading of the *Holy Sonnets* as instances of religious melancholy in the pathological sense explained by Robert Burton in his *The Anatomy of Melancholy*, see Roger B. Rollin, "'Fantastique Ague': The Holy Sonnets and Religious Melancholy," in Claude Summers and Ted-Larry Pebworth (eds.), *The Eagle and the Dove: Reassessing John Donne* (Columbia: University of Missouri Press, 1986), pp. 131–46.

9 Petrarch, *Petrarch's Lyric Poems: The Rime Sparse and Other Lyrics*, ed. and trans. Robert M. Durling (Cambridge MA: Harvard University Press, 1976), p. 582.

10 Robert Durling, "Petrarch's 'Giovene donna sotto un verde lauro,'" *Modern Language Notes* 86 (1971), 19. For other accounts of Petrarch's adaptation and transformation of Augustinian conversion, see John Freccero, "The Fig Tree and the Laurel: Petrarch's Poetics," *Diacritics* 5 (1975), 34–40; Giuseppe Mazzotta, "The *Canzoniere* and the Language of the Self," *Studies in Philology* 75 (1978), 271–96; Kenelm Foster, "Beatrice or Medusa: The Penitential Element in Petrarch's 'Canzoniere,'" in C. P. Brand, K. Foster, and U. Limentani (eds.), *Italian Studies presented to E. R. Vincent* (Cambridge: W. Heffer & Sons, 1962), pp. 41–56. The phrase "Christian anguish" is Erich Auerbach's and is cited in Thomas M. Greene, *The Light in Troy: Imitation and Discovery in Renaissance Poetry* (New Haven, CT: Yale University Press, 1982), p. 316 fn. 4.

11 St. Augustine, *Expositions on the Book of Psalms*, Nicene and Post-Nicene Fathers of the Christian Church, ed. Philip Schaff, vol. VIII, ser. 1 (Grand Rapids, MI: Wm. B. Eerdmans, 1996), p. 133.

12 Petrarch, *Petrarch's Lyric Poems*, Sonnet 342, p. 538.

13 See the Introduction for an explanation of how this distinction is understood in the exegetical tradition.

14 Siegfried Wenzel, "Petrarch's Accidia," *Studies in the Renaissance* 8 (1961), 38. For a Freudian reading of Petrarch's *accidia* that is closely related to my approach, see Gordon Braden, "The Petrarchan Career," in Joseph H. Smith and William Kerrigan (eds.), *Pragmatism's Freud: The Moral Disposition of Psychoanalysis* (Baltimore, MD: Johns Hopkins University Press), p. 145.

15 Petrarch, *Secretum*, cited in Braden, "The Petrarchan Career," p. 145.

16 Ronald Corthell cites Clay Hunt's 1954 study to make this point. See Ronald Corthell, *Ideology and Desire in Renaissance Poetry: The Subject of Donne*

(Detroit, MI: Wayne State University Press, 1997), pp. 62–63. See also, Ilona Bell, "The Role of the Lady in Donne's *Songs and Sonets*," *SEL* 23 (1983), 113–29.

17 Arthur Marotti, *John Donne: Coterie Poet* (Madison: University of Wisconsin Press, 1986), p. 78.

18 William Kerrigan, "What was Donne Doing?" *South Central Review* 4 (1987), 12.

19 Patricia P. Pinka, *This Dialogue of One: The Songs and Sonnets of John Donne* (Alabama: University of Alabama Press, 1982), p. 27. Leonard D. Tournay makes much the same point in "Donne, the Countess of Bedford, and the Petrarchan Manner," in Gary A. Stringer (ed.), *New Essays on Donne* (Salzburg: Universität Salzburg, 1977), p. 50.

20 Robert Southwell, *Marie Magdalens Funeral Teares*, A4.

21 Pinka, *Dialogue of One*, p. 27.

22 William Kerrigan and Gordon Braden, "Milton's Coy Eve: *Paradise Lost* and Renaissance Love Poetry," *ELH* 53.1 (1986), 32.

23 Cited in ibid., 32.

24 Arthur L. Clements, *John Donne's Poetry*, 2nd edn. (New York: W. W. Norton, 1992), p. 42.

25 Petrarch, *Petrarch's Lyric Poems*, p. 50.

26 See, for example, Donald L. Guss, *John Donne, Petrarchist: Italianate Conceits and Love Theory in the Songs and Sonets* (Detroit, MI: Wayne State University Press, 1966), p. 150. For a reading of the poem in the context of the metaphysics of love tradition, see H. M. Richmond, "The Intangible Mistress," *Modern Philology* 56.4 (1959), 217–23. Richmond admits some confusion over "how seriously Donne intends this curious poem," noting that unlike "Ronsard, he does not even admit the folly of his point of view" (219).

27 Such a reading is consistent with Donne's description of Petrarchism as "Whining poetry." For quote see Kerrigan and Braden, "Milton's Coy Eve," 33.

28 Freccero, "Fig Tree," 34.

29 In fairness to Petrarch, several scholars have insisted that this claim to monumentality is consistently thwarted within the *Rime Sparse* itself and that Freccero is overstating his case. See for example, Mazzotta, "The *Canzoniere*," and Marguerite R. Waller, *Petrarch's Poetics and Literary History* (Amherst: University of Massachusetts Press, 1980).

30 For a Freudian-inflected discussion of Petrarchism as increasing the play of desire through the cultivation of obstacles, see Kerrigan and Braden, "Milton's Coy Eve," 38.

31 Braden, "The Petrarchan Career," 145.

32 This sense of permeability between self and other would seem to be the thesis of Donne's "The Ecstasy," not to mention many other poems.

33 Donne, *Devotions*, p. 26.

34 In terms of the basic structures I am analyzing here there is no substantial difference between discourses of Petrarchism and discourses of courtly love. As John Freccero notes, "Far from repudiating verse forms of his predecessors,

[Petrarch] brought them to technical perfection and established them as models for future generations of poets ... In content, [the *Canzoniere*] are familiar, not to say banal, for they elaborate with spectacular variations a tired theme of courtly love: the idolatrous and unrequited passion for a beautiful and sometimes cruel lady" ("Fig Tree," 34).

35 Slavoj Žižek, *The Metastases of Enjoyment: Six Essays on Woman and Causality* (New York and London: Verso, 1994), p. 96.

36 Ibid., p. 90.

37 Ibid., p. 96.

38 Jacques Lacan, *The Ethics of Psychoanalysis: Seminar VII*, ed. Jacques-Alain Miller and trans. Dennis Porter (New York: W. W. Norton, 1986), p. 151.

39 Roberto Harari, *Lacan's Seminar On 'Anxiety': An Introduction*, trans. Jane C. Lamb-Ruiz, revised and ed. Rico Franses (New York: Other Press, 2001), p. 36.

40 Understood here in the generally dialectical sense described in the opening to this chapter.

41 Slavoj Žižek, *On Belief* (London: Routledge, 2001), p. 47.

42 Slavoj Žižek, *The Fragile Absolute – Or, Why is the Christian Legacy Worth Fighting For?* (New York and London: Verso, 2000), p. 127.

43 Petrarch, *Petrarch's Lyric Poems*, p. 226.

44 Ibid.

45 Petrarch, *Secretum*, cited in Braden, "The Petrarchan Career," p. 145.

46 Robert Burton, *The Anatomy of Melancholy*, ed. Floyd Dell and Paul Jordan-Smith (New York: Tudor Publishing Co., 1927), p. 9.

47 Julia Kristeva, *Black and Sun: Depression and Melancholy* (New York: Columbia University Press, 1989), p. 12. For a discussion of how this "wound" gets configured in the poetry of tears tradition, see my discussion of Marvell in Chapter 3.

48 Richard Hooker, *A Learned and Comfortable Sermon of the Certaintie and Perpetuitie of Faith in the Elect* (Oxford, 1612), pp. 9–10. For a brilliant discussion of this passage from Hooker in relation to Herbert's representation of despair, see William Flesch, *Generosity and the Limits of Authority: Shakespeare, Herbert, Milton* (Ithaca, NY: Cornell University Press, 1992), pp. 39–40.

49 Strier makes this point about "Oh My Blacke Soule" in "Awry and Squint," 374.

50 Daniel Dyke, *The Mystery of Selfe-Deceiving Or A Discourse of the Deceitfulnesse of Man's Heart* (London, 1614), pp. 76–77.

51 Ibid., p. 77.

52 Mary Ann Radzinowicz, "'Anima mea' Psalms and John Donne's Religious Poetry," in Summers and Pebworth (eds.), *Bright Shootes of Everlastingness*, p. 45.

53 Dyke, *Mystery of Selfe-Deceiving*, p. 75.

54 John Donne, *The Complete Poetry and Selected Prose of John Donne*, ed. Charles M. Coffin (New York: Modern Library, 1952), pp. 168–69, lines 25–27.

55 C. S. Lewis, *A Preface to Paradise Lost* (Oxford: Oxford University Press, 1942), p. 100.

56 John Donne, *John Donne: The Divine Poems*, ed. Helen Gardner 2nd edn. (Oxford: Clarendon Press, 1978), p. 13. For an overview of this sonnet's manuscript transmission history and modern editing history, see *The Variorum Edition: The Holy Sonnets*, pp. 75–77.

57 Mary Ann Radzinowicz suggests that "O Might Those Sighes and Teares" uses the psalmic device of "Anima mea" "directly" (p. 41). I am qualifying her reading by suggesting that the poem does not open up as clear a dialogue with the soul as an immanent form of otherness in as direct a way as other *Holy Sonnets*, especially "If Faithfull Soules," which concludes with a clearer articulation of difference between the interlocutors involved. This structural difference, I am suggesting, registers a difference in the regenerate status of the speaker for which Radzinowicz does not account.

58 Koory, "'England's Second Austine,'" 142.

59 Stachniewski "John Donne: The Despair," 693.

60 Strier, "Awry and Squint," 376. Though I do not see the poems as being quite as autobiographical as he does, my reading of how some of the *Holy Sonnets* express confusion over competing theological and devotional traditions builds on Strier's authoritative essay, "Awry and Squint."

61 Victoria Silver, *Imperfect Sense: The Predicament of Milton's Irony* (Princeton, NJ: Princeton University Press, 2001), p. 76.

62 For a discussion of the different epistemologies informing Protestant and Ignatian meditative traditions, see Frank L. Huntley, *Bishop Joseph Hall and Protestant Meditation in Seventeenth-Century England: A Study With the Texts of The Art of Divine Meditation (1606) and Occasional Meditations (1633)* (Binghamton, NY: Center for Medieval and Early Renaissance Studies, State University of New York, 1981), pp. 3–12 and Louis Martz, *The Paradise Within: Studies in Vaughan, Traherne, and Milton* (New Haven, CT: Yale University Press, 1964), pp. 17–34. For a discussion of how "Batter My Heart" is caught between competing soteriologies, see Strier, "Awry and Squint," 374–77 and the conclusion to Gary Kuchar, *Divine Subjection: The Rhetoric of Sacramental Devotion in Early Modern England* (Pittsburgh, PA: Duquesne University Press, 2005).

63 See Peterson's thesis that the sonnets dramatize the speaker's progression from fear of punishment to love of God, "John Donne's Holy Sonnets," 506, and Cefalu's discussion of the distinction between filial and servile fear, "Godly Fear," 72.

64 Matthew 27:45, Mark 15:33, Luke 23:44–48.

65 Augustine, *Confessions*, book 3, chapter 6, paragraph 11. It is worth noting here that Freud and Otto Rank argue that the immortal soul is the most primordial instance of the *unheimlich* because it is "probably ... the first 'double' of the body," an "energetic denial of the power of death." Sigmund Freud, "The Uncanny," *Art and Literature*, trans. James Strachey (New York: Penguin, 1985),

p. 356. See Otto Rank, *The Double: A Psychoanalytic Study*, trans. Harry Tucker, Jr. (Chapel Hill: University of North Carolina Press, 1971), pp. 49–68.

66 Michel de Certeau, *The Mystic Fable: The Sixteenth and Seventeenth Centuries*, trans. Michael B. Smith (Chicago: University of Chicago Press, 1992), p. 195.

67 See my reading of "Batter My Heart" in the conclusion to *Divine Subjection*.

68 Cited in John S. Tanner, *Anxiety in Eden: A Kierkegaardian Reading of Paradise Lost* (Oxford: Oxford University Press, 1992), p. 30.

69 Dubrow, *Echoes of Desire*, p. 227.

70 For a closely related reading of *The Anniversaries*, see Marshall Grossman, *The Story of All Things: Writing the Self in English Renaissance Narrative Poetry* (Durham, NC: Duke University Press, 1998), chapter 5.

71 Stachniewski, "John Donne: The Despair," 686. For a related view of the poem in the context of sacramental theory, see Theresa DiPasquale, "Ambivalent Mourning: Sacramentality, Idolatry, and Gender in 'Since She Whome I Lovd hath Payd her Last Debt,'" *John Donne Journal* 10 (1991), 45–56.

72 *De Doctrina Christiana*, 3.10.16, cited in David Jeffrey (ed.), *A Dictionary of Biblical Tradition in English Literature* (Grand Rapids, MI: William B. Eerdmans, 1992), p. 130.

73 Martin Luther, "Preface to Romans," in *Martin Luther: Selections from his Writings*, ed. John Dillenberger (New York: Anchor, 1962), p. 25.

74 Petrarch, *Petrarch's Lyric Poems*, p. 542, lines 1–3, 7–9.

75 Joy L. Linsley, "A Holy Puzzle: John Donne's 'Holy Sonnet XVII,'" in Raymond-Jean Frontain and Frances M. Malpezzi (eds.), *John Donne's Religious Imagination: Essays in Honor of John T. Shawcross* (Conway, AR: UCA Press, 1995), p. 204, rightly cites Romans 8 in order to account for this sonnet, though she does not situate it within an explicitly Reformation context as I do.

76 As cited in St. Augustine, *On the Trinity Books 8–15*, ed. Gareth B. Matthews and trans. Stephen McKenna (Cambridge: Cambridge University Press, 2002), p. 168, (book 15, chapter 2).

77 Petrarch, *Petrarch's Lyric Poems*, p. 542, lines 13–14.

78 Jean-Luc Marion, *God Without Being: Hors Texte*, trans. Thomas A. Carlson (Chicago: University of Chicago Press, 1991), p. xxiv.

79 "If Poysonous Mineralls, and If That Tree," lines 11–12.

80 Frank Kermode cited in *The Variorum Edition: The Holy Sonnets*, p. 431; Lewalski, *Protestant Poetics*, p. 273.

CHAPTER 6

John Donne and the poetics of belatedness: Typology, trauma, and testimony in An Anatomy of the World

If "Since She Whome I Lovd" enacts the impossibility of writing a Petrarchan elegy in the wake of Reformation soteriology, then *An Anatomy of the World. The First Anniversary* does something similar but on a scale that is both formally and thematically much grander. Where the beloved's death in "Since She Whome I Lovd" instigates a personal crisis of mourning and conversion for the speaker, the death of Elizabeth Drury in the 1611 elegy instigates a crisis of mourning and regeneration for the entire world. In *An Anatomy*, Drury's death is presented as having annulled all possible forms of sacramentalization – dividing asunder all "commerce twixt heaven and earth" (399). In the process of mourning this desacralization, Donne's elegy exemplifies how questions about the experience of testimony are often posed in and articulated through the language of religious sorrow. Just as Peter's experience of bearing witness to Christ and Herbert's experience of searching for God occur by their understanding how their sorrow speaks to them of an other within themselves, so Donne's attempt to bear witness to the spirit of his would-be patron's daughter unfolds as an anatomy of the world's melancholy.

At the furthest level of generality, *An Anatomy* presents itself as an effort to assimilate the significance of Drury's untimely death into the meta-narrative of Christian history. What is most remarkable and least understood about the poem's effort to interpret Drury's death within the framework of Christian history is the way it unfolds as a meditation on belatedness that puts on trial the redemptive power of Reformation typology and soteriology. Throughout *An Anatomy*, the speaker tries to recover the conditions for a godly sorrow rather than a desacralized despair by describing the world as belated in at least four key senses: (1) as having separated from purer origins and hence as historically and onto-logically belated, as though it were living the kind of afterlife or *viva morte* we saw in relation to Southwell's Magdalene and Shakespeare's Richard II; (2) as possibly past the time of justifying grace and hence as soteriologically

184

late; (3) as in mourning for the death of a child and hence as psychologically belated in the sense that a father should not outlive his child; (4) and literarily belated in the same way as "Since She Whome I Lovd" – in the sense that Drury's death occurs after the point at which the female beloved can function as a mediatrix conjoining earthly and heavenly orders. The speaker's near-despairing sense of belatedness involves a rigorous, at times even heretical, questioning of the recuperative power of sacred history, particularly as it gets configured in the post-Reformation context.

What is intriguing about the poem's treatment of typology is that it does not simply assume the validity or recuperative power of figurative narrative. On the contrary, it submits typology to rigorous questioning by confronting the Pauline theme that faith is an affront to reason and experience. In this respect, *An Anatomy* is similar to Godfrey Goodman's *The Fall of Man* (1616), which it appears to have influenced. According to Goodman, the experience of faith is so incongruous with reason that it is difficult to comprehend how the God of the Gospels is the same God who created the world; one has to be credulous, he indicates, to believe the typological structure of revelation without admitting that it contradicts experience:

religion, seemes wilfully to oppose it selfe against the current and streame of mans nature; it propounds precepts and rules of practise, contrary to mans owne inclination; mysteries of faith, ouerthrowing the grounds of reason; hope beyond all coniecture and probabilitie: as if man could conspire against himselfe, or that the testimonie of the whole world could preuaile against the cabinet-counsel and knowledge of his own soule; as if that God which reueales the mysteries of grace, were not the same God which first laid the foundations of nature. To whom shal a man giue credit and trust, if the inward light of his owne soule shall serue as a meanes to delude him? ... Man, according to the measure of his own know-ledge, giues his assent or dissent; to be credulous and easie of beleefe, is no token of the greatest wisedome.[1]

By questioning the typological legibility of history in the wake of Drury's death in a way that is similar to Goodman, Donne's speaker will arrive at an ethics of testimony that is predicated on recognizing a certain impossibility of testimony as such. The act of bearing witness to Drury's absence and the process of "enrolling her fame" is inherently bound up, for the speaker, with the process of admitting (in the double sense of confess and assimilate) his and his reader's mortal finitude and epi-stemological limitations. Such a process entails an existential as well as a cognitive recognition of the limits of testimony – a recognition that the act of bearing witness to Drury is, at a certain fundamental point, "incomprehensible." In the process of reiterating, both purposefully and unintentionally, the desacralizing effects of Drury's death, the speaker encourages himself and his "wise reader" to come to an increasing awareness that bearing witness to her means confronting one's own submersion in the corrupt world that one seeks to transcend. In this respect, the poem's depiction of the work of mourning consists not only of an (impossible) effort to "emprison her" in language (470), but more fundamentally it consists of an effort to convey the experience of what it feels like to have outlived her and thus to have overlived one's own time. This experience unfolds through a logic of repetition, in which Drury's death is configured as an event that reiterates the founding traumas of Christian history, the falls of Satan and Adam. Through this structure of repetition, *An Anatomy* puts into question the recuperative power of the narrative of redemption at the heart of the Christian story, even as the poem will ultimately come to rely upon typology for its own efficacy as an elegy.

The reading of typology in *An Anatomy* that I am proposing should be distinguished from the one offered by Barbara Lewalski. While Lewalski argues that Donne poeticizes the Protestant tendency to personalize biblical patterns as reflecting the motions of one's own soul, I am suggesting that a certain ambivalence attendant upon Reformation typology constitutes an unsettling problem that the speaker is trying to work through. Where Lewalski sees Protestant typology as a static context informing the poem's theology, I see the Reformation tradition of *figura* as constituting part of the desacralizing problem the poem records. Thus, if Lewalski views typology as the mechanism of recuperation and redemption operating in the poem, I view the poem as questioning the recuperative power of typological forms of historical narration, even as it seeks to enact the recuperative force of typology. Moreover, I see this questioning of typology as a crucial feature of the poem's power of fascination, its ability to enthrall readers with its depiction of the experience of traumatic loss. In short, I think the relationship between Donne's poem and Protestant traditions of typology is more dynamic and more vexed than her reading would lead us to believe.[2]

THOU MIGHTST HAVE BETTER SPAR'D THE SUNNE

From the poem's opening, Drury's death registers not only as a sorrow bordering on world despair, but as a feeling of grief that registers as de-animation. The grievous feeling of belatedness is so profound that it is experienced as a state of being spectral, of being posthumous to oneself.

This ghostly *viva morte* means that the world has somehow been rejected from the reality of death, as though in the subjective experience of death the world is being objectively deprived of death's substance. This sense of being in a posthumous state is first explicitly expressed when the speaker's meditation on Drury's death brings to mind, in a somewhat oblique fashion, Adam's original sin and the sacrifice of the "Son/Sunne" that is thought to have redeemed it:

> Her death did wound, and tame thee than, and than
> Thou mightst have better spar'd the Sunne, or Man;
> That wound was deepe, but 'tis more misery,
> That thou hast lost thy sense and memory.
> T'was heavy then to heare thy voyce of mone,
> But this is worse, that thou art speechlesse growne.
> Thou hast forgot thy name, thou hadst; thou wast
> Nothing but she, and her thou hast o'erpast. (25–32)

These lines implicitly associate Drury's death with the deep wound of the "Sunne's" sacrifice for Man's first sin; more than that, they syntactically conflate Christ's sacrifice, Drury's death, and Adam's primal sin. "That deep wound" of line 27 is ambiguous, referring not only to Drury's demise but to the (now pointless?) death of the Son/Sunne and the original sin it redeemed. While deictic indicators such as "than," "then," and the pronominal "that," normally help individuate spatial, temporal, and conceptual differences, here they complicate matters. The confusing repetition of deictic terms works to conflate the different "wounds" to which the speaker is referring and the times in which they occurred, just as the word "moan" blurs with the word "man" in a morbidly clever play on homonyms. Most importantly, this conflation of Drury's death with Christ's wound and thus Adam's sin reveals the poem's most significant recurring structure, namely the pattern of traumatic *repetition* itself. Indeed, the speaker's oblique conflation of Drury's death with Adam's fall and Christ's sacrifice is symptomatically repeated over the course of the elegy itself. Following the claim that the temporal origin of Drury's death cannot be confidently located, the speaker recounts the two prior events which caused time to become "out of joint." Around line 100 he offers a sardonic summary of Adam's original sin and then approximately one hundred lines later he offers an oblique account of the fall of Lucifer and his minions. This recursive movement into and then prior to human prehistory is symptomatic of the way the speaker experiences Drury's death as a traumatic repetition of original sin, a repetition of the founding traumas of Christian history. This repeated fall into the vortex of

Christianity's founding traumas threatens the poem's stated aims, even as it generates a morbidly fascinating effect.

I use the word "trauma" in the precise structural sense that psycho-analysis gives to this term. In psychoanalytic theory, an event is traumatic insofar as it is not fully experienced at the time it occurs. In trauma, significant aspects of the event bypass the psyche's regular forms of memorialization and mediation. As Cathy Caruth puts it, a trauma consists "in the *structure of its experience* or reception: the event is not assimilated or experienced fully at the time, but only belatedly, in its repeated *possession* of the one who experiences it. To be traumatized is precisely to be possessed by an image or event."[3] The belated world described in Donne's poem is haunted in just this way by the trauma, first of Drury's death, and second, by the way this death repeats, and thus makes the speaker relive in hyperbolic and – apropos of Ben Jonson's famous quip about the poem – symptomatically heretical ways, the more primordial trauma of original sin.[4] By depicting Drury's death as a repetition of original sin, Donne's poem necessarily calls into motion the redemptive efficacy of Christian typology – the practice of interpreting New Testament events or persons as fulfilling the promise of Old Testament events or persons, as in the case of reading Christ as a new, redeemed, Adam. Yet, rather than simply investing Drury's death with transcendent meaning, by framing it within the narrative of typological redemption, Donne's poem begins by calling into question the very efficacy of the typological narrative upon which it is relying for its recuperative power. As we shall see, the poem's interrogation of typology is an effect of, among other forces, Reformation critiques of medieval traditions of *figura*. Thus, just as the Reformation critique of Augustinian notions of flesh unsettled the process of mourning and conversion in "Since She Whome I Lovd," so related critiques of medieval traditions of typology unsettle the process of mourning and regeneration in *An Anatomy*. Yet in both poems, the desacralizing forces set in motion do not serve a simply demystifying function; on the contrary, they constitute an integral part of the texts' aesthetic structures and the Reformation visions expressed through these structures. In other words, the desacralizing forces recorded in these two poems do more than disturb the work of spiritual regeneration being pursued; such forces are central to the rhetorical power the poems possess as well as the (ambivalent) Reformation view they forward. Because doubt occurs within the horizon of the faithful life, functioning as one possible structuring attitude within a Christian *Weltanschauung*, as we saw Goodman explain, so despair occurs within the horizon of religious sorrow. *An Anatomy* takes full advantage of the way despair emerges at the furthest horizon of godly sorrow's failure, flirting with the dangers of excessive sadness as a way of enhancing the rhetorical effect of the poem.

SICKE WORLD, YEA DEAD, YEA PUTRIFIED

If the obsession with posthumous existence in *An Anatomy of the World* exhibits the uncanny power of fascination and thematic significance that I believe it does, then it is because the poem's depiction of belatedness is articulated through a structure of repetition which overdetermines the theme and experience of being belated, endowing it with ontological, soteriological, psychological, as well as literary-historical meaning. First and foremost, Drury's death registers as ontological belatedness. Following a view of world history as entropic, that had become increasingly influential in England by the end of the sixteenth century, the poem presents the world as having lost its vitality through a process of separation from its divine source.[5] The world is thus configured variously as lethargic, dying, or already dead. While this ontological decay constitutes the most central poetic conceit in the poem, it presents only one modality of belatedness depicted in *An Anatomy*. Accompanying this ontological sense that the world has died or decayed, is the soteriological sense that the world is under threat of having lived beyond the time of redemption as intimated in the speaker's declaration, "Sicke world, yea dead, yea putrified, since shee / Thy'ntrinsque Balme, and thy preservative, / Can never be renew'd, thou never live" (56–58). The idea that the world is under threat of having lived beyond the point of spiritual regeneration is earlier expressed in the image of the world having languished in a bath of its own tears and blood: "in a common Bath of teares it bled, / Which drew the strongest vitall spirits out: / But succor'd then with a perplexed doubt, / Whether the world did loose or gaine in this" (12–15). What is in question here and throughout the poem as a whole is the very legibility of the theological assumptions inherent in Christian elegy: the incarnational assumption that loss is a form of gain and that temporal death is a prelude to eternal life. Rather than tracing the sublation of downward-moving tears to the upward swing of a transcendent *visio Dei* as we saw in Crashaw and Alabaster, Donne's speaker calls into question the very possibility of such transcendence. To begin with, the world's tears are represented as "common," indicating not only "universal" (*OED*) but also "secular, or not holy" (*OED*), as well as "indiscriminate" and "inferior"

(*OED*). While this imagery of tears and blood clearly suggests that "like Christ on the cross the world in its agony feels itself deserted by God,"[6] the speaker has cut off the route to transcendence which *lacrimae Christi* normally take in sacred poetry. This is not, I would emphasize, an empty "conventional" gesture; it is a real question that arises as a result of the competing soteriological and typological theories available to Donne in 1611. What is on trial in Donne's poem is the very process of working through an empirically traumatic event by means of the kenotic paradoxes – of loss in gain, of life in death – organizing Christian elegy and the typological narrative supporting the genre. The speaker wants to interpret the emptying of the world's vital spirits as a paradoxical prelude to its spiritual regeneration, but the kenotic process of emptying in order to become fulfilled is in question. And as a result, it leads to "a perplexed doubt, / Whether the world did loose or gaine in this" (14–15). The fundamental doubt signaled in this opening sequence is whether God's abundant grace has exhausted itself or not.

The "perplexed doubt" in question in the poem rests on the concern over soteriological belatedness that Luther expresses in his highly influential *Commentary on Galatians* – a concern shared by many English Calvinist writers of the 1590s. As Dayton Haskins observes, in the "Lutheran scheme, to live through anguished experiences of personal turmoil and inward affliction, and to pass through 'the time of the law' into the 'time' of abundant grace, was to be, finally, on time. Only those whose lives did not ultimately manifest the pattern were too late."[7] And as Michael Davies has argued, warnings about the soteriologically belated status of sinners was a favorite theme of English conformist divines in the 1590s: "According to preachers such as Gervase Babington, one of the greatest problems facing Elizabethan Protestants was the erroneous presumption ... that 'unreformed children' and 'unruly friends' can repent whenever they wish, not realizing that the time to do so is short and that, indeed, the 'day of grace' may have already passed them by."[8] The anxiety of being without grace manifests in Lutheran and Calvinist traditions as an anxiety that the limited atonement may have exhausted itself by the time one seeks God's grace. The uncanny power of Donne's poem rests on the way it exacerbates this Reformation concern with belatedness by expressing it in unusually hyperbolic terms. Even those "weedless paradises," who are said at the outset to be the poem's elect readers, are under threat of global reprobation.

While the soteriological modality of belatedness is by far the most threatening, its theological and imaginative power is occasioned by the

more existentially immediate event of a child's death. The hyperbolic
sense of grief expressed in the poem undeniably transgresses the universal
prohibition against excessive grief in early modern England, thus cor-
roborating the thesis that "deaths of adolescents ... were deeply felt" in
the period.[9] Even in light of William Drummond's famous assertion that
Donne claimed to be mourning the *Idea* of woman and not the girl as she
was, we should not deny the obvious psychological relevance of
belatedness in a poem about the death of a child. What is the parental
experience of mourning for a child other than feeling that one has lived
too long by outliving one's child? This feeling clearly lies at the heart of
Donne's poem and the strange power it possesses.

The combination of this psychological feeling of overliving and the
theme of ontological decay, in which the world is figured as striving to
return to the nothing from which it came, is revealingly paralleled by
psychoanalysis' attempt to theorize trauma in relation to parental grieving
and the death drive. In her discussions of repetition and trauma, Caruth,
like Donne, links a Father's reaction to his child's death with the phenomenon of *Todestriebe*. As Caruth observes, what Freud defines as the
death drive "could be seen generally as a sense that death is late, that one
in fact dies only *too late*. And what could it mean to die *too late*, except to
die *after one's child*?"[10] Like Freud's work on trauma, Donne's *An Anatomy*
thematically links the parental experience of having lived too long in the
wake of a child's death with a desire for oblivion that gets expressed
through a compulsion to repeat: "We seeme ambitious, Gods whole
worke t'undoe; / Of nothing he made us, and we strive too, / To bring
our selves to nothing backe; and we / Doe what wee can, to do't so soone
as hee" (155–58). While the ontological and soteriological modalities of
belatedness may take conceptual priority over the psychological, they are not,
finally, separable from it. The ethics of testimony articulated in the poem
emerge most fully when read alongside the poem's depiction of the psychological experience of mourning for a child. Such an experience, the poem
insists, involves accepting an existence forever determined by the structure of
belatedness – an existence forever marked by having outlived a death that can
never be fully witnessed or responded to.[11]

Though the poem is laced with intersecting senses of ontological,
soteriological, and psychological modalities of belatedness, it is also, like
"Since She Whome I Lovd," a meditation on literary belatedness. As
Marshall Grossman has argued, *An Anatomy* records a moment of literary-
historical desublimation, what Harold Bloom would identify as the
retroactive emptying of a precursor's poetic vitality:[12]

Elizabeth Drury has died – as, indeed, Beatrice and Laura had died before her –
but her death structures these earlier deaths as autonomous repetitions. Whereas
the deaths of Beatrice and Laura are decisive in the literary texts of Dante and
Petrarch – textual events that become metalyptically formative of their authorial
personae – the death of Elizabeth Drury resists symbolic incorporation. Because
her death does not signify and cannot be made to mean, it retrospectively hollows
out and empties these previous literary sacrifices.[13]

In Grossman's reading, Drury's death comes too late within the literary history of epideictic idealism to be successfully mourned via poetic
beatification in the way Laura and Beatrice were. While Grossman
interprets Donne's desublimating poetics within the history of epideictic
idealism and the Aristotelian epistemology underwriting it, the poem
itself thematizes Drury's death in relation to the problem of original sin
and the *figural* tradition believed to redeem that originary wound. Thus in
order to account for the overdetermined articulation of belatedness in the
poem we must attend to its interrogation of Christian typology and its
recurring use of traumatic repetition as its central structural strategy. By
doing so, we will come to see that what is at stake in the question of
belatedness is not only the perceived efficacy of typological modes of
interpretation, but the ethics of testimony that emerges at the furthest
limits of typology's legibility. At its heart, *An Anatomy's* project of reading
the world in typological terms is part and parcel with its effort to recover
the conditions of godly sorrow; its quest is to ensure that sorrow continues
to signify the status of the world's soul. By interrogating the world's grief,
or its lack of, Donne's speaker hopes to recover the signs of justifying
grace.

IT LABOUR'D TO FRUSTRATE EVEN GODS PURPOSE

As I have suggested, Donne's speaker depicts Drury's death as a symptomatic repetition of Adam's fall and Adam's fall as a repetition of Satan's
fall. By doing so, Donne's poem bears out Jean Laplanche's observation
that "it always takes two traumas to make a trauma."[14] Because traumatic
events are, by definition, too terrifying to be fully experienced either
affectively or conceptually, they cannot be processed until a subsequent
event re-ignites, so to speak, the terror that was avoided in the first
instance. In this respect, events that are traumatic cannot be interpreted or
understood until they are, in effect, re-experienced, as though for the first
time. Freud called this process deferred action, the re-experiencing of an
event as traumatic which originally did not register within the psyche as a

conscious phenomenon.[15] The logic of deferred action helps explain why Donne's speaker seeks to make the world feel, as though for the first time, the terrifying absence of Drury as a necessary prelude to positioning her memory within what the speaker refers to as "the book of destiny." By getting the world to "admit" Drury's death, it will come to learn the traumatic lesson "That this worlds generall sicknesse doth not lie / In any humour, or one certaine part; / But, as thou sawest it rotten at the hart" (240–42). Donne thematizes the idea that Drury's death resists interpretive assimilation in the manner of a trauma in "A Funerall Elegie," which prefaced *An Anatomy* in the original 1611 edition of the poem, and which followed it in the 1612 version of the poem:

> He which not knowing her sad History,
> Should come to reade the booke of destiny,
> How faire and chast, humble and high shee'ad beene,
>   Much promis'd, much perform'd, at not fifteene,
> And measuring future things, by things before,
>   Should turne the leafe to reade, and read no more,
> Would thinke that eyther destiny mistooke,
>   Or that some leafes were torne out of the booke. (83–90)

As Rosalie Colie suggests, Donne here "describes the process of *figura*, that is, how one reads present events as the fulfillment of an actual and symbolic event from the past, in terms of his dead maiden."[16] Yet Colie understates the skeptical force of this call for post-figurative analysis; Drury not only demands typological interpretation, but, like the events of Shakespeare's *Richard II*, she resists such interpretation. These lines indicate that in the translation from Drury's historical life to the typological meaning her life possesses within the text of sacred history as a whole, something has fallen out. As *An Anatomy* testifies, this gap in the book of destiny arises because Drury's death is not experienced as simply one moment within a larger typological history, but is configured as an *event* that calls into question the very legibility of sacred history. As a result, Drury's death touches upon the broader cultural anxiety regarding original sin and the precise mechanism of grace believed to resolve it that is in question in the Reformation, and that was of considerable preoccupation for the Catholic-raised Donne, who was in the process of coming out publicly as a Protestant around the time of the poem's publication.[17]

Heather Anne Hirschfeld explains the traumatic character of original sin when she remarks that the theological efficacy of this foundational doctrine "is frustrated by the traumatic consequences that the precept itself underwrites." The primal trauma in the garden "is the scene around which Christian typology is structured, and which it exacerbates even as it attempts to rectify it. That is, although the past reality and future promise of Christ's sacrifice are meant to allay the bitter loss entailed in Original Sin, the devastations of this loss are inculcated precisely by the same Christological claims meant to subdue it."[18] In Hirschfeld's account, Christian typology is constantly under threat of a catastrophic regression because the recuperative event of Christ's Crucifixion fails to annul, even runs the risk of exacerbating, the lived experience of loss and suffering that the concept of original sin tries to explain. *An Anatomy of the World*, I am arguing, derives its uncanny power from exacerbating exactly this compulsive tendency within the lived experience of Augustinian Christianity to pick at the scab, as it were, of its founding traumas. To put this more precisely, the depiction of Drury's death as instigating the loss of justifying grace in the world runs the risk of reversing the progressive terms of *figura* – relocating the ultimate moment of historical meaning, not in the Resurrection of Christ with its promise of future redemption, but in the originary loss of paradise in the Garden. In other words, the hyperbolic depiction of desacralizing grief in the poem runs the risk of disclosing the possibility that history is structured as trauma, not as typology – where it is the past event rather than the future promise that determines the shape of human destiny.

The speaker will prevent this catastrophic regression from taking over his poem not by confidently repairing the tear in the book of destiny through poetic sublimation, but by coming to accept the contingency of such a process as the very condition of faith as lived experience. The work of mourning and testimony in the poem does not take place through a triumphal symbolization of the gap between temporal and eternal orders – not through the "fame" he will enroll – but by the fragile and contradictory process of living out the lost promise of Drury's virtue. As "A Funerall Elegie" indicates, this process occurs at the level of lived experience rather than through the symbolizing operations of human thought: "if after her / Any shall live, which dare true good prefer, / ... They shall make up that booke, and shall have thankes / Of fate and her, for filling up their blanks" (97–98, 101–2). The work of filling in the book of destiny occurs through exemplary action, not at the level of representation. What is thus accomplished in the poem is a kind of articulation of the conditions proper to faith as lived in the confrontation with the untimely death of a child and, through it, with the untimeliness of death as such. As the poem concludes, such conditions are, at a certain fundamental level, incomprehensible.

Another way to look at this is to see the poem as striving towards the kind of understanding the Reformers associated with a justified view of the world. Victoria Silver summarizes such a view in relation to Book 1 of Calvin's *Institutes*:

once confronted with the incoherence or incongruity that suffering exposes in the world, we are compelled to acknowledge a disparity between what we imagine for ourselves and our actuality, and so to rethink our position in the light of such felt discrepancy. And we do this in order to create a more viable and coherent picture of the world as we find it, which must incorporate the fact of contradiction ... the conflict of worlds and value embodied in our lives and pictured in the suffering Christ [or dead Drury] compels us to reflect upon and to alter our ideas even as we persist in the painful predicament this anomaly intrudes upon us. And according to the reformers, in doing this, we are justified before God.[19]

Whatever else *An Anatomy* does, it enacts the process of incorporating "the fact of contradiction" into the speaker's and reader's experience of the world. Tarrying with the incomprehensibility of a child's death, and through it to the untimeliness of death as such, the poem flirts with the same possibility expressed in *Richard II* – the possibility that the world simply doesn't give itself to be read in typological terms.

The anti-typological pressure registered in the poem is felt most clearly in the speaker's quasi-heretical accounts, in which Drury's death is figured as a repetition of the two primordial falls from grace. In both cases, the speaker depersonalizes the force of corruption, making sin an inherent, predetermined aspect of creation rather than an active choice made by a free subject. For instance, the fall from Eden is depicted as a result of the impersonal force of ruin which "labour'd to frustrate / Even Gods purpose; and made woman, sent / For mans reliefe, cause of his languishment" (100–2). If this brief account seems to take away both Eve's and, remarkably, God's agency with respect to the fall, then the account of Satan's transgression a hundred lines later also seems to displace responsibility for the force of corruption: "before God had made up all the rest / Corruption entred, and deprav'd the best: / It seis'd the Angels: and then first of all / The world did in her Cradle take a fall" (193–96). These accounts of the origins of evil border on heresy to the extent that they personify the force of sin as a power whose origin cannot be located in the subjective acts of individual agents, including God. By situating the origins of corruption in a past that was never present as such, and by personifying it as an impersonal force at work within the cosmos, Donne's poem flirts with the Manichean heresy that evil is an active force separate from God's will. Donne thus calls attention to the possibility that evil is a substantial presence in the cosmos rather than a pure negation of divine will as Augustine established for future orthodoxy. By entertaining this heresy, Donne's speaker alludes to the possibility that it is beyond the power of God to recuperate the originary loss being mourned in the poem. Ben Jonson's claim that Donne's poem is full of blasphemies notwithstanding, we should note that Donne's speaker is betraying the spiritual corruption that he claims to be diagnosing. In other words, Donne's speaker is revealing as much about his melancholic and near-despairing attitude as he is about the world outside of him.

By personifying sin as a force that logically and temporally precedes even Lucifer himself, Donne's poem creates the conditions for experiencing Christian typology as exacerbating rather than alleviating the fall it is designed to negate. The impersonal nature of corruption circulating in the poem opens an interpretive possibility that orthodox Christianities wish to silence, namely that the force of cosmological "ruin," which the Genesis story puts into motion, cannot be recuperated by a subsequent event, but is a force there at the beginning of things, indeed prior to the beginning of things. Donne's poem derives some of its emotional and rhetorical power from gesturing at, if not actually advocating, such an interpretive possibility.

By exacerbating the structural weaknesses of Christian typology, the poem registers how Reformation critiques of medieval interpretations of *figura* rendered such structural weaknesses more apparent. Thus, in order to properly contextualize the poem's poetics of belatedness, a brief detour through Reformation critiques of medieval traditions of typology is in order.

Although Luther resuscitated much of Augustine's soteriology through a re-reading of the doctrine of original sin, the German Reformer significantly critiqued Augustine's concept of *figura*. And it is through this critique of *figura*, as much as through the revisiting of the question of grace, that Luther intensified the narrative of historical decline that Donne's speaker tarries with in *An Anatomy*. As Lisa Freinkel has demonstrated, Luther offered "a sustained and rigorous critique of Medieval traditions of *figura* . . [a critique] that Luther pursues to its logical conclusions, radically undermining any notion of the flesh's temporal, figural fulfillment."[20] By emphasizing the Pauline idea that the promise of grace emerges out of a past that was never present as such, Luther unsettles the progressive Augustinian model of typology in which flesh is fulfilled by, rather than radically opposed to, spirit. This shift is signaled in Luther's *The Deuteronomy of Moses*, when he asserts that "The New Testament is the older one, promised from the beginning of the world, yes, 'before the times of the world.'"[21] Thus, after Luther and the magisterial Reformation, the symmetry of the Old Testament letter fulfilled by the New Testament spirit is complicated as the Old Testament spirit "now appeared *simul* in its letter, that is, in its inviolable promise of the future, unconditioned by the law of Moses and the failure of Israel."[22] In this historically unprecedented and hermeneutically destabilizing view of sacred history, the "teleological narrative from Judaism to Christianity" that characterized Augustinian typology is replaced by the "ceaseless ambivalence" of a system in which the Old Testament letter already hosts within it the spirit of the Gospel.[23] This typological perspective is part and parcel of Luther's anti-progressive view of human history. As Heinrich Bornkamm argues, "Luther saw human history not as natural progress, but as a progressive separation from purer beginnings. That was why God had to communicate once again with particular clarity his natural law through Moses."[24] The historical vision of world decay expressed in *An Anatomy* is "Lutheran" in this precise sense.

According to J. S. Preus, Luther challenged Augustinian and later medieval traditions of typological interpretation by resituating the "'hermeneutical divide' between letter and spirit" from its "traditional law-grace, Old Testament – New Testament terms" within the Old Testament itself.[25] Despite his efforts to render the word of God transparent, Luther's view of typology is hermeneutically destabilizing insofar as it produces an impossibly paradoxical relationship between letter and spirit – between an Old Testament literality that is simultaneous with, even as it is wholly other than, a Christological spirit. For Luther, as Preus explains, "there is already a deep theological divide among Old Testament words themselves, between its earthly, temporal provisions and the eternal covenant of faith made with Abraham." Luther asserts this divide when he claims that although Abraham's descendants "did not yet have the revealed faith, which directs one immediately to God through Christ, nevertheless, what they had was *not a naked letter*, but a letter which was hiding those things which are spirit."[26] Such a "letter" is stranger than anything patristic or scholastic theology ever entertained, for it collapses what had long been a conceptually symmetrical division between Old and New Testaments. Luther thus rendered the relationship between spirit and letter more strangely intimate than ever before, even as he insisted that the two oppositions were to be understood as irredeemably differentiated.

By insisting upon the radical difference between letter/spirit, even while emphasizing their necessary coexistence within the revelation of Gospel,

Luther's typology results in what Freinkel speaks of as a "ceaseless ambivalence, [a shuttling] back and forth between mutually exclusive alternatives: flesh/spirit, law/gospel, damnation/salvation, slavery/freedom," to which we might add *deus absconditus/deus revelatus.*[27] Preus anticipates Freinkel's point when he remarks "that the Old Testament promises always *sound* 'temporal,'" even when "they are intended to be *understood* spiritually," resulting in "a certain irreducible ambiguity."[28] What emerges from this reshifting of hermeneutic terms is a growing sense that Lutheran typology unleashes the threat of what we would now identify as the Derridean supplement, "the possibility of a catastrophic regression and the annulment of progress"[29] from Gospel to law, from spirit to letter, from promise to shadow, and ultimately from salvation to damnation. Donne's poem not only registers this hermeneutically destabilizing view of Reformation typology through its depiction of Drury's death as a traumatic and hyperbolic repetition of the origin of sin, but it also derives its uncanny aesthetic power *from this threat.* It is in this precise and rather disturbing sense that we should speak of *An Anatomy* as an instance of Protestant poetics.

OUR ANATOMEE . . . SHOULD MORE *AFFRIGHT*, THEN PLEASURE THEE

Throughout *An Anatomy,* anti-typological pressures arise from the way Drury's death is not assimilated emotionally or interpretively. Ronald Corthell comments on the world's inability to render Drury's death meaningful when he describes it as melancholic in the Freudian sense that the "world knows whom has been lost, but not what has been lost in her."[30] This observation brings to mind the fact that trauma and melancholy are parallel phenomena insofar as both occur when the subject does not consciously assimilate and thus cannot interpret the terror of an event that is psychically overwhelming.[31] The speaker thematizes the world's failure to "admit" Drury's death when he accuses the world of trying to repress her absence and its desacralizing effects. Early on in the poem, the speaker diagnoses the world as being in "a general thaw," implying that it remains stuck in a state of numbness and denial:

> . . . as in states doubtfull of future heyres,
> When sickenes without remedy, empayres
> The present Prince, they're loth it should be said,
> The Prince doth languish, or the Prince is dead:
> So mankind feeling now a generall thaw,

...
Thought it some blasphemy to say sh'was dead;
Or that our weakness was discouered
In that confession; therefore spoke no more
Then tongues, the soule being gone, the losse deplore.
                                    (43–47, 51–54)

Repressing the disjointing effects of Drury's death, the world has fallen into a
state of delusion where confessing the reality of her absence is confused with
"blasphemy" – a threat the speaker expresses further when he flirts with the
Manichean heresy moments later. Drury's death cannot be grieved through
the articulation of her loss because the "soul [is] gone." As a result, her death
can simply be "deplored" – given up as hopeless, as reason to despair. This
failure to confess the desacralizing effects of Drury's death precludes the
possibility of bearing witness to her spectralized presence. And this is crucial
because the stated burden of the speaker's anatomy is to bear witness to
Drury's spirit, and by doing so to fully acknowledge what it feels like to have
survived her, thereby re-establishing the conditions for godly sorrow and
spiritual regeneration. This process of admitting her loss involves the same
terrifying recognition of experiencing the Law that Luther speaks of when he
says the spiritual purpose of the Law is "to reveal unto a man his sin, his
blindness, his misery, his impiety, ignorance, hatred and contempt of God,
death, hell, the judgment and deserved wrath of God."[32] The poem's various
refrains seek to terrify the world in precisely this way: "Shee, shee is dead;
shee's dead: when thou knowst this, / Thou knowst how wan a Ghost this
our world is: / And learnst thus much by our Anatomee, / That it should
more affright, then pleasure thee" (369–72). The poem as a whole works by
trying to inspire in its readers a feeling of anxiety, even of terror, that is
consequent upon living in a world mired by sin. For such experiences are
prerequisite to the redemptive sorrow the speaker seeks to generate.

   In other words, *An Anatomy* seeks to heal the loss of typological legibility
resulting from Drury's death by means of traumatically shocking the world
into seeing the reflection of its own sinfulness in the image of the poem
itself. This process might be understood by looking forward to the aesthetic
and ethical vision that Walter Benjamin sees at work in the "traumatic" and
modernist poetics of Baudelaire, rather than just backwards to Reformation
theology. According to Benjamin, Baudelaire "placed the shock of
[traumatic] experience at the very center of his artistic work."[33] Baudelaire's
poems are ethical, Benjamin explains, insofar as they identify a gap within
experience as historically legible in order to make it available to consciousness in the form of *Erfahrung* – experience as consciously assimilated

into a larger, shared context. For Benjamin, Baudelaire's aesthetic of trauma is "modern" because it is symptomatic of the loss of historically communicable experience. Kevin Newmark explains Benjamin's reading of Baudelaire when he says that modernity "names the moment when the thinking subject can no longer be said to be completely in control or conscious of the actual events that necessarily comprise 'his' own past, an experience in which the subject is not able to provide the necessary links or connections between individual and collective patterns of memory."[34] While it is somewhat difficult to imagine an historical moment that is not definable in these terms, what we are speaking of in the context of Donne's and Baudelaire's poetry are two respective moments when this breakdown in experience became chronic enough to necessitate being thematized as a central problem for poetic expression and/or religious thought. Thus, while drawing Donne and Baudelaire together may seem anachronistic, the most famous passage in Donne's poem makes clear that an early modern form of the breakdown in experience in the form of *Erfahrung* is precisely what *An Anatomy* expresses. Moreover, through the process of articulating the implications of this breakdown between temporal experience and publicly shared metanarrative, Donne's speaker will envision an ethics of testimony that takes the impossibility of ever fully expressing our experience of the connections between these two orders as its condition of proceeding:

> So did the world from the first houre decay,
> That evening was beginning of the day,
> And now the Springs and Sommers which we see,
> Like sonnes of women after fifty bee.
> And new Philosophy cals all in doubt,
> The Element of fire is quite put out;
> The Sunne is lost, and th'earth, and no mans wit
> Can well direct him, where to looke for it.
> And freely men confesse, that this world's spent,
> When in the Planets, and the Firmament
> They seeke so many new; they see that this
> Is crumbled out againe to his Atomis.
> 'Tis all in peeces, all cohærence gone;
> All just supply, and all Relation:
> Prince, Subject, Father, Sonne, are things forgot,
> For every man alone thinkes he hath got
> To be a Phœnix, and that then can bee
> None of that kinde, of which he is, but hee. (201–18)

Reacting to the corrosive force of sin, the speaker reaches back into human prehistory in search of an original sin that put time out of joint in

the first place. But the amnesia causing individuals to experience themselves as autonomous beings disconnected from the divinely instituted
order that grounds them without their knowing it, is so developed that no
man's wit, nor the earth itself, can locate the justifying grace of the "Son/
Sunne." Original sin is thus a decisive theme for understanding both the
poem's meaning and its rhetorical form because the doctrine provides the
conceptual terms for articulating exactly how experience can exceed
consciousness in the way that Benjamin and others identify with
"modernity." For example, Luther says in his commentary on Romans
that the iniquity of original sin "exists whether I perform it or even know
about it. I am conceived in it, but I did not do it. It began to rule in me
before I began to live. It is simultaneous with me."[35] And as we saw in the
previous chapter, faith has "her privy operations secret to us ... yet
known to [God] by whom they are."[36] Donne's *An Anatomy of the World*
anticipates a modern poetics of trauma precisely insofar as it hyperbolizes
the way that original sin, and with it the world of flesh, can be part of
experience but not part of consciousness. By depicting the human subject
as constituted by a blind spot between past sin and future promise,
between sinful forgetting and impossible remembering, the poem diagnoses the forces that lead the speaker to call into question the typological
– cosmological – social order grounding the Elizabethan "World Picture."
This hyperbolization of the disjointing force of sin is an integral part of
the poem's questioning of the recuperative force of typological interpretation; for such hyperbolization leads the speaker to an ethics of testimony that is predicated on the tear in the book of destiny that it,
paradoxically, seeks to mend. In other words, the process of bearing
witness to Drury's absence entails confessing the disjointed condition of
the world in the wake of her death: to bear witness to Drury means fully
admitting what it feels like to have overlived her.

The thesis I am forwarding is as concerned with the poem's formal
structure as its thematic content. Donne's phenomenology of original sin
is literarily, rather than just theologically, compelling *because he does not
exclude his speaker from it.* Lewalski misinterprets this aspect of the poem
when she claims that although "the speaker admits his and our involvement in [the world's corrupt] condition, he retains his achieved stance of
superiority to the natural order and invites his audience to adopt the
perspective of 'wise, and good lookers on.'"[37] The entire thrust of the
poem is characterized by the way the speaker is constantly succumbing to
the world of the flesh that he is diagnosing. This self-reflexive paradox is
not a symptom of the poem's failure, but rather it indicates that the "wise,

and good lookers on" are those who know and experience the corruption within and about them. The force of Law as Luther and the Reformers expressed it demands such an awareness of sin as the paradoxical pre-condition and expression of faith. As a result, the speaker unwittingly reiterates the force of corruption, even as he seeks a way out of it. The form of "superiority" achieved by the speaker is not characterized by a transcendence of sin, in the sense that he is immune from it and is thus able to achieve a Platonic *visio*. Rather, the speaker achieves a fragile sense of authority by undergoing a growing existential awareness that sin exists within the deepest part of the human creature, and that incomprehension conditions faith. Only through the power of justifying grace expressed as faith, does one overcome the sin to which one is simultaneously subject. Paradoxically, however, this grace appears absent from the world of the poem. *An Anatomy* consistently forces us to face this paradox as its basic condition of proceeding. Failing to recognize the (im)possibility of the poem's own condition of proceeding renders one something other than "a wise, and good looker on."

The reflexive paradox characterizing the poem's motions is encapsu-lated in the speaker's assertion that "thou hast but one way not t' *admit* / The world's infection, to be none of it" (245–46, my emphasis). The word "admit" must be read in the double sense of "allow in" and "confess." Throughout the poem, Donne's speaker does exactly this, betraying his immersion in a world that he seeks to transcend through faith. Donne's speaker thus enacts what Godfrey Goodman admits at a rather remarkable moment in *The Fall of Man*, when he interrupts his analysis of original sin by confessing: "I forget my selfe, I forget my selfe, for, speaking of mans corruption, I am so far entangled, that I cannot easily release my selfe; being corrupted as wel as others, me thinkes whatsoeuer I see, whatsoeuer I heare, all things seeme to sound corruption."[38] The disjunctions between meaning and intention in Donne's poem enact exactly the self-reflexive entangling that Goodman thematizes.

The speaker's submersion in the world that he seeks to transcend becomes particularly legible at the very moment he proposes his anatomy: "I (since no man can make thee live) will trie, / What we may gaine by thy Anatomy" (59–60). The tentative tone here changes dramatically, even manically, as the speaker shifts into making the optimistic assertion that those who are "Elemented" by the "stuff" of Drury's virtue constitute "weedlesse Paradises" immune to "hom-borne intrinsique harm" (79–80). These "weedlesse Paradises" are the poem's ideal readers referred to at the beginning, those who do not lodge "an In-mate soul," but who "see,

judge, and follow worthiness" (4–5). As a result of their virtue, such readers
are said to be vulnerable to "forraine Serpent[s]" but not to the more
uncanny "hom-born harme[s]" (84). As Edward W. Tayler emphasizes, *An
Anatomy* as a whole is organized around a distinction between those who
follow Drury's worthiness and those who are constitutively incapable of
doing so.[39] What Tayler does not mention, though, is that the basis for this
structuring distinction is qualified the moment it is made and is undercut
later:

> Yet, because outward stormes the strongest breake,
> And strength it self by confidence growes weake,
> This new world may be safer, being told
> The dangers and diseases of the old:
> For with due temper men do then forgoe,
> Or covet things, when they their true worth know. (85–90)

The very confidence inherent in being a "weedless paradise" can itself be a
"hom-born" illness, one that might undermine the soul from within in
the same way concupiscence can. Thus just as the poem uses the theory of
correspondence between microcosm and macrocosm in order to mourn
the loss of correspondence, so the distinction between ideal and vulgar
readers is deployed as a way of conveying the impossibility of coherently
sustaining such a distinction in the corrupt world being anatomized. This
is not to say that the distinction has no meaning, but that it is a distinction that cannot be sustained by reason unaided by justifying grace,
and it is exactly the question of justifying grace as spiritual aid that is in
question in *An Anatomy*. The poem takes this situation more seriously
and poeticizes its implications more rigorously than most readings of *An
Anatomy* recognize.

Later in the text, the assertion that we are in a decaying Thomistic
world, in which reason and will play a role in fending off corruption, is
explicitly undercut as corruption is said to be not a matter of "foreign
serpents" but "home-born harms." By this point, the Thomistic anthro-
pology shifts into a conspicuously Lutheran–Calvinist one:

> And that, not only faults in inward parts,
> Corruptions in our braines, or in our harts,
> Poysoning the fountaines, whence our actions spring,
> Endanger us: but that if every thing
> Be not done fitly'nd in proportion,
> To satisfie wise, and good lookers on,
> (Since most men be such as most thinke they bee)
> They're lothsome too, by this Deformitee. (329–36)

The threat of sin is no longer a mere matter of "foreign serpents," it is now an issue of "faults in inward parts, / Corruptions in our braines, or in our harts." The further the poem moves on, the more the speaker cannot help but "admit" the corruption he and his world are subject to. This sequence, like the poem as a whole, enacts the extent to which there is no outside to the corruption that the speaker diagnoses except that offered by the divine grace that is itself in question in the poem.

The mourning of a Thomistic *analogia entis* unfolding in the sequence on proportion and in the poem as a whole is not simply a comment on the New Philosophy, but also on the attack against analogical thinking taking place within Reformation discourse. As Alister McGrath observes, Luther's *theologia crucis* "represents a programmatic critique of the analogical nature of theological language."[40] For instance, while Augustine presumed "a direct correlation between human and divine justice," Luther "was convinced that human concepts of justice *were contradicted* by divine justice."[41] An inescapable, if not wholly intended, result of Luther's critique of the theological use of analogy is the "hermeneutical circle" that results when Protestants seek to know themselves as reflections of deity. If one is entirely circumscribed by "flesh" then one cannot gain perspective on oneself long enough to know if one is in a state of sinfulness or grace, spiritual illness or health.[42] As Goodman puts it, "To whom shal a man giue credit and trust, if the inward light of his owne soule shall serue as a meanes to delude him?"[43] The constant reiteration of sin through the speaker's symptomatic submersion within the flesh is a poetic response to this non-analogical view of the human subject's relationship to the cosmos and to God. It is Donne's way of having his speaker signal how he is entangled in the process that he is diagnosing, how he implicitly declares: "I forget myself, I forget myself." The only way of becoming disentangled from the world's corruption is by paradoxically admitting one's constitutive entanglement within it. And perhaps not even then.

A highly remarkable example of the speaker inadvertently enacting his submersion within the world occurs during his rather perverse summary of the Incarnation: "This man, whom God did woo, and loath to attend / Till man came up, did down to man descend, / This man, so great, that all that is, is his, / Oh what a trifle, and poor thing he is!" (167–70). The speaker syntactically conflates "Christ" and "this man," first in the phrase "This man" in line 169 and then in the following phrase "what a trifle, and poor thing he is" in line 170.[44] The result is a strangely sordid grammatical enactment of the Incarnation, one that alerts us to the speaker's near-despairing view of the divine will. The speaker's inability to distinguish between Christ's divinity and man's depravity discloses how the speaker stands within the diseased hermeneutic circle that he seeks to cure. This diseased quality of the speaker's discourse is encapsulated in the word "trifle" that is used to denote mankind and Christ, for it implies not only shallow or unserious (as it still does today) but it also intimates "false or idle tale, told (*a*) to deceive, cheat, or befool, to divert or amuse; a lying story, a fable, a fiction; a jest or joke; a foolish, trivial, or nonsensical saying" (*OED*). The speaker's tone is that of the religious melancholic slipping into a state of deep despair; he experiences the narrative of redemption as a "trifle" – a foolish story that belies belief in its sheer absurdity. The speaker's relation to the narrative of redemption borders on that of denegation – a form of repression in which an event is cognitively available to memory, but is emotionally inaccessible.

NOR COULD INCOMPREHENSIBLENESSE DETERRE

While the poem as a whole puts enormous pressure on the recuperative power of Christian narrative, even to the point of heresy, it ends by seeking to reconstitute that power. It does so not by overcoming the limitations of reason and will enacted in the poem, but by consciously assuming and accepting such limits as the condition of faith itself. Like Marvell's "Eyes and Tears," *An Anatomy* does not end by denying the insuperable conflict between explanation and transcendence, between reason and faith, but by seeking to accept such conflict as the condition of the bond between God and humankind. This assumption of an abyss between divine authority and human knowledge is exactly what the apophatic move concluding the poem accomplishes. In the concluding sequence, the speaker accepts the limits he has been bumping up against throughout the poem: "Nor could incomprehensiblenesse deterre / Me, from thus trying to emprison her. / Which when I saw that a strict grave could do, / I saw not why verse might not doe so too" (469–72). The poem as a whole is placed under erasure in these final lines. Such an erasure constitutes an admission that no amount of poetic expression or "watchtower" experience could properly accommodate Drury; no act of verbal testimony could adequately memorialize her. Drury's spirit, he tells us, cannot be comprehended in the form of a propositional belief, but can henceforth only be experienced in the act of faith itself.

The typological structure through which Drury's death is acknowledged, though not "comprehended," is established by means of the speaker's allusion to the song of revelation at the end of Deuteronomy:

> ... if you
> In reverence to her, do thinke it due,
> That no one should her prayses thus reherse,

As matter fit for Chronicle, not verse,
Vouchsafe to call to minde, that God did make
A last, and lastingst peece, a song. He spake
To *Moses* to deliver unto all,
That song: because he knew they would let fall,
The Law, the Prophets, and the History,
But keepe the song still in their memory. (457–66)

While many critics have observed the basic parallels between Moses and the speaker here, none have emphasized how this allusion reiterates the theme of belatedness.[45] To review the parallels: Donne's speaker re-reveals the message of the Law to a sinful people in verse form, just as Moses does in the conclusion to the Pentateuch. The allusion thus establishes *An Anatomy of the World. The First Anniversary* as a re-revelation of the Law, thereby identifying the anticipated *Second Anniversary* as concerned with the revelations of Gospel. Luther establishes the basic Protestant reading of Deuteronomy, which Donne is assuming when he interprets Moses' death before entry into Canaan, as signifying the gap between Law and Gospel: "Moses is the minister of the Law, which does not lead to ful-fillment, that is, to righteousness, but shows sin and demands grace, which it does not confer."[46] Donne's speaker thus positions himself as a belated Moses, re-revealing what is in Deuteronomy itself, a second revelation of the Law. The speaker ends by standing with Moses in the gap between temporal and eternal orders, in the space between a now doubly-belated historical reality and an impossibly distant future promise of grace. But more is going on here than this basic typology implies.

As a gloss in the Geneva Bible indicates, the word "Deuteronomy" signifies "second law." The Greek term, *deuteronomion* (and its Latin equivalent Deuteronomium), as well as the Hebrew, *Mishneh Torah*, all mean "repeated law."[47] The term indicates that the Book of Deuteron-omy as a whole is a belated reiteration of the commandments given at Sinai in Exodus. Donne's speaker thus presents himself as a belated re-revealer of what is in the Old Testament already a late reassertion of the Law. By evoking the final book of the Pentateuch, Donne draws further attention to the theme of desacralization at the heart of the poem. As the commentators of the *New Interpreter's Bible* observe, Deuteronomy "may be held to have desacralized [Jewish] religion, removing much of the mystical and quasi-magical notions of cultic power. As such, it promotes a rather 'secularized' interpretation of religious commitment."[48] This sum-mary makes clear why Deuteronomy was a favorite text of Reformers: it provides biblical authority for the critique of magical thinking that

Protestantism carried out – the kind of thinking Donne's speaker mourns when he declaims:[49]

> What Artist now dares boast that he can bring
> Heaven hither, or constellate any thing,
> So as the influence of those starres may bee
> Imprisond in an Herbe, or Charme or Tree,
> And doe by touch, all which those starres could doe?
> The art is lost, and correspondence too. (391–96)

But like Deuteronomy, Donne's poem does more than express a process of desacralization; *An Anatomy* articulates a form of faith that is less committed to sensual experience than the analogically organized Thomistic world it mourns – though it does so with greater reluctance than its biblical archetype. Although Deuteronomy advocates a certain desacralization of Israelite religion, "it can [also] be held to have spiritualized a wide range of everyday activities, spiritualizing their significance." Deuteronomy is the most quoted text in the New Testament because it anticipates the internalization of religious faith in the form of conscience.[50] By drawing its own recuperative power from an allusion to Deuteronomy, Donne's poem identifies itself with the work of spiritualization and desacralization so crucial to the Reformation. In this respect, the poem's relationship to Deuteronomy is not transumptive in the Bloomian sense of being metaleptic; it does not "ruin" the sacred truths as Marvell worried Milton's epic would. Rather, the speaker's identification with Moses constitutes a perspectival trope in which Donne positions his own text as resting upon the authority of his model. By identifying his poem with the song of revelation in Deuteronomy, Donne's speaker implies that his poem participates in the work of desacralizing spiritualization initiated by Deuteronomy and realized by the Reformation itself. Yet, the poem's hyperbolic account of desacralization and its obsessive thematization of belatedness render the process a melancholic and thus fragile one. In this respect, if the poem is discernibly Protestant then it is, like the *Holy Sonnets*, ambivalently so. And as with the *Holy Sonnets*, this ambivalence accounts for the poem's apparent "modernity" and thus its recognizable aesthetic force.

For Donne, the process of coming to terms with the traumatic loss "of commerce 'twixt heaven and earth" involves coming to terms with an emotional state that registers as conceptually distorting grief. While this state of holy mourning is conceptually paralyzing, it serves as a nonpropositional call to the infinitely constitutive otherness of deity that is immanent within the world even as it is radically in excess of the language of analogy, proportion, and symmetry. The poem registers the irreducible relation between the orders of grace and nature by collapsing and qualifying its structuring distinctions, particularly the distinction between intended and unintended readers. This self-consuming structure leads to the poem's articulation of the basic aporia upon which it has unfolded, where the term aporia must be read not simply as paralysis, but as "the condition of proceeding, of making a decision, of going forward. The aporia is not simply a negative stop."[51] Incomprehensibleness will not deter.

Although *An Anatomy* begins by doubting the applicability of incarnationist paradoxes to the experience of Drury's death, it ends by trying to preserve the paradoxes of kenosis. It does so, however, in an entirely different way than Crashaw's "The Weeper" or Alabaster's *Penitential Sonnets*. Where Crashaw's and Alabaster's poems aspire towards a sacramental communion with God through a contrite emptying of the self, Donne's poem laments the loss of the conditions of possibility for experiencing one's tears as an ambiguous sacrament. (Donne reserves such a sacramental vision of tears for his secular verse, most notably "A Valediction: Of Weeping.")

The ethics of testimony articulated in the poem's conclusion return us to the psychological modalities of trauma and belatedness at work in the poem. As I indicated earlier, the overdetermined theme of belatedness in the poem is occasioned by the lived experience of Robert Drury's grieving for his daughter and the poetic–ethical experience of having to bear testimony to the untimely death of a child. While Donne's poem has been criticized, both in its own time and in ours, for its representation of an excessive response to Drury's death, critics tend to overlook the phenomenological verisimilitude of the poem's representation of traumatic loss. Part of the reason for this is that until recently there has not been a sustained phenomenological account of psychic pain. Juan-David Nasio's 1996 work, *Le Livre da La Douleur et de L'Amour*, fills this gap with an account of psychic pain that brings into relief the phenomenological veracity of Donne's depiction of *la douleur* and the ethical vision resulting from it.

According to Nasio, the pain of separation one experiences in melancholy is intensified by the process of overinvestment that accompanies it. Such an account reads like a paraphrase of *An Anatomy* and thus helps explain its hyperbole:

the prototypical [form of psychic] pain is the pain of separation ... such a pain is made more intense ... by a second pain, which consists in reinvesting the image of the lost loved one. The ego, in this first paradoxical situation, continues to love the one who has been lost more than ever before, magnifying the image of the loved one beyond all reasonable proportions, thus inducing an overexcitation and an exhaustion of the ego ... [T]he paradox is that the pain does not lie in the loss but in the fact that we love the one who has been lost as never before ... "*Pain is not due to a detachment but to an overinvestment.*" It is an overinvestment of an object "within," because it is no longer without ... [T]he pain is not that of an absence, but of an excessive presence.[52]

In other words, melancholic pain involves a twofold movement, a disinvestment in the world and an overinvestment in the image of the lost other. The process of mourning thus consists of rebalancing this radical shift in psychic energy through a slow reversal of the process – a reinvestment in the world through a gradual disinvestment in the image of the other. Nasio's phenomenological account of pain allows us to see that whatever symbolic value one might ascribe to Drury or to the idea of *Idea* being substituted for her, the poem depicts a phenomenologically accurate expression of psychic pain. The apparent overinvestment of value ascribed to Drury is wholly consistent with actual experiences of traumatic forms of loss. As a result, Donne's poem depicts one of the most unsettling features of mourning, namely that in the experience of grief we often feel the beloved's gaze more intensely following her death than we do in her life. This is because "her gaze" is no longer external but internal, no longer "foreign" but "home-born." After death, the departed other is experienced, not as "nowhere," but as "everywhere," not as altogether absent, but as terribly overpresent. Such is the modality of Drury's spectral presence in a world that has been emptied of meaning due to the ongoing and unintelligible experience of her death.

The poem's depiction of how one experiences time in the wake of a traumatic loss is also consistent with Nasio's account of sudden or untimely loss. According to Nasio, if "the loss of the loved one is sudden and unexpected, the pain is brutal and upsets all references of space, time, and identity."[53] Like *Hamlet*, Donne's *An Anatomy* constitutes an extended meditation on the *time of mourning* – the uncanny sense that one cannot accurately locate the origin of one's grief and the time of the other's death. Just as Hamlet appears unable to determine the time of his father's death, so the speaker of *An Anatomy* is at a loss to determine the exact moment of Drury's departure from the world: "Some moneths she hath beene dead (but being dead, / Measures of times are all determined) / But long shee'ath beene away, long, long, yet none / Offers to tell us who it is that's gone" (39–42). In both *Hamlet* and *An Anatomy*, the experience of loss unsettles the phenomenon of time as a linear process – throwing the mourner back upon himself in the impossible effort of bearing witness to the other's death. Therein, I would suggest, is where the ethical vision of Donne's poem is to be located: the speaker does not triumphantly turn Drury's death into something that is "fit for Chronicle," something one can coherently position within a typological framework, but rather he openly admits to the impossibility of bearing witness to her death and thus the "incomprehensibility" of testifying fully to her memory. As a result, "verse" is the proper form of testimony rather than "Chronicle," because poetry does not make a direct claim to empirical verisimilitude, but, as Philip Sidney proclaimed, it expresses the dimension of desire, the optative dimension of subjective experience. Chronicle takes place in the indicative, while poetry occurs within the subjunctive. Only in verse can the limits of experience and the impossibility of testimony be expressed in the very process of bearing witness. Only in a poem, the speaker concludes, can one convey how the experience of testimony is founded on its incomprehensibility.

In the incomprehensible process of trying to bear witness to Drury's memory the speaker is consistently thrown back upon himself in such a way that he *feels* the force of his finitude more profoundly than ever before. It is this experience of finitude and the implications it has for the speaker's understanding of testimony that the poem articulates in its ethics of mourning. Donne's ethical vision implies that what the speaker cannot comprehend in the death and absence of the child, becomes the basis of his very identity as witness – as poet-prophet. By the end of the poem, the speaker's identity as poet is determined by the inability to ever fully comprehend the moment and meaning of her death.[54] The gap in the book of destiny is not written over as Chronicle, as truth within the indicative, but as poem which has "a middle nature," that is to say, one mediated by time, sin, and death, and the limitations of the human creature.

The ethics of testimony articulated in the poem is thus predicated on the experience of unintelligibility surrounding death as such. This state of unintelligibility is registered in the poem in various ways: through the speaker's tortured motions of reflexivity and the acts of misprision arising from them; through his incapacity to render world events typologically legible; and through his depiction of the uncanny dimensions of the phenomenology of grief. All these formal and thematic dimensions are a function of the speaker's grappling with the delimitations of the human will and the experience of working through traumatic loss. Moreover, the formal structures which unsettle the conditions of possibility for the speaker's anatomy disclose how Protestant theology, especially the skeptical effects of Luther's thought, do not constitute a static context which the speaker poeticizes as though he passively accepts such doctrine. On the contrary, the destabilizing effects of Reformation thought are a dynamic problem being enacted and grappled with in both *An Anatomy of the World* and the *Holy Sonnets*. This process of working through the existential implications of doctrinal commitments takes place most often in the English Renaissance through the experience of grief – in the case of *An Anatomy*, a grief that registers in the strange modality of overliving and which is confirmed as both a source of and a proper matter for poetry.

NOTES

1 Godfrey Goodman, *The Fall of Man, or The Corruption of Nature* (London, 1616), p. 8.
2 See Barbara Lewalski, *Donne's Anniversaries And the Poetry of Praise: The Creation of a Symbolic Mode* (Princeton, NJ: Princeton University Press, 1973).
3 Cathy Caruth, *Unclaimed Experience: Trauma, Narrative, and History* (Baltimore, MD: Johns Hopkins Press, 1996), p. 4. For an explanation of how Ruth Leys' critique of Caruth's work in *Trauma: A Genealogy* (Chicago: University of Chicago Press, 2000) is based on a distorting misreading, see Shoshana Felman, *The Juridical Unconscious* (Cambridge MA: Harvard Universtiy Press, 2002), pp. 175–82.
4 As the *Variorum* editors indicate, William Drummond recorded Jonson's critique of the poem along with Donne's reaction: "Dones Anniversarie was profane and full of Blashphemies that he told Mr. Donne, if it had been written ye Virgin Marie it had been something to which he answered that he described the Idea of a Woman and not as she was," *Variorum Edition: Anniversaries*, p. 240. Like many readers after him, Jonson's view belies a fundamental misunderstanding of how the poem works by thematizing its belatedness and by having the speaker become entangled in the corrupt world he seeks to diagnose.
5 See Victor Harris, *All Coherence Gone* (Chicago: University of Chicago Press, 1949); George Williamson, "Mutability, Decay, and Seventeenth-Century Melancholy," *ELH* 2.2 (1935), 121–50; Catherine Gimelli Martin, "*The Advancement of Learning* and the Decay of the World: A New Reading of Donne's *First Anniversary*," *John Donne Journal* 19 (2000), 163–203; and Achsah Guibbory, *The Map of Time: Seventeenth-Century English Literature and Ideas of Pattern in History* (Urbana: University of Illinois Press, 1986), pp. 69–104.
6 Frank Manley, cited in the *Variorum Edition: Anniversaries*, p. 373.
7 Dayton Haskin, "Bunyan, Luther, and the Struggle with Belatedness in *Grace Abounding*," *University of Toronto Quarterly* 50.3 (1981), 300–13.

8 Michael Davies, "Falstaff's Lateness: Calvinism and the Protestant Hero in *Henry IV*," *Review of English Studies* 56.225 (2005), 351–78.

9 Ralph Houlbrooke, *Death, Religion, and the Family in England 1480–1750* (Oxford: Clarendon Press, 1998), p. 236.

10 Caruth, *Unclaimed Experience*, p. 143.

11 For a different psychoanalytic approach to Donne and the question of the death drive, see Donald R. Roberts, "The Death Wish of John Donne," *PMLA* 62 (1947), 958–76.

12 See Harold Bloom *The Anxiety of Influence: A Theory of Poetry*, 2nd edn. (New York: Oxford University Press, 1997), pp. 77–92.

13 Marshall Grossman, *The Story of All Things: Writing the Self in English Renaissance Narrative Poetry* (Durham, NC: Duke University Press, 1998), pp. 179–80.

14 Cited in Heather Anne Hirschfeld, "Hamlet's 'First Corse': Repetition, Trauma, and the Displacement of Redemptive Typology," *Shakespeare Quarterly* 54.4 (2004), 424.

15 See Freud's classic case study, "The Wolf-Man," in *Case Histories II* (New York: Penguin, 1991), pp. 227–366; and Jean Laplanche's *Life and Death in Psychoanalysis* (Baltimore, MD: Johns Hopkins University Press, 1993), pp. 41–44, p. 48.

16 Rosalie Colie, "'All in Peeces': Problems of Interpretation in Donne's Anniversary Poems," in Peter Amadeus Fiore (ed.), *Just So Much Honor: Essays Commemorating the Four-Hundredth Anniversary of the Birth of John Donne* (University Park: Pennsylvania State University Press, 1972), p. 211. Although the post-figurative view of *figura* expressed by Donne is more akin to allegoresis than the concretely historical view of *figura* Auerbach forwards in "Figura," in *Scenes From the Drama of European Literature* (New York: Meridian Books, 1959), pp. 11–76, it is still typological in the sense that the present event/person is only legible in relation to a prior event that it/he/she realizes.

17 Donne's first published prose work was the 1610 anti-Jesuitical treatise urging Catholics to take the Oath of Allegiance, *Pseudo-Martyr*, in which he self-identifies as a conforming Protestant. In 1611 he had *Ignatius His Conclave*, another conformist work of religious controversy, published.

18 Hirschfeld, "Hamlet's 'First Corse," 427, 446.

19 Victoria Silver, *Imperfect Sense: The Predicament of Milton's Irony* (Princeton, NJ: Princeton University Press, 2001), p. 76.

20 Lisa Freinkel, *Reading Shakespeare's Will: The Theology of Figure From Augustine to the Sonnets* (New York: Columbia University Press, 2002), p. 119.

21 Cited in Heinrich Bornkamm, *Luther and the Old Testament*, trans. Eric W. and Ruth C. Gritsch, ed. Victor I. Gruhn (Philadelphia, PA: Fortress Press, 1969), p. 81.

22 J. S. Preus, *From Shadow to Promise: Old Testament Interpretation from Augustine to the Young Luther* (Cambridge, MA: Belknap Press, 1969), p. 268.

23 Freinkel, *Reading Shakespeare's Will*, p. 138.

24 Bornkamm, *Luther and the Old Testament*, p. 128.

25 Preus, *From Shadow to Promise*, pp. 267–68.

26 Ibid., p. 208; Luther, cited in ibid., p. 209.

27 Freinkel, *Reading Shakespeare's Will*, p. 138.

28 Preus, *From Shadow to Promise*, p. 206.

29 Jacques Derrida, *Of Grammatology*, trans. Gayatri Chakravorty Spivak (Baltimore, MD: Johns Hopkins University Press, 1976), p. 298.

30 Ronald Corthell, *Ideology and Desire in Renaissance Poetry: The Subject of Donne* (Detroit, MI: Wayne State University Press, 1997), p. 125. While Corthell's concern is to trace the way that the critical history of *The Anniversaries* symptomatically repeats the poem's enigmatic depiction of Drury, mine is to focus attention on the formal, thematic, and theological treatment of traumatic repetition within the poem itself.

31 Freud notes the parallels between melancholia and trauma in "Beyond the Pleasure Principle," in *On Metapsychology: The Theory of Psychoanalysis*, trans. James Strachey (New York: Penguin, 1991), p. 282.

32 Martin Luther, "Commentary on Galatians," in *Martin Luther: Selections From His Writings*, ed. John Dillenberger (New York: Anchor Books, 1962), p. 140.

33 Walter Benjamin, *Illuminations*, trans. Harry Zohn (New York: Schoken Books, 1968), p. 163.

34 Kevin Newmark, "Traumatic Poetry: Charles Baudelaire and the Shock of Laughter," in Cathy Caruth (ed.), *Trauma: Explorations in Memory* (Baltimore, MD: Johns Hopkins University Press, 1995), p. 238.

35 Martin Luther, *Luther's Works*, vol. 25: *Lectures on Romans*, ed. Hilton C. Oswald (Saint Louis, MO: Concordia, 1972), p. 274.

36 Richard Hooker, *A Learned and Comfortable Sermon of the Certaintie and Perpetuitie of Faith in the Elect* (Oxford, 1612), p. 9.

37 Lewalski, *Donne's Anniversaries*, p. 256. Although Edward Tayler criticizes Lewalski on a number of points pertaining to the poem's epistemology and theology, he shares her view that the speaker presents himself as transcending the "natural order." And although Tayler offers the most historically informed reading of the poem's distinction between ideal and vulgar readers, he does not recognize any self-consuming dimensions to the poem and thus, in my view, misreads it. By insisting on the Thomistic – Augustinian nature of the poem, Tayler misses what I see as its ambivalent relationship to Reformation theology. See Edward. W. Tayler, *Donne's Idea of a Woman: Structure and Meaning in the Anniversaries* (New York: Columbia University Press, 1991). Even Ronald Corthell, who is rigorously post-structural in his interpretation, remains uncritical about the way the poem asks the reader to identify with "an elite soul mate" – largely ignoring how the poem destabilizes the conditions of possibility for such an identification. See Corthell, *Ideology and Desire*, p. 130. And while my reading is indebted to Grossman's *Story of All Things*, chapter 5, in several respects, he is unconcerned with how the poem's theological contexts inform its self-consuming structure. The one

essay that most closely anticipates my reading of the poem's self-consuming structure is Zailig Pollock's "The Object and the Wit: The Smell of Donne's *First Anniversary*," *English Literary Renaissance* 13 (1983), 301–18. Pollock concludes that "if anything is clear by the end of the poem, it is that the smell which the poet's wit seems to detect in the course of its 'punctuall' anatomy of the world is no more nor less than the smell of its own corruption," (317). While I agree with the particularities of Pollock's reading, I do not think the poem's epistemology is reducible to Thomism, nor do I think the question at stake here is simply a matter of rhetorical decorum. As I go on to show, I think *An Anatomy* blends Thomistic and Lutheran anthropologies in the same ambivalent way that many of the *Holy Sonnets* do. Moreover, I think the rhetorical power of the poems derives from such blending of theologies. For an approach to the question of the reader in the poem that is different from, but compatible with mine, see Kathleen Kelly, "Conversion of the Reader in Donne's 'Anatomy of the World,'" in Claude J. Summers and Ted-Larry Pebworth (eds.), *The Eagle and the Dove: Reassessing John Donne* (Columbia: University of Missouri Press, 1986), pp. 147–56.

38 Goodman, *Fall of Man*, p. 81.

39 Tayler, *Donne's Idea of a Woman*, p. 43. Tayler makes the distinction between types of readers sound more specific to Donne's poem and patronage situation than it really is. The distinction between virtuous and unvirtuous, informed and ignorant, readers is quite conventional; it is found in many poems and religious treatises in the early modern period and before. What is significant about Donne's poem is the way that it questions the conditions for making and sustaining such a distinction.

40 Alister E. McGrath, *Luther's Theology of the Cross: Martin Luther's Theological Breakthrough* (Oxford: Basil Blackwell, 1985), p. 159; See also Preus, *From Shadow to Promise*, pp. 252–53.

41 Alister E. McGrath, *Reformation Thought: An Introduction* (Oxford: Basil Blackwell, 1988), pp. 82–83. See also, Goodman, *Fall of Man*, p. 33.

42 McGrath, *Luther's Theology*, p. 135.

43 Goodman, *Fall of Man*, p. 8.

44 John Shawcross points out the syntactical conflation of line 169, *Variorum Edition: Anniversaries*, p. 398.

45 See ibid., pp. 448–49.

46 Martin Luther, *Luther's Works*, vol. 9: *Lectures on Deuteronomy*, ed. Jaroslav Pelikan (Saint Louis, MO: Concordia, 1960), p. 284.

47 I follow Moshe Weinfeld's discussion in *The Anchor Bible: Deuteronomy 1–11: A New Translation with Introduction and Commentary* (Toronto: Doubleday, 1991), vol. 5, p. 1.

48 *New Interpreter's Bible* (Nashville, TN: Abingdon Press, 1998), p. 285.

49 For a study of Reformation critiques of magical thinking, see Keith Thomas, *Religion and the Decline of Magic* (New York: Charles Scribner's Sons, 1971).

50 *New Interpreter's Bible*, pp. 284–85. Grossman, *Story of All Things*, p. 185, makes a related claim, though one largely aloof from the Reformation context

I am emphasizing here, when he argues that Donne's poem connects the passing of the person of Moses into the shared idea of the Israelite community to the passing of *visio* into voice, the passing, "that is of the homogenous spatial repetitions of macrocosm and microcosm into the linear reiterations of memory."

51 Jacques Derrida, "Epoché and Faith: An Interview with Jacques Derrida," in Yvonne Sherwood and Kevin Hart (eds.), *Derrida and Religion* (New York: Routledge, 2005), p. 43.

52 This citation is from the translator's introduction to Juan-David Nasio, *The Book of Love and Pain: Thinking at the Limit with Freud and Lacan*, trans. David Pettigrew and François Raffoul (Albany, NY: State University of New York Press, 2004), p. 4.

53 Ibid., p. 41.

54 My articulation of the poem's ethics of testimony is informed by Caruth's development of Lacan's reading of the "burning child" dream in Freud's *The Interpretation of Dreams*. See Caruth, *Unclaimed Experience*: "What the father cannot grasp in the death of his child, becomes the foundation of his very identity as father," p. 92.

Conclusion

This book has sought to demonstrate the religious and literary consequences following from the idea that godly sorrow is understood in the early modern period as a kind of language, indeed a kind of poetry. I have argued that because sacred grief is viewed in the period as linguistic in nature, the discourse of godly sorrow often functions as a medium for thinking through some of the most pressing theological, metaphysical, and literary questions at issue in the post-Reformation period. The verbal character of religious sorrow also means that it is thought to require close analysis, an awareness of figuration, and a critical recognition that Christian affects often signify in a way that has nothing or little to do with intention – as though such affects come to the supplicant from an immanent otherness that is "within" the soul but is not part of the self as such. In this respect, godly sorrow is a symptom of the fact that we are, as Augustine argues, "mysterious, even to ourselves."[1] Yet, even as godly sorrow is an expression of our own opacity to ourselves, it is also thought to help mitigate such opacity – providing a way out of our epistemological limitations and narcissistic inclinations.

Because godly sorrow is a mode of confession that happens at the furthest reaches of one's intention, one encounters it as a kind of text – indeed a sort of divine poem, in which one sees oneself from the point of view of an other. While the soul may receive the poetry of grief, while it may even have a small hand in shaping it, the soul does not "author" the divine language of Christian sorrow in any modern sense of the term. This passive attitude towards grief is suggested by Augustine's conception of man as *homo significans*, by which he not only means that man is a speaking being, but also that man is a being that is spoken: "[God] spoke, and we were made; but we are unable to speak of Him."[2] Above all else, the experience of religious sorrow reveals the implications behind the belief that the Christian person is a creature that is spoken into existence by an Alien Word. Godly sorrow is the trace of that Word's otherness in the soul.

In the process of trying to testify to the traces of the Word in the soul, early modern poets produce remarkably counter-intuitive and rhetorically complex conceptions of affective experience in post-Reformation England. This is because the question of how such traces are to be read undergoes intense scrutiny in the early modern period. Debates over how sin deforms and how godly sorrow reforms the soul give rise to the kinds of questions and anxieties we have considered in the preceding chapters. Such debates also help explain why poets continually re-envision the moment of the fall, be it through an ironic account of Venus' tears over Adonis, a near-despairing reaction to the death of a child, or through an actual retelling of Genesis. In *An Anatomy of the World. The First Anniversary*, for example, Donne not only worries about how to interpret the world's sinfulness, he also expresses terror at the thought that Drury's death may have instigated an epoch in which elegiac sorrow no longer expresses the kenotic paradoxes of incarnational theology. By expressing the experiential consequences of living in the crucible between competing soteriologies and vying figural traditions, *An Anatomy* does more than express the complications of religious grief in the period; it questions the very legibility of grief in a world that has lived beyond its time. Donne's poem thus seeks to diagnose, even as it acknowledges itself as a symptom of, the spiritual problems arising from cultural debates about soteriology – about the limitations of reason and will arising from original sin. In the process, Donne's *An Anatomy* offers the most disturbingly vivid account of the *viva morte* that we have seen now in a number of works, particularly *Richard II, Venus and Adonis*, "Marie Magdalens Complaint at Christs Death," and *Paradise Lost*. Donne's anxiety that godly sorrow has become illegible and unregenerative is a symptom of the encroaching threat of spiritual death facing the speaker and his world – a threat, I have suggested, which should be understood as a creative response to theological transformation as well as to Drury's death.

For Milton, no less than for Donne, the experience of spiritual death that arises from the failure of godly sorrow to regenerate the soul is primarily felt as a weakening of the faculties, especially understanding and will. As Milton explains in *Of Christian Doctrine*: "This death consists, first, in the loss or at least the extensive darkening of that right reason, whose function it was to discern the chief good, and which was, as it were, the life of the understanding … secondly, in that extinction of righteousness and of the liberty to do good, and in that slavish subjection to sin and the devil which is, as it were, the death of the will."[3] Milton offers an originary account of such a state in Adam's first soliloquy after the fall.

Echoing Satan's parody of Psalm 51 in the opening to the Niphates speech, Adam's soliloquy shows him facing into the abyss of spiritual death; and in the wake of such "extensive darkening" he begins to sound like Satan both formally and thematically:[4] "Oh miserable of happy! ... / Why do I overlive, / Why am I mocked with death, and lengthened out / To deathless pain?" (10.720, 773–75). While Shakespeare's Venus expresses life after the fall of Adonis as a grievous state of division between individuals, Adam knows that the real divisions instituted by sin occur within the soul, as indicated when he admits that in the act of falling his "will / Concurred not to [his] being" (10.746). This diagnosis indicates that he will henceforth be subject to the Pauline condition, expressed in Romans 7:15, of pursuing that which he abhors and avoiding that which he loves. This book has sought to explain how the poetry of religious sorrow derives much of its power of fascination from enacting this sort of disjunction between will and being and the disjunctions between meaning and intention arising from it.

Although the consequences of Adam's fallen subjectivity become increasingly audible as he descends further into the devolutions of "sin's round," his speech also faintly demarcates the way towards the "paradise within." His speech thus constitutes an originary account of the kind of dialectical confession that we have seen is characteristic of the poetry of religious sorrow. He reveals the hope of regeneration in the very process of experiencing the gulf between will and being: "if here would end / The misery, I deserved it, and would bear / My own deservings; but this will not serve; / All that I eat or drink, or shall beget, / Is propagated curse. Oh voice once heard / Delightfully, *Increase and Multiply*, / Now death to hear! For what can I increase / Or multiply, but curses on my head?" (10.725–32). What differentiates Adam's voice from Satan's, and thus what separates his sorrow from the archfiend's, is the willingness to remain in the interrogative mode. While Satan quickly forecloses all questions about future reconciliation, Adam's interrogatives intimate that he remains more open to the possibility of some form of reconciliation with God. Adam's questions continually pile up in the speech, leaving him open to further revelation and subsequent change rather than fixing him in place. Thus even when he picks up Satan's image of the labyrinth as a figure for his cognitive and affective motions (10.1829–31), we get a distinct sense that the way out of "sin's round" is emerging in the folds of his speech, and in the oscillations of his grief.

This latent sense of hope within Adam's near-despair becomes particularly discernible when the first patriarch wants to save his offspring from the effects of sin: "fair patrimony / That I must leave ye, sons; oh were I able / To waste it all myself, and leave ye none! / So disinherited how would ye bless / Me now your curse! / Ah, why should all mankind / For one man's fault thus guiltless be condemned, / If guiltless?" (10.818–25). Even when Adam's questions may appear to be instances of Luther's view that "It is an Execrable and Damnable Monosillable, '*Why*'" to query God's will,⁵ they are nonetheless genuinely interrogative: Adam truly wants an answer. And by seeking a genuine response from God, Adam remains open to an encounter with the divine – an encounter the reader anticipates in the very structure of the interrogative. Satan, on the other hand, tends to pose what we now speak of as "rhetorical questions" – questions that have the effect of reinforcing a previously-held conviction rather than opening up a dialogical encounter. Adam thus speaks, for the first time in the epic, much like we saw Southwell's St. Peter speak when the Apostle declares that "My threnes an endlesse Alphabet do find, / Beyond the panges which *Jeremy* doth paint" (37–38): he says more than he intends. Such speech is a function of the rupture between will and being that Adam diagnoses as both the cause and effect of the fall. It is out of this rupture, or what Marvell calls a "Sluice," that the possibility of godly sorrow emerges and the much of the literary power of penitential poetry rests.

The Miltonic bard signals the beginning of Adam's hope for repentance in the final lines of the soliloquy, which provide an originary account of the *anima mea* tradition so central to the Psalms and to the poetry of religious sorrow more generally: "O conscience, into what abyss of fears / And horrors hast thou driven me; out of which / I find no way, from deep to deeper plunged!" (10.842–44.) Although this split within the self echoes Satan, it is – like Donne's "if Faithfull Soules" – the mark of a possibly genuine rather than inauthentic *soliloquium animae*. Adam's speech thus initiates the beginning of godly sorrow as a heavenly language. At the opening of Book 11, Christ translates this language for the Father, thereby reconciling creatures and Creator: "Prevenient grace descending had removed / The stony from their hearts, and made new flesh / Regenerate grow instead, that sighs now breathed / Unutterable, which the spirit of prayer / Inspired, and winged for heaven with speedier flight / Than loudest oratory" (11.3–8).

As I already indicated, the state of *viva morte* that Adam identifies as one possible future for himself is the same state that threatens both Southwell's Magdalene and Donne's speaker, and which entirely consumes Shakespeare's Richard II and Milton's Satan. The depiction of near-despair in Donne's *An Anatomy* unfolds in much the same way as it does in *Richard II* in the sense that excessive grief is figured in both texts as the affective correlative to the world's desacralization. In each of these works, the world's desacralization occurs through a breakdown in typological structures. Biblical patterns no longer appear to map onto the lived experience of suffering and loss. Sadness becomes despair when it is no longer legible in typological terms, when it no longer bears the structure of scripture. In *Richard II*, this breakdown is expressed by having Richard demonically invert the kind of divine language Augustine envisions in *De Trinitate*. When Richard pits the word against the word, he dialectically reverses the divine signifier Augustine theorizes when the Bishop of Hippo asserts that God's Word

cannot be uttered in sound nor thought in the likeness of sound, such as must be done with the word of any language; it precedes all the signs by which it is signified, and is begotten by the knowledge which remains in the mind when this same knowledge is spoken inwardly, just as it is. For the sight of thought is very similar to the sight of knowledge. For, when it is spoken through a sound or through some bodily sign, it is not spoken just as it is, but as it can be seen or heard through the body. When, therefore, that which is in the knowledge is in the word, then it is a true word, and the truth which is expected from man, so that what is in the knowledge is also in the word, and what is not in the knowledge is not in the word; it is here that we recognize, "Yes, yes; no, no" [*Matthew* 5:37]. In this way the likeness of the image that was made approaches, insofar as it can, to the likeness of the image that was born, whereby God the Son is proclaimed as substantially like the Father in all things.[6]

Where the likeness of the Son to the Father is expressed in the transparent language of "Yes, yes; no, no," Richard II's difference from the Son is hauntingly captured in his response to Bolingbroke's question "Are you contended to resign the crown?": "Ay, no. No, ay" (4.1.201). Richard's chiastic inversion of Matthew 5:37 perfectly encapsulates the difference between the iconic Word of Christ and the equivocal word of the poet-king. This linguistic difference reflects and arises from the difference between Christ's perfect suffering and Richard's self-involuting despair. In *Richard II*, as in *Paradise Lost*, language most shows a man precisely insofar as what language shows is the character of his grief.

The iconic form of signification that Augustine imagines in *De Trinitate* is what Crashaw pursues at the end of "The Weeper." Crashaw tries to poeticize the kind of sign that Augustine theorizes – a sign that grounds and thus precedes all other signs. Although Donne, Marvell, and Herbert do not try to predicate such a sign, they do seek to identify its effects.

In "Affliction III," for example, Herbert retrospectively locates the divinity of his grief through the absence of despair, which is discerned by the fact that his "unruly sigh had [not] broken [his] heart." In other words, it is through the process of negation that Herbert identifies the trace of God's presence in his grief: "My heart did heave, and there came forth, *O God!* / By that I knew that thou wast in the grief, / To guide and govern it to my relief, / Making a sceptre of the rod: / Hadst thou not had thy part, / Sure the unruly sigh had broke my heart" (1–6). Instead of being destroyed by grief, this speaker has been transformed by affliction in the way Herbert explains in *The Country Parson*, when he suggests that the minister must undergo "the benefit of affliction which softens and works the stubborn heart of man."[7] By tracing the motions of his grief, Herbert's speaker is assured that it arises from, and is thus spoken by, the Alien Word. Although Shakespeare's Richard is also an apophatic poet of the negative, his lugubrious peregrinations never produce the experience of assurance Herbert's speaker finds.

For Herbert, as for Marvell, this process of tracing one's grief often occurs through a deepening of the difference between the poetic sign and the divine Word. The failure of poetic language to mimetically imitate or incarnate the divine sign is figured in Herbert as a way of clearing a space for godly sorrow to speak in its "mystic voice." In "Grief," as in "The Search," for example, the speaker's attempt to find God through sorrow must first take a failed detour through the world: "My grief hath need of all the watry things, / That nature hath produc'd. Let ev'ry vein / Suck up a river to supply mine eyes" (3–5). The post-Petrarchan hyperbole, so reminiscent of Southwell's tear poetry, indicates that this speaker is off the mark both thematically and formally. The formal failure here is expressed in the poem's rhyme scheme in which "the first 16 lines rhyme *ababcdcd*, etc.; [and where] lines 17 and 18 form a couplet; [while] the nineteenth and last line rhymes with nothing. Ironically, however, this last line – 'Alas, my God!' – is a quintessentially poetic recognition, and one of mortal silence, which points toward the redemption."[8] The speaker of "Grief" is thus most godly at the very moment the formal failure of his poetry gives way to an alternative order of understanding, one that is no less poetic for being out of tune with the prosody of previous lines.

One of the key things revealed by the end of "Grief" is the close association that is often made in early modern religious poetry between the experience of godly sorrow and the birth of the Christian poet as such – an association we first saw in relation to Southwell's "A Vale of Teares." "Grief" poeticizes the psalmic idea that in the process of becoming truly repentant one becomes God's instrument and thus a genuine poet. Herbert returns to this theme in "Ephes. 4.30," where the process of becoming contrite signifies Christ's presence within the soul – a presence that makes one a poet in the most meaningful Christian sense: "Oh take thy lute, and tune it to a strain, / Which may with thee / All day complain. / There can no discord but in ceasing be" (19–22). If "Grief" locates the truest poetic utterance in the sacred silence carved out by formally flawed poetry, then "Ephes. 4.30" locates such a divine utterance in the music of grief – in the idea that true grief is Christ speaking/singing through one's affects. In both poems, though, the very idea of poetry is identified with the expression of godly sorrow. For Herbert, poetry is inconceivable without the category of devout melancholy informing it because the true penitent is, in effect, a living poem. Such an association rests on the relation between weeping and singing that we see Donne refer to when he observes that "when it is said *Tempus cantus, The time of singing is come*, it might as well be rendered out of the Hebrew, *Tempus plorationis, The time of weeping is come (SD 4.343)*" – an association that concludes Herbert's "Joseph's Coat": "I live to show his power, who once did bring / My *joys* to *weep*, and now *my griefs to sing*" (13–14).

No Herbert poem associates godly sorrow with poetic utterance as closely as "A True Hymn" – the title of which intimates the idea that being repentant is the highest form of poetry. The two final stanzas of the poem indicate that devout poetry is dialogical in the same way as devout melancholy – in it one is speaking as well as being spoken to:

> He who craves all the mind,
> And all the soul, and strength, and time,
> If the words only rhyme
> Justly complains, that somewhat is behind
> To make his verse, or write a hymn in kind.
>
> Whereas if th'heart be moved,
> Although the verse be somewhat scant,
> God doth supply the want.
> As when th' heart says (sighing to be approved)
> *O could I love!* and stops: God writeth, *Loved.* (11–20)

Perhaps the most fascinating and unusual thing Herbert implies here is that the very process of writing poetry transforms the poet. The poet is not figured as transcendent from the poem, as though he were documenting a past experience that is complete; nor does he figure himself as a *vates* – creating his poem in a way that is analogous to God's creation of the world in Genesis. On the contrary, the poet is figured as being made by the poem as much as he makes it. In this respect, poetry and grief are exactly analogical. One must interpret one's own poem in the process of making it in the same way one must interpret the character of one's "sighs and tears": one must listen for the otherness emerging from it, remaining vigilantly sensitive to the other voice that is immanent within one's "own" verse. Even more remarkably, Herbert implies that grief and poetry can help reveal or complete one another. By presuming a dynamic relation between poet and poem – a relation in which the poet's soul as an image of God is revealed to himself by the poem as a divine sign – Herbert implies that poetry works as a way of accessing and interpreting the nature of one's grief as a way to God. For Herbert, then, penitential poetry is experimental rather than mimetic, genuinely searching rather than strictly documentary.

This remarkably dynamic way of configuring the relationship between poet and poem is the theme of "The Quiddity" which further exemplifies Herbert's apophatic poetics. Like "The Search" and "Grief," "The Quiddity" works by negation. It tells us what poetry is not, as a way of clearing a space for revealing what poetry is. Searching out the question of the "essence" or "quiddity" of poetry, we are told that verse is not "a crown ... or gay suit, hawk, or banquet, or renown ... nor yet a lute" (1–3, 4). Recalling the anti-Catholic literary criticism of "Grief," we are also told that "It never was in *France* or *Spain*" (6). In the third and final stanza, however, the negations give way as Herbert offers a definition of poetry in terms of its effects on the poet: "But it is that which while I use / I am with thee, and *Most take all*" (11–12). Herbert not only implies that the poem is ultimately a creation of God and thus must return to him, but he also works out the compositional implications of this view. Because the poem is not wholly of the poet's own making, the process of "writing" (though not "authoring" it) reveals the other power at work in the poetic process. The ultimate end of poetry, then, is to help the poet turn toward God in the very act of writing itself. This, it would seem, is the thesis of Herbert's "Sion," which ends by claiming that penitential "sighs and groans" are the most perfect offering one can make to God: "And truly brass and stones are heavy things, / Tombs for the dead, not temples fit for thee: / But groans are quick, and full of wings, / And all their motions upward be; / And ever as they mount, like larks they sing; / The note is sad, yet music for a king" (19–24). As this and other poems imply, godly sorrow is analogous to poetry – in a certain sense *is* the truest poetry – insofar as both are dialogical processes in which one enters into conversation with the immanent otherness of God.

Herbert's view that the poet is not transcendent from the poem, but is changed in the very process of writing, theorizes a dimension of poetic voice that we have seen throughout this book. Herbert, in effect, draws out the implications of what it means to write from the subjective point of view that Milton's Adam discovers in his soliloquy from Book 10 – a point of view where will and being are constitutively at odds such that intention and meaning are always at risk of becoming discontinuous. To put this another way, Herbert theorizes the gap between utterance and significance that Southwell expresses through the dramatic monologue structure. As we saw, St. Peter's voice is characterized by the way he confesses more than he knows, by the way his language conveys how the experience of compunction takes him beyond the limits of the will to the point of excessive wonder. While Southwell enacts the limitations of poetic authority that Herbert thematizes, his Jesuit poetic precludes him from adopting the personally dynamic and individually transformative view of verse characteristic of *The Temple*: Southwell tends not to write himself into his poems to the same degree that Herbert does; or when he does, it is from a point of view of recollection where the act of writing is not figured as actually changing the direction of his soul at that moment of writing.

The poetic voice Herbert theorizes is thus consistent with the view of poetry often associated with Milton's account of Renaissance narrative verse – an account Paul Stevens articulates when he observes that for Milton

Spenser is a better teacher than Scotus or Aquinas (*Paradise Lost* than the *Christian Doctrine*) because poetry unlike prose enables the reader to know good by evil, to confirm truth by scanning error ... Poetry is able to place the reader in a situation which simulates the field of this world where "the knowledge of good is so involv'd and interwoven with the knowledge of evill, and in so many cunning resemblances hardly to be discern'd" that the reader is forced into the exercise of virtue: he is forced to reason, to choose, to read actively – otherwise he finds himself in the Devil's party without knowing it.[9]

In practice, Herbert and Milton actually go one step further than this; they not only presume that the reader's soul is in question in the process of reading, but they also presume that the poet/narrator is actively at risk in the writing process itself. For instance, in the invocation to light in Book 3, Milton's narrator expresses relief at the fact that he did not go mad in the process of depicting Hell in Books 1 and 2, relating how

> I ...
> Escaped the Stygian pool, though long detained
> In that obscure sojourn, while in my flight

> Through utter and through middle darkness borne
> With other notes than to the Orphéan lyre
> I sung of Chaos and eternal Night,
> Taught by the heavenly Muse to venture down
> The dark descent, and up to reascend.
> Though hard and rare: thee I revisit safe. (3.14–21)

The descent into the eternal despair of Hell is figured as an accomplishment realized with great risk to the narrator's own soul. There was a very real possibility, the narrator warns, of becoming afflicted by the despair that he related in Books 1 and 2. The question of the poet's inspiration can only be answered retrospectively: having re-ascended from the abyss of despair the narrator is more assured that the divine muse is, indeed, within him and that he can continue with the story of all things.[10]

Although Herbert does not presume to justify the ways of God to man in the cosmological terms to which Milton aspires, he does see the writing of grief as entailing considerable risk. In "Affliction IV," for example, Herbert's speaker is at risk of devolving into his afflicted thoughts in the same way that Milton's Satan and Shakespeare's Richard do. Like *St Peters Complaint*, Herbert's "Affliction IV" offers a series of images and tropes which signify both terrible anguish and redemptive hope at one and the same time. It is up to the reader as well as the narrator to identify the redemptive trace lurking in the speaker's "sighs and tears," while simultaneously remaining on guard for signs of reprobation. The opening stanza of Herbert's poem operates in much the same way as Southwell's prefatory letter to the reader. It indicates that the meaning of individual lines tend to signify in two opposing ways, as they hover "Betwixt this world and that of grace": "Broken in pieces all asunder, / Lord, hunt me not, / A thing forgot, / Once a poor creature, now a wonder, / A wonder tortur'd in the space / Betwixt this world and that of grace" (1–6). The poem's motions encapsulate the basic dialectic that I have been analyzing in this book – the oscillation between despair and compunction. This oscillation happens across as well as within individual lines. The petition, "Lord, hunt me not," is defensive in its desire to hide from *ira dei*, even as it is hopeful in its implicit appeal for mercy, an appeal that becomes more audible following the line: "A thing forgot." Like the speaker of Donne's "O Might Those Sighes and Teares," Herbert's speaker seeks for mercy without the humiliation of judgment and as a result he timidly hopes God will take him into his presence but not overwhelm him in the process. Yet even when the line "A thing forgot" is read as developing the previous line, thus articulating a desire to be in God's merciful presence, it might also be discontinuous with the previous line as though the speaker were sighing and thus breaking off from rather than completing his previous thought. Such a discontinuity would be consistent with the opening line's description of him as "Broken in pieces all asunder." He both desires and fears God, just as he both completes and leaves off his own thought. Through this oscillating movement of continuity and discontinuity of thought we hear the traces of a regenerative sorrow. This basic pattern continues in stanza 2, but the focus now is on the opposition between trope and image: "My thoughts are all a case of knives, / Wounding my heart / With scatter'd smart, / As watring pots give flowers their lives. / Nothing their fury can control, / While they do wound and pink / my soul" (7–12).[11] While the catachresis, or mixed metaphor, suggests that the speaker is devolving further into his own delusions rather than moving towards the otherness of God, the flower imagery communicates the potentially regenerative motions the speaker is experiencing even in the midst of such apparent devolution. What is crucial here, though, is that the solipsistic pull of catachresis expresses the risk Herbert believes himself to be taking in the very act of writing his grief as a way of reading it. Like the Miltonic bard's descent into despair, Herbert's speaker does not presume to know that the pilgrimage into grief that he takes in *The Temple* is finished before it begins. This risk is a central if generally overlooked feature of how Herbert theorizes religious poetry.[12]

As I have tried to show throughout this book, the power of fascination elicited by poetic depictions of repentance, both authentic and parodic, lies in the way they presume a highly active, invested, even experimental relation to the reader. By experimental I mean that the status of the reader's own soul is believed to be at stake in the encounter with works such as Herbert's *The Temple*. As a result, the reader's investment in the poetry of sorrow is sometimes thematized in much the same way that Herbert thematizes the risks and investments the poet takes in becoming a new psalmist. Crashaw, for example, describes the active, devotional appropriations that Herbert's *The Temple* invites in "On Mr. G Herberts Booke Intituled the Temple of Sacred Poems, Sent to a Gentlewoman." The poem begins by emphasizing the dynamically sacramental relation between reader and text, a relation in which the animated, iconic book comes alive through the reader's gaze. By receiving and accepting Herbert's *The Temple*, Crashaw's unnamed gentlewoman participates in the creation of a devotional community consisting of author, book, reader, and giver: "Know you faire, on what you looke? / Divinest love lyes in this booke: / Expecting fire from your eyes, / To kindle this his sacrifice" (lines 1–4). The flame that will kindle the book as a way of forging this community of believers is the reader's mourning sighs: "When your hands unty these strings, / Thinke you have an Angell by th' wings. / One that gladly will be nigh, / To wait upon each morning sigh" (lines 5–8). *The Temple* calls for more than interpretation, it demands devotional appropriation and an existentially committed form of identification, even as it requires a highly critical ear.

"On Mr. G Herberts Booke" concludes with a similarly active assimilation of the book into the soul of the reader with which it begins, as Crashaw takes ownership of *The Temple* for his own devotional (and perhaps poetic) uses: "And though *Herberts* name doe owe / These devotions, fairest; know / That while I lay them on the shrine / Of your white hand, they are mine" (lines 15–18). Like the end of "The Weeper," this poem emphasizes the communal dimensions of reading poetic accounts of godly sorrow: Crashaw figures himself as a mediator between the sacrificer, Herbert, and the gentlewoman who is in the role of communicant – making the process of reading *The Temple* implicitly Eucharistic.

Thomas Carew offers a different but equally revealing poetic account of how the early modern poetry of religious sorrow was read in his 1637 lyric "To My Worthy Friend Master GEO. SANDS, on his Translation of the Psalms." Where Crashaw emphasizes how Herbert's book forges a relationship between readers, Carew takes the newly translated Psalms as an occasion for revisiting the Petrarchan scenario of conversion that Donne explores in "O Might Those Sighes and Teares." Carew focuses particular attention on the destructively creative power of penitential tears: "Prompted by thy example then, no more / In moulds of clay will I my God adore; / But teare those Idols from my heart, and write / What his blest Sprit, not fond Love shall indite."[13] The act of reading Sands' translation of the psalms is figured here as leading to a private reformation of the soul in which Carew's tears tear him away from the idols of his Petrarchan/ courtly past. By entering into Sands' translation of the psalms, Carew begins to move from the Church porch – where his muse had humbly (though judging by the tone not too humbly) stayed – into the Church itself. Like Donne's conversion poem, the question of Carew's sincerity haunts and unsettles his confession. Only the issue of insincerity is more explicitly thematized by Carew as he opens by admitting a distaste for Church attendance and for the composition of devotional verse: "I Presse not to the Quire, nor dare I greet / The holy place with my unhallowed feet."[14] Despite the differences between Carew's courtly disavowal of courtly verse and Crashaw's sincere piety, both men follow Herbert in linking authentic acts of poetic composition to genuine experiences of grief. The very idea of Christian poetry is intrinsically bound up in early modern England with Paul's conception of grief as an *apologia*.

Because godly sorrow often mediates early modern English conceptions of religious poetry, the soteriological controversies surrounding the theme often bleed into literary traditions. This process gives rise to the kinds of agonistic relations I have traced in this book: the articulation of theological cruxes by means of godly sorrow generally involves rewriting some prior text with alternative theological commitments. In the case of *Paradise Lost*, the depiction of Satan's despair in Book 9 unfolds through a parody of the Catholic literature of tears tradition. Through this parody, Milton creates the effect that the tradition associated with Southwell's Jesuit mission emerges as a result of Satan's demonic mission in Eden. In Crashaw's "The Weeper," godly sorrow is depicted in a highly sacramental manner through a rewriting of Herbert's "Grief," in which the private, meditative mode of Herbert's Calvinist aesthetic is reconceived in more liturgical terms and in the light of a Laudian emphasis on the Real Presence of Christ in the Eucharist. In turn, Marvell's "Eyes and Tears" reforms the devotional and poetic vision of "The Weeper," thereby continuing the project Herbert began in *The Temple*. In *Salve Deus*, Lanyer not only combines an unofficial Catholic tradition with Protestant ecclesiology, she also rewrites Philip Sidney's gendering of poetic authority through his account of the art/nature distinction. In Donne's *Holy Sonnets*, godly sorrow is figured by reconceiving Petrarch's ambivalent attitude towards conversion in the *Rime Sparse* within the devotionally and theologically amorphous context of Jacobean England. And in *An Anatomy*, godly sorrow is figured through a self-consciously belated response to Deuteronomy's meditation on belatedness.

Another important theme I have traced in this book is the gendering of sacred sorrow as feminine. From Donne's *An Anatomy*, to Crashaw's "The Weeper," to Lanyer's *Salve Deus*, and in many, if not most, other early modern works dealing with godly sorrow, the point of sacramental contact between heavenly and earthly grief is figured as feminine in nature. This means that the process of mourning unfolding in the poems I have analyzed generally involves a movement from a "masculine" resistance to confessing one's weakness in the moment of loss, to kenotically opening up to such weakness in a "feminine" manner. As Lanyer's poem discloses, this kenotic process constitutes one of the few domains in early modern culture where women could claim to possess greater authority than men. Just as Milton's *Paradise Lost* offers an originary account of the *viva morte* theme, so too it offers an account of how godly sorrow came to be gendered as feminine. In Book 10, Milton explains the gendering of godly sorrow by depicting Eve as a type of the penitent sinner, specifically the woman of Luke 7, who was thought, in the Renaissance, to be Mary Magdalene. As many scholars have observed, Milton's Eve foreshadows both the woman of Luke 7 and the Virgin Mary, who brings forth the redeemer whom Eve also mirrors. After being rejected by Adam, Eve pleads for mercy – falling to her knees in a gesture which clearly recalls the woman thought to be Magdalene: "Eve, / Not so repulsed, with tears that ceased not flowing, / And tresses all disordered, at his feet / Fell humble, and thus proceeded in her plaint" (10.909–13). By the end of her speech, an unprecedented form of "peace" emerges – one that Adam will come to recognize as the fruit of devout grief: "She ended weeping, and her lowly plight, / Immovable till peace obtained from fault / Acknowledged and deplored, in Adam wrought / Commiseration" (10.937–40).

This reconciliation between Adam and Eve initiates the fuller recognition Adam makes following Eve's temptation to *Todestriebe*: "Eve, thy contempt of life and pleasure seems / To argue in thee something more sublime / And excellent than what thy mind contemns" (10.1013–15). Adam thus perceives Eve in much the same way Elizabethan prose dilations of John 20 ask us to perceive Magdalene at the empty tomb: he sees her as being in possession of knowledge of which she is unaware. This is the moment in human history, Milton's narrative tells us, when a distinction emerged between "heart-knowing" and "head-knowing." Through Eve, Adam comes to know the difference between an enunciation and the position of enunciation – between what is said and the position from and attitude in which it is said. Eve exemplifies how a truly contrite complaint must be spoken such that the position of speech is as important as the speech itself. In other words, Milton offers this scene as his archetype for the moment that godly sorrow clears the soul in the form of a Pauline *apologia*.

The gendering of godly sorrow as feminine is part of the larger context by which early modern culture turned to the discourse of devout melancholy as a way of conceiving difference as such. In the cases of *Paradise Lost* and *Salve Deus*, godly sorrow is deployed as a way of accounting for the difference between the sexes as well as the difference between human and divine. Similarly, in "Eyes and Tears," "The Weeper," and Herbert's "Grief," godly sorrow serves as the medium by which the difference between human and divine is expressed in poetic form. In all of these cases, the question of difference is thematized through the question of godly sorrow – which is understood in the period as a unique phenomenon in which spiritual things are given to be "seen."

Perhaps the most original depiction of the relation between human and divine in the context of godly sorrow is Thomas Traherne's Christian humanist celebration of man in "Admiration" – a poem that recalls even as it radically rewrites the incarnationist poetics of seventeenth-century tear poetry. Stanza 3 of the poem reconfigures the Magdalenian scene of the penitent weeper shedding tears on Christ's feet in a shockingly new, highly spiritualized, way:

> The Lilly and the Rosy-Train
>   Which, scatter'd on the ground,
> Salute the Feet which they surround,
>   Grow for thy sake, O Man; that like a Chain
>   Or Garland they may be
>   To deck ev'n thee:
>   They all remain
>   Thy Gems; and bowing down their head
>   Their liquid Pearl they kindly shed
> In Tears; as if they meant to wash thy Feet,
> For Joy that they to serv thee are made meet.[15]

In this passage, "man" is to nature as Christ is to the weeping Magdalene. Yet the scenario is more complex than this as nature is also identified with Christ through the images of the lily and rosy-train, traditional images of the Incarnation derived from the Song of Songs. This chiastic relation of God and world is conveyed through the word "meet," which has several meanings here, indicating the somewhat archaic "made an equal," as well as "made suitable to" (*OED*). Perhaps more importantly, it also carries a Eucharistic pun on "meat," implying a gift of grace. Through these figures, Traherne completely transforms the scene of godly sorrow in Luke 7 into a communion with God in the temple of nature. The result is that the poem celebrates the immanence of God in man by positioning man in the place of Christ within an archetypal scene of divine love: man is to nature as Magdalene is to Christ. For Traherne, Luke 7 authorizes natural theology more than it exhorts one to sorrow. Being remarkably uninterested in repentance, Traherne turns the tears of contrition into tears of gratitude, retaining the thematics of communion while eschewing the regimen of guilt so central to the discourse of godly sorrow. By this very late point in the English tradition of tear poetry, then, the Magdalenian scenario has become wholly metamorphosed – a symbol of

Communion rather than a prescript of repentance. By this stage in the poetry of early modern religious sorrow, we are well on our way to eighteenth-century natural theology.

One of the key things that emerges from this study is a recognition that the language of godly sorrow spoken in early modern England is arguably more subtle than anything we are likely to encounter in current contemporary discourses of grief, be they critical, clinical, or religious. In this respect, the varying tenses of devout melancholy available to seventeenth-century writers differentiates early modern culture from our own historical moment. Part of the reason for this is that the grammar of tears loses much of its cultural relevance after the Enlightenment. As Traherne's "Admiration" testifies, the archetypal scenes of godly sorrow begin to speak in new ways as poets become less concerned with the authenticity of repentance and more concerned with how nature reveals or does not reveal the Godhead. By the time the discourse of godly sorrow became less culturally determinative, however, it reached a remarkable level of theological, literary, and philosophical complexity. Such complexity is a function of the fact that seventeenth-century poets had the benefit of nearly two millennia's worth of elaborations on St. Paul's distinction between godly and worldly sorrow in 2 Corinthians 7, from the Eastern tradition of *penthos*, to patristic diagnoses of *accidia*, to scholastic views of despair and penance, to Reformation accounts of the *ordu salutis*. Benefiting from this long history, the poems examined in this book constitute the moment when the discourse of devout melancholy had reached its highest degree of self-consciousness, thus rendering possible accounts of its origins such as we see in *Paradise Lost*.

NOTES

1 John Rist, *Augustine: Ancient Thought Baptized* (Cambridge: Cambridge University Press, 1994), p. 88.
2 Cited and translated in Marcia L. Colish, *The Mirror of Language: A Study in the Medieval Theory of Knowledge* (New Haven, CT: Yale University Press, 1968), p. 35.
3 *"Of Christian Doctrine,"* in *Complete Prose Works of John Milton Volume VI* (New Haven, CT: Yale University Press, 1973), p. 395 (book 1, chapter 12).
4 The similarity between the opening of Adam's speech in Book 10 and the beginning of Satan's in Book 4 has been observed by Jason Philip Rosenblatt, "The Law in Adam's Soliloquy," in Diana Trevino Benet and Michael Lieb (eds.), *Literary Milton: Text, Pretext, Context* (Pittsburgh, PA: Duquesne University Press, 1994), pp. 180–201.

5 Cited in Brian Cummings, *The Literary Culture of the Reformation: Grammar and Grace* (Oxford: Oxford University Press, 2002), p. 402.

6 St. Augustine, *On the Trinity: Books 8–15*, ed. Gareth B. Matthews and trans. Stephen Mckenna (Cambridge: Cambridge University Press, 2002), pp. 188–89 (book, 15, chapter 11).

7 *George Herbert*, Slater (ed.), p. 219.

8 Mark Taylor, *The Soul in Paraphrase: George Herbert's Poetics* (The Hague: Mouton, 1974), p. 46.

9 Paul Stevens, *Imagination and the Presence of Shakespeare in Paradise Lost* (Madison: University of Wisconsin Press, 1985), p. 95.

10 Gordon Teskey provocatively describes Milton's tendency to present himself as having undergone the experiences he describes in his poetry as a feature of his "delirious" poetics in *Delirious Milton: The Fate of the Poet In Modernity* (Cambridge, MA: Harvard University Press, 2006).

11 Such a reading also offers further evidence that the word "pink" works better than the word "prick" in line 12 as it signifies both puncture and adorn, thus encapsulating the dialectical motions of the poem more effectively than the less dialectical "prick" that appears in some manuscript versions of the poem. Slater chooses "prick," while Hutchinson, *The Works of George Herbert* (Oxford: Clarendon Press, 1941) has "pink." I have thus emended Slater's version.

12 For other accounts of Herbert's views on poetry, see Mark Taylor, *The Soul in Paraphrase*; Richard Todd, *The Opacity of Signs: Acts of Interpretation in George Herbert's The Temple* (Columbia: University of Missouri Press, 1986); Elizabeth Clarke, *Theory and Theology in Herbert's Poetry: "Divinitie, and Poesie, Met"* (Oxford: Clarendon Press, 1997).

13 Thomas Carew, "To My Worthy Friend Master GEO. SANDS, on his Translation of the Psalms," in Edward W. Tayler (ed.), *Literary Criticism of Seventeenth-Century England* (New York: Alfred A. Knopf, 1967), p. 223, lines 29–32.

14 Ibid., lines 1–2.

15 Thomas Traherne, *Centuries Poems and Thanksgivings*, ed. H. M Margoliouth (Oxford: Clarendon Press, 1958), lines 23–33.

Index